W E S T E R N W A S H I N G T O N S T A T E C O L L E G E

P R O G R A M I N E A S T A S I A N S T U D I E S

Occasional Paper No. 7

中國經濟史

AN ECONOMIC HISTORY OF CHINA

by

Chou Chin-sheng

A Translation in Précis

by

Edward H. Kaplan

1974

Editor:

Henry G. Schwarz

Western Washington State College
Bellingham, Washington 98225

Originally published in Chinese in 1959

Library of Congress Cataloging in Publication Data

Chou, Chin-shêng, 1907-
An economic history of China.

(Program in East Asian Studies, Western Washington State College. Occasional papers, no. 7)
Translation of Chung-kuo ching chi shih.
1. China--Economic conditions--Early to 1644.
2. China--Economic conditions--1644-1912. I. Kaplan, Edward H., 1936- II. Title. III. Series: Washington (State). Western Washington State College, Bellingham. Program in East Asian Studies. Occasional paper, no. 7.
HC427.6.C5513 330.9'51 74-620032
ISBN 0-914584-07-3

The publication of this volume has been assisted by a generous grant from Western Washington State College.

PREFACE

This translation is a severely abbreviated version of the 1,200-page Chinese original text. The principles I have followed in deciding what to omit and how to summarize the author's original argument are set out in the translator's introduction. Professor Chou may not, of course, be held responsible for the infelicities of style, distortions and errors which must inevitably appear in a work which has gone through the double process of translation and abridgment.

I have assumed that readers of this text already have some basic knowledge of Chinese political and cultural history. Hence I have pruned rather drastically from Professor Chou's original text material not directly relevant to economic phenomena. I have, however, appended a dynastic table keyed to Professor Chou's periodization of Chinese economic history.

Special Chinese terms for economic institutions have, wherever possible, been translated into English equivalents and explained at their first occurrence in the text. The English terms are cross-referenced to their Chinese originals (with ideographs placed next to the transliterations) in the glossary-index. I have also appended a separate list of Chinese weights and measures. Given the wide variation in Chinese measures with identical names over space and time, the English equivalents of these terms should be taken only as approximations.

Though not included in Professor Chou's original text, I have added what I hope is a representative selection of traditional style woodblock illustrations of economic activities, taken from Ming and Ch'ing dynasty illustrated encyclopedias, so as to provide a pictorial equivalent of the kind of Chinese perspective on

Chinese economic history given by the text.

Finally I would like to thank Professor Chou for graciously consenting to the publication of my translation. My thanks also to the undergraduate students in my senior seminar at Western Washington State College during the last two years who have given me highly useful comments on earlier drafts of this translation.

TABLE OF CONTENTS

LIST OF ILLUSTRATIONS

Sources:

Figs. 10, 12, 13, 17, 18, 19, 20, 21, 22, 24, 25, 26: Ch'en Meng-lei and Chiang T'ing-hsi (comps.), Ku-chin t'ushu chich'eng Shanghai: T'ushu chich'eng chü, 1884 reprint of the Yung-cheng era movable type edition);
Figs. 1, 2, 3, 4, 5, 6, 7, 8, 9, 11: Wang Ch'i, San-ts'ai t'uhui (Taipei: Ch'eng-wen ch'upanshe, 1970 reprint of the 1565 edition);
Figs. 14, 16, 23: Sung Ying-hsing, T'ien-kung k'ai-wu (Taipei: Chunghua shuchü, 1955 reprint of the 1637 edition);
Fig. 15: P'eng Hsin-wei, Chungkuo huopi shih (Shanghai: Jenmin ch'upanshe, 1964).

TRANSLATOR'S INTRODUCTION

Given the paucity of works in English on Chinese economic history, particularly for the earlier periods, there is perhaps no particular need to offer elaborate justification for a translation, even in abbreviated form, of a work which has for more than a decade enjoyed so wide a popularity on Taiwan and among many foreign students of Chinese economic history. It is, however, necessary to indicate the several audiences to which this translation is addressed and the limited uses to which it may prudently be put.

The first draft of this translation was made in sections week by week for my undergraduate seminar in Chinese economic history during the fall of 1972. It was to serve in lieu of a current textbook survey which did not at that time exist.[1] I also hoped it could illustrate one of the modes of understanding China's economic history now current within the Chinese intellectual sphere, as opposed to one of the Western points of view toward non-Western economic experiences which are all too accessible to students in our part of the world.

Subsequently, it occurred to me that such a work might also serve as useful supplementary reading in my own, and perhaps in other people's, survey courses in pre-twentieth-century Chinese history, introducing Chinese economic history from a particular Chinese perspective in a way similar to what Derk Bodde's translation of Fung Yu-lan's Short History of Chinese Philosophy does for Chinese intellectual history, though on a considerably more modest scale.

This translation may perhaps also be of some use to students of the Chinese language who are interested in learning the vocabulary of economic history through reading all or part of the original Chinese text. I hope that this greatly abbreviated version preserves enough of the substance of the original to serve as a guide to or at least as a set of detailed hints as to the original's content, and that hence it can ease the student's path through it without doing so much of the work for him as to tempt him completely away from the original Chinese version.

Finally, this translation may be of interest to economists and economic historians who, for linguistic reasons, lack direct access to the original and who wish, in some of their reading at least, to minimize the inevitable distortion of Chinese perspectives which takes place when Chinese works are filtered through alien sensibilities in monographic works by Westerners.

All three of the above potential audiences should, however, be aware of the limitations of this translation lest they judge Professor Chou's work as inadequate on the basis of its shortcomings. I trust that the subtitle, A Translation in Précis, adequately indicates these limitations. The order and the major elements of Professor Chou's argument have been preserved, and all of his chapter headings have been retained. In the process of reducing the 1,200 pages of the Chinese original to about one-sixth of that amount, however, literal or close translation (at least to the degree that any translation can be considered literal) much of the time had to give way to summaries.[2] Even in these summaries, I have attempted to preserve something of the idiosyncratic flavor of the original and nearly all of its judgments and the mode of understanding on which they are based. I have also left out most of Professor Chou's bibliographic apparatus, for the most part consisting of lists of books at the end of each section, except for general indications of whom he is quoting at certain points. In almost all cases a reader would have to know Chinese to effectively exploit these sources. For those readers it should, however, be relatively easy to use this translation as a key to Professor Chou's original and the bibliographic apparatus it contains.

The two-volume[3] original on which this translation in précis is based has been virtually the standard work in the Republic of China on Chinese economic history since its publication in 1959. It was reprinted in 1970, and a one-volume abridgement appeared in 1973.[4] Its preeminence is, no doubt, partly due to the quasi-official standing of its author and to the somewhat delicate status of its subject, it being necessary for writers on Taiwan to avoid even the appearance of using Marxist interpretations, particularly in economic matters. The work, however, is quite capable of standing on its own merits, and its quasi-official status renders it sufficiently archetypical to be in itself of interest to the foreign student who wishes to discover the range of viewpoints extant within the modern Chinese intellectual community.

It will be evident from the very first page that Professor Chou is actively committed to the system of political economy built around Sun Yat-sen's concept of People's Livelihood (民生 min sheng), the third of Dr. Sun's Three People's Principles (三民主義 san min chuyi). Such an attachment must seem almost quaintly archaic outside of the Republic of China on Taiwan. How seriously, after all, are the economic principles of Henry George (the inspiration, unacknowledged in this work, for most of Dr. Sun's own economic ideas) taken in the West these days? Indeed on Taiwan itself, avowal of the Three Principles has, especially in recent years, become for most people, a pro forma exercise designed to show one's political respectability rather than evidence of a deeply held ideological position informing the whole of a writer's viewpoint in whatever he writes. To some extent this is true even of Professor Chou's work, though he appears to make more whole-hearted use of Sun's worldview than do most contemporary serious Taiwan scholars. Nevertheless People's Livelihood is not sufficiently profound a concept to dominate a work so wide in scope as Chou's and, whever necessary, he simply rises above principle so as to do justice to a particular topic. He is in this respect more fortunate than his compatriots within the People's Republic of China who are obligied by their governing authorities to apply the Marxist-Maoist orthodox ideology deeply to the whole course of their studies. Because Marxism-Maoism is far more ambitious than Sunism, this results in distortions far more severe than do the more eclectic nineteenth-century liberal doctrines of Dr. Sun.

In particular, Chinese Marxists have far greater difficulties than does Professor Chou in accepting the very considerable accomplishments of the traditional Chinese economy, and while this attitude of acceptance occasionally leads Professor Chou into a perhaps excessive complacency,[5] this is not necessarily to be despised. It is likely rather nearer the truth than many of the libelous statements made during the last generation about even China's more remote past by respectably patriotic Chinese Marxists. At heart it is also psychologically healthier than the Marxist position and hence more likely to lead further toward the truth in future investigations. Most schools of psychology tell us that a patient cannot begin to plumb the truth of his own nature until he has fully accepted a priori his own worth as an individual. As for the individual, so for society. Whatever else is right with it, Marxist China has yet to accept, in its own terms, the worth of China's pre-Marxist past. Whatever else is wrong with it, Nationalist China has so accepted its past.

To be sure, neither Chou nor his mentor Sun sees China's tradition entirely in that tradition's own terms. Both must ultimately be placed in the camp of the Westernizers in that most agonizing of nineteenth- and twentieth-century China's intellectual dilemmas, the clash between Westernizers and Purifiers of the Chinese tradition. But even in their own terms, the Western economists' and economic historians' very claims to universality prevent any serious assertion by either Chinese or Westerners that a Chinese economic historian is in some sense betraying his own culture if he applies the "laws" of economics to its history. There is nothing peculiarly Western about these laws except for the historical accident of the region where they were discovered. As one of the greatest of modern economists, Ludwig Von Mises, asserts, "the a priori sciences," among which he includes economics, "aim at a knowledge unconditionally valid for all beings endowed with the logical structure of the human mind."[6] At this level there is no room for what Von Mises dismisses as the "polylogical" approach, there are no more grounds for asserting a peculiarly Chinese economic science than there were for Hitler to assert the existence of (and cruelly persecute) a pecularly Jewish science or, for that matter, for Marxists to assert the existence of (and, when they can, persecute) a peculiarly bourgeois economics.[7]

Economic <u>history</u> and what for lack of a more currently fashionable term must be labeled political economy are, however, quite another matter. It is evident that there must be an idiosyncratically Chinese economic history, though the narration of its course and the analysis of its inner logic must never contradict the laws of valid economic science. It may initially be less or not at all evident that there can be one or more idiosyncratically Chinese versions of political economy, but to deny this would be to assert that political science and political philosophy are sciences in the same a prioristic sense as are logic or economics. The range of behavior in the realm of politics, the range of variant values that underlies the many varieties of political philosophy alone guarantee at least the potential existence of many political economies in all but the simplest of human cultures. Of course, a particular political philosophy may require use of modes of economic activity which economic science determines cannot achieve the ends at which they aim. All this means, however, is that not all things are possible to attain within any given political system no matter what its partisans may claim.[8]

It is in his political economy that Professor Chou may justly be labeled idiosyncratically Chinese and Chinese of a particular sort for which the label "neo-traditional" is appropriate. It is unfortunate that such a label in these times carries with it an aura of the "reactionary." I should have preferred to use the words "radical" or "revolutionary," or at least have substituted the word "new" for the prefix "neo-," but the former would have been inaccurate and the latter would have been awkward. Though he is in many respects a man of the twentieth century, Professor Chou shares with the mainstream of traditional Chinese political economy an abiding concern with the ethical norms of equality (or at least equity) and harmony[9] and the assumption that it is the duty of a well-organized state to attempt to realize these ideals in the life of the society it governs. This traditional benevolent statism is in some measure accentuated by Professor Chou's allegiance to the Kuomintang's ideal (typical of most of the left- and right-wing movements aiming at national liberation and development which have characterized our century) of using the power of the state to make or at least encourage the creation of a modern industrial society.

Hence Chou applauds Emperor Wu of Han for the purity of intent of his statist policies, but while Chou deplores their excesses he does not ascribe them to this inherent statism. He clearly implies that the Kuomintang would not have gone so far, particularly in frustrating the legitimate activities of merchants. A disciple of the "Austrian" school of economists might deny the <u>economic</u> efficacy of even the more limited Kuomintang interventionism, but in doing so he would simply be exposing one of the differences between his own and Professor Chou's political economy. For Chou state intervention is an ethical imperative.

Chou's statism is, however, also balanced or at least rendered ambivalent by its logical opposite: an attraction toward laissez-faire. Of course, something akin to laissez-faire seems actually to have been present within both the Confucian and Taoist traditions, and this trend is faithfully reported by Chou. This traditional anti-statism appears to have been reenforced in Professor Chou's mind by his exposure to the Western classical economic tradition. Hence he depicts the early Confucians, particuarly Mencius, as overt advocates of laissez-faire and concludes that philosophical statism is a Han and post-Han distortion of this aspect of the original Confucian tradition.

This tendency to view the thinkers of the classical period as more "modern" than their successors during the imperial era is, of course, an old habit among modern Chinese intellectuals, conspicuous at least since K'ang Yu-wei, and was, as Joseph Levenson has argued, a stage in modern Chinese intellectuals' transcendance of their tradition.[10] Chou's tendency to occasionally take too literally such putatively early literary sources as the Chou Li 周禮 (The Rites of Chou) is another aspect of the earlier stages of this transition but one which appears, particularly among scholars on Taiwan, to be coming (with some justification) back into fashion in recent years.

Also reminiscent of the traditional historiography is Chou's tendency on occasion to practice "appropriate concealment" (諱 hui),[11] as by separating discussion of some of the key flaws of Wang An-shih's reforms from his narrative of them and celebration of their and Wang's virtues. Of greater significance, though much of it is lost in this necessarily abbreviated version, is Chou's retention of the traditional practice of knitting the narrative together with extended quotations from all relevant primary sources.

Giving due weight to its weaknesses, Chou's neo-traditional point of view nevertheless retains the virtue of enabling him and, through him, us to see the past in terms more nearly congruent with its own values than can be done through currently more fashionable points of view. If he misses insights obvious to the latter, the converse is also the case, and in many situations he allows us to see the same seeming novelties as does the latter, but domesticated into the normal fabric of Chinese history. A good example of this sort of shift in perspective is the issue of land tenure. Mark Elvin asserts that manorialism and serfdom were key aspects of the Sung land system. These two labels seem to jar us with their novelty when placed in an explicitly non-feudal context. The institutions which these terms represent seem less odd and can be more easily accepted as normal parts of the Chinese economy during certain periods in Chou's treatment. Chou's treatment of manors and their tenants thus helps us place Elvin's view of these phenomena within a fully Chinese context.

Of the limited number of general economic histories of China available in English, only Mark Elvin's book is comparable in currentness, scope and detail of treatment to even this translation in précis of Chou's work. Though it is a highly controversial work, based largely on only one of the two main opposing schools of thought among Japanese students of key aspects of Chinese economic history[12] and has so far met with a mixed reception among economists and economic historians of China, Elvin's book is nevertheless an important addition, and indeed the only one in English since E. Stuart Kirby's 1954 work, to the literature in the field. In many respects, including its most controversial conceptual innovations, it represents a significant advance from Chou's work, and thus at least its main ideas ought to be available to readers of this translation, particularly undergraduates for whom this is their first sustained exposure to Chinese economic history. Hence I have appended a précis of the main line of Elvin's argument.[13] Particular attention ought to be paid to Elvin's view of the nature of Sung-Ming "manorialism" and "serfdom," the most controversial elements in his work, and his concept of a "high level equilibrium trap" which he asserts kept late Ming and Ch'ing China from breaking through to an industrial economy.

To complete the survey of the range of contemporary views of China's economic history, I have also appended a translation in précis of a Chinese work contemporary with Chou's and typifying an orthodox Chinese Marxist view of the course of economic history of the imperial era. To place this work within a larger framework, it should be noted that the currently orthodox Marxist view of ancient China's economic history makes Shang and Western Chou the Marxist Slave Society stage of development; the Spring-Autumn period of Eastern Chou considered the transition between Slave Society and Feudalism; the Warring States the first, fragmented stage of Feudalism; and Ch'in-Han the beginning of the two-millenia long epoch of Centralized Feudalism, within which "sprouts" of capitalism eventually appeared well before and independent of the intrusion of Western capitalism into Chinese economic life.

Detailed comparison of the views of Chou, Elvin, and Fu and Li is an exercise perhaps best left to the reader.

NOTES TO THE TRANSLATOR'S INTRODUCTION

1. Last spring saw the appearance of Mark Elvin's The Pattern of the Chinese Past (see Appendix A), the first book-length economic history of China in English since E. Stuart Kirby's Introduction to the Economic History of China in 1954. As will be argued below, however, Elvin's work reflects somewhat monolithically the point of view of only one school of Japanese historians of the Chinese economy and hence cannot be viewed as preempting the field.

   The few other extant English-language general economic histories of China were all either out-of-date or too limited in scope or concept to merit consideration as texts in such a course. Mabel Ping-hua Lee's The Economic History of China (New York: Columbia University Press, 1921) is out-of-date both factually and conceptually, giving little sense of China's continuing economic development after classical antiquity. Chi Chao-ting's Key Economic Areas in Chinese History (London: Allen and Unwin, 1936) was a fundamentally new contribution in its time and is still well worth reading but, given its focus on hydraulics as the determining factor in both economic and political change, it is a monograph rather than a general economic history. E. Stuart Kirby's book, cited in note 1, is, as its title avows, merely a bibliographic introduction to its subject rather than the general economic history he promised (p. 14) to eventually produce but which has never appeared.

2. Some sub-chapters have been compressed, some are rather closer to the length of the original. I have also compared my text with Professor Chou's own one-volume Chungkuo chingchi shih kang 中國經濟史綱 (Outline of Chinese Economic History) (Taipei: Huan-yu ch'upanshe, 1973).

3. Four paperbacked volumes, two volumes in hardback.

4. Cf. note 2 above.

5. In his preface to Chou's Chungkuo chingchi shih kang, Chang Kuo-wei 張果為 fairly summarizes the moral underlying Chou's narrative: One may judge the health of a society's economy by its results. "For the last thousand years or so the land of China has nourished an incomparably large population, and there has been a somewhat equal distribution of wealth. This demonstrates the talents and wisdom of the Chinese people" (p. 4).

6. Ludwig Von Mises, Human Action (New Haven: Yale University Press, 1949), 57.

7. Von Mises, 5, 6, 75-89.

8. Hsün Tzu aptly made this point: "When men acquire something, they never get only what they desire and nothing more; when men reject something, they never rid themselves only of what they have and nothing more." Burton Watson, tr., Basic Writings of Hsün Tzu (New York: Columbia University Press, 1963), 153.

9. The Chinese terms are chün 均 and ho 和 respectively. Yang Lien-sheng has argued that these two ideals underlie all legitimate traditional Chinese economic statecraft. Cf. his Excursions in Sinology (Cambridge: Harvard University Press, 1969), 231-233.

10. Cf. his Confucian China and Its Modern Fate. Vol. II: The Problems of Historical Significance (Berkeley: University of California Press, 1965).

11. Cf. Yang Lien-sheng, "The organization of Chinese official historiography," in W. C. Beasley and E. G. Pulleyblank, eds., Historians of China and Japan (London: Oxford University Press, 1961), 49, 51. One example of perhaps unconscious "appropriate concealment" practiced by Chou is his treatment of Wang An-shih's field survey and equal-tax law. In the section dealing with Wang's reforms, Wang is praised for spending only twelve years on the field survey as compared with eighteen years required for a similar cadastral survey in Napoleonic France, but only in the later section on Sung taxation is it mentioned that only half of the land had been in fact surveyed during those twelve years.

12. Cf. the discussion of these schools in Evelyn Sakakida Rawski, Agricultural Change and the Peasant Economy of South China (Cambridge: Harvard University Press, 1972), 240, n. 68.

13. Originally prepared for a panel on Elvin's work which I led at the Northwest Regional Seminar on China, held at the University of British Columbia on November 3-4, 1973. I should note that the consensus of the participants was considerably harsher toward Elvin than the judgment expressed here.

Section I

PREFACE

An Overview of China's Economic History

Subjective idealism, whether Chinese or European, boils down to spiritualism. Pre-Marxist materialism boils down to the reduction of man to a thing, as it fails to recognize that not only does the natural environment (sunspots, China as a continental rather than a seacoast-dominated geographic entity) act on man, but that man reacts on his environment too. The same is true of the school of social or economic materialism founded by Marx. At best, materialism provides the objective element in history; the spiritual element must remain history's motive force. Mind and matter must interact in history. In earliest times the material forces predominated in man's history, but the trend has been for the immaterial forces to grow in strength with time until now they can (as in the accomplishments of modern science) reshape the material forces themselves. Only the historical viewpoint of Sun Yat-sen's "People's Livelihood" adequately synthesizes the strong points of spiritualism and both varieties of materialism, making them inseparable facets of itself, the center of human history. It sees human progress as a spiritual process, but one inextricably linked to continuous improvement in material production.

According to Sun, mankind's search for its livelihood is the basis for social progress and is the center of history. Men first seek sustenance. Government arises to assure just distribution of scarce sustenance. With sustenance assured, culture can appear. Hence economics is the foundation for both government and culture and determines their nature. Marx erred in not noting that tools, though the basis for economics, are themselves the products of human volition in the search for the People's Livelihood. Hence only Sun's philosophy avoids the partiality of the other three views.

The Stages of Chinese Economic Development

All economic development rests on the interaction of natural, social, and technical factors. The natural factor, predominant in earlier epochs, steadily yields to human intervention. Environment determines a people's character. Social organization is linked to the political structure, which in turn affects the economy. Hence all economics is in some sense political economics. Technology is what has put men above the animals. Werner Sombart judges economic ideas, economic organization, and technology to be the three most important factors in studying economic history.

China is somewhat unusual for its physical isolation, not only from the rest of the world, but from some of its own frontier regions, like Sinkiang and Mongolia. Hence its economy, like other aspects of its culture, evolved in isolation. Its economic center has tended to shift south and east from the Wei River-Yellow River area to the Yangtze.

Exploitation of mineral deposits has not been important until the recent industrial age. Given a static technology, population has tended to vary in proportion to the dynastic cycle. Only technological progress offers hope of escape from this Malthusian trap.

Since ancient times the Chinese impulse has been to organize society in accord with what was viewed as the dictates of nature. Confucianism reenforced this. Confucius himself was misinterpreted by later generations. When he said righteousness was for the "gentleman" (chüntzu) and profit for the "mean fellow" (hsiaojen), he meant "ruler" and "common man," respectively, not "good" and "evil" man. Mencius' statement that producers must nourish rulers has been similarly distorted by later Confucians who have also formally discriminated against "secondary" merchants in favor of "primary" farmers. The Confucian motto was to use the past to transform the present, as in their perpetually unsuccessful advocacy of a return to the well-field system. Not until Chiang Kai-shek put Sun's land reform proposal into practice in 1952 was the two millenia old land question finally solved.

Chou feudalism was organized on the model of an enormously extended family. So too, with some differences, was the imperial system since Ch'in-Han times, though the trend was to centralize power in the hands of the emperor and his non-related personal servants, like the eunuchs. There has also been a tendency for the official class to become the greatest landed and commercial capitalists and to perpetuate their power through the various examination systems.

Chinese science, though now backward, was quite developed through the middle ages. Chinese thought was most fertile during the late Eastern Chou and Han whose writers also forged many works purporting to belong to high antiquity. Astronomy and medicine were founded then. Metallurgy, hydraulics, salt manufacture showed great progress in the epochs of the Warring States Ch'in and Han. T'ang saw mathematical advances, and Sung built much on them. In addition to obvious contributions to world culture like the compass and gunpowder, Han China exported silk cultivation, and Sung and Yüan contributed porcelain and movable-type printing.

Progress halted only in Ming and Ch'ing. Since then the scientific and industrial revolutions have come at the initiative of the West. Economic development is now a function of man's social initiative, and henceforth we must look to man's efforts as the key to future progress.

There are various ways to periodize Chinese economic history. One is to start with high antiquity (everything up to Spring-Autumn), move to middle antiquity (Spring-Autumn to the coming of the West in the nineteenth century)and conclude with modern times (since mid-nineteenth century). Another method is: prehistoric to Hsia (founding period); Shang-Western Chou (feudal monarchy); Spring-Autumn and Warring States (monarchical period); Han-Ch'ing (imperial period).

This book treats the prehistoric through Hsia as the mythical period; Shang-Western Chou as the founding period of the Chinese economy; Spring-Autumn and Warring States as the metamorphosis of the economy; Ch'in-Han up to Wang Mang as the period of its flourishing; Eastern Han, Chin, Northern and Southern Dynasties as the age of troubles of the economy; Sui, T'ang, and Five Dynasties as the period of reestablishment of the economy; Sung as the period of the economy's renewal; Liao, Chin, and Yüan as the period of the economy's destitution; Ming as the period of the economy's revival; Ch'ing as the period of the modern economy's fermentation.

An Outline of the Evolution of the Chinese Economy

The Chinese people have been welded together from diverse local groups over the past five thousand years but largely by peaceful means rather than conquest. Though nomads have had to be fought off in the north since Ch'in-Han, there has been steady absorption of agricultural peoples to the south, and these southerners have become fully integrated with the Chinese people. Nomad invaders of the north have also been assimilated.

Internal migration from north to south China usually proceeded gradually and for economic reasons to take advantage of favorable conditions for agriculture in the south. External migration to the northern frontiers was usually artifically induced by government policy, and such emigrants were on the front lines of the millenia-long process of assimilating nomadic peoples, as, for example, the three centuries of struggle with the Hsiungnu in Ch'in-Han times. But by the time the Hsiungnu were driven off, Han was too weak to repopulate the northern frontier and thereafter until Sui-T'ang, successive waves of nomads engulfed much of northernmost China.

The T'ang reunification was based on an agriculturist-nomad alliance. T'ang soon broke with and defeated its Eastern Turkic allies and, like Han, filled empty areas in the north with farmers. T'ang weakness after the An Lu-shan Rebellion allowed the Khitan to enter the north like the Turks and others before them. The Khitan, like the Jurched after them, were soon sinicized, even though they conquered much of north China.

The trend toward greater scope of barbarian conquests, which began in 755, was not reversed until the founding of Ming in 1368. The Mongols were expelled before they had been much sinicized. This allowed them to remain nomads confronting China from their original homeland right through the Ming period. Subsequently the Manchus were able to take advantage of late Ming decadence to conquer China, obliging the Chinese agriculturists to devote two centuries of time and blood to absorbing them. This absorption, however, was eventually all but complete; only a few thousand now remain who call themselves Manchus. The great size and long tenure of the Ch'ing finished the job of politically absorbing frontier peoples. Most remained culturally unassimilated. The long peace and consequent great growth in population during Ch'ing removed the necessity for official pressure to induce migration; natural forces now made people move.

It has taken five thousand years since the Yellow Emperor founded our civilization, but in blood and culture all nomads have now been absorbed into our agricultural people.*

As Chiang Kai-shek has written in Chungkuo chihmingyün (CHINA'S DESTINY), after the Three Kingdoms period China's

---

*This formula which ignores the existence of nomadic and sedentary non-Chinese within China and which furthermore asserts, contrary to common knowledge, that "all nomads" (what about sedentary non-Chinese?) have lost their identity within the Chinese majority is typical of but not unique to the Kuomintang world view. (EHK)

economic center moved from the Yellow River to the south and east. The closure of Central Asia after the fall of the Yüan ruined the cities of the west, and the coming of the Europeans eventually raised the power of the cities of the east. Until the Republic, the tendency was for the wealth of the southeast to nourish the soldiers of the northwest. Now all parts of the country patriotically support the entire nation.

The earliest period saw the basic techniques (stone, then copper tools, animal domestication, sericulture, agriculture, finally building of palaces and walled cities) established. The founding period (Shang-Western Chou) began with the natural economy of feudalism, evolved to the beginning of the use of iron tools, saw the evolution of the first monetary systems and the beginnings of monarchical methods of government. The age of metamorphosis (Spring-Autumn and Warring States) was characterized by intellectual freedom, political conflict, the influence on all aspects of economic life of extensive use of iron tools, replacement of the well-field system by private property in land, hydraulic works, rise of commerce, commercial urbanism and increased use of money.

In the flourishing epoch (Ch'in-Han), the first stages of a national economy appeared once feudalism had been more fully transcended by the Ch'in-Han imperial system. Constant warfare during the age of troubles (late Han through Northern and Southern Dynasties) retarded the economy. North Chinese agriculture weakened; the money system was thrown into disorder. The barbarian invasions of the north shifted the economic center to the south, while economic influence gradually sinified the northern barbarians. The Equal Fields systems and shifts in forms of private ownership which appeared during this period were to have varying consequences for the future.

The age of reestablishment (Sui, T'ang, and Five Dynasties) saw a broadening of the economy as compared to that of Ch'in-Han. Population increased, cities grew bigger, hydraulic projects were of wider scope, new handicraft industries appeared (e.g., cotton weaving), coal came into use as did new metallurgical techniques. There was increased use of porcelain, tea, and sugar to improve the everyday standard of living. Fiscal resources increased. Printing developed, increasing the reach of the national culture. The Grand Canal united north with south. Seaborne commerce with India, Arabia, Annam, Korea and Southeast Asia became important as it had never before been. The tea and salt trades were tied to the government's fiscal system. Ever-normal granaries were established. The An Lu-shan Rebellion was only a temporary setback midway through this period.

The age of renewal (Sung) saw difficulties in the north, but under Sung seaborne trade was encouraged to make up for this. Navigation by the stars, sun, and compass came into use. Gunpowder played a role in the Sung-Chin wars. Movable type printing appeared. Wang An-shih's policies affected the economy to no small extent. It is one of the great tragedies of Chinese economic history that the innovations of this period did not bear consequences similar to those of modern Europe's economy.

The fiscal policies of the Mongols had grave effects on the economy of the age of destitution, but technological innovations continued, especially in methods of warfare (the cannon), paper money was broadly used, and overseas and overland commerce with the outside world continued to develop.

The age of revival (Ming) saw the return of Chinese control over the economy and the end of the previous era's state management of the economy. That taxes were now paid in cash and salaries to aristocrats were no longer paid in land, shows the growth of the money economy. Overseas trade continued to develop.

The age of fermentation (Ch'ing) made little contribution to the economy. But for the Manchu conquest the Chinese economy might have continued to grow. In the West, the age of the industrial and democratic revolutions eventually tied the whole world together, but the Western pioneers retained their initial advantage while the Manchus stagnated until loss of the Opium War in 1842 began to rouse the Chinese people to catch up.

Section II

THE MYTHICAL PERIOD: FROM THE PREHISTORIC TO THE HSIA

Outline

Details of the history of the 2,000 years from the Yellow Emperor to the founding of Hsia are obscure, but this period set the stage for the later feudal order. Material life was characterized by hunting, fishing, herding and the use of stone tools. Economic organization was based on family ties. The division of labor had begun and warfare occurred, but the economy was localistic and elaborate government had not yet appeared. Various animals, like the elephant, now restricted to the south, were then common in north China.

Evidence for Economic History from Mythical Accounts

Evidence is derived from excavated artifacts (usually fragmented) and from literary sources (often recorded in distorted form much later). Stone tools found in association with Peking Man (ca. 400,000-500,000 B.C.) and elsewhere in northwest China indicate that Paleolithic life was very primitive. Though the use of fire was known, early man's life appears to have been barely distinguishable from that of the animals. Neolithic stone tools are found widely in China. Pottery appeared. The site of Yangshao, in Kansu, yields the most notable artifacts. The earliest Neolithic remains apparently date ca. 5,500 years ago, a few hundred years before the Yellow Emperor.

Literary sources permit little to be said about political organization. Even in Confucius' time little was known of the mythical period. Many border peoples of later times claim descent from one or another of the tribes mentioned in literary accounts of mythical times. This shows that despite differences in ways of life, all the peoples of modern China are blood relatives. The China of mythical times constituted present-day Shensi, Shansi, Honan, southern Hopei, eastern Kansu, and northern Anhui.

Society and Economy

Society was organized collectively along clan lines and economic life revolved around nomadic gathering, fishing and hunting, especially in the hilly and wooded west. To the east, in the central plain, a more settled agricultural existence was possible on the fertile loess soil. Literary accounts permit only a vague general account of the life of these times, as in the various later accounts of culture heroes like Shen Nung, who was said to have invented agriculture to make up for the growing scarcity of wild animals.

In the process of inventing material culture, culture in general was evolved, thereby distinguishing man from the animals. Agriculture not only produced a larger and more stable population but reverence for the ancestors who pioneered this more profitable way of life was also engendered, and this characteristically Chinese trait further distinguished our ancestors from the surrounding peoples.

Bronze appeared early. Tradition ascribes it to the Yellow Emperor. This is probably too early, but bronze had likely appeared by Hsia times. Some unadorned bronzes excavated in Kansu (traditionally the Hsia homeland) may be of Hsia origin. Tradition holds that Yü, Hsia's founder, had nine bronze tripods cast.

Commerce, Science and Technology

Tradition ascribes the first markets to Shen Nung, and establishment of weights and measures to the Yellow Emperor. Yao is said to have regulated the division of labor and consequent barter among practitioners of the trades. Salt was easily manufactured along the east coast and would have been ideal as an object of trade. The calendar was said to have appeared by the Yellow Emperor's time. Writing, already well developed by Shang times, must have appeared earlier.

Section III

THE FOUNDING PERIOD: YIN-SHANG AND WESTERN CHOU

Outline

The thousand years of Shang and Western Chou constitute the founding period of Chinese economic history. The feudal economic institutions then established were influential long after.

Feudal Polity and Economy

Shang's economic influence much exceeded its political reach (centering in northern Honan), covering much of the area of modern China. Western Chou more or less controlled politically much of North China. Traditional sources estimate its population at 13,700,000. Though its political capital was in the Sian area west of the great bend of the Yellow River, Western Chou's cultural and economic capital was in the Loyang area, amidst the fertile loess plain. Under Chou feudalism, Shansi concentrated on agriculture. Hopei and Shensi, dominated by non-feudalized barbarians, saw development of commerce.

Pre-Shang feudalism was more an ethical-political bond among local leaders than an economic institution. Shang's feudalism, based on conquest, was (according to the literary sources) a centrally directed militarized hierarchy. It served as the model for the later more extensive Chou conquest-feudalism. Western Chou had a systematic hierarchy of fief and sub-fief holders. Each lord's land was divided into his personal land and that parcelled out as sub-fiefs. The whole system was organized as a complex family, each lord owing allegiance, tribute and service to the king as the family's head. The king was to periodically check up on the lords and punish them for various offenses. In Chinese feudalism, the king had more power than in the later European variety.

Shang's initial clan-based society evolved toward a private-property-holding family system, especially after P'an-keng's reign (tr. 1403-1373 B.C.). This was because of the greater complexities introduced into the system of property distribution by the increase of wealth.

The Land System and Agricultural Labor

Before P'an-keng's reign there were frequent shifts of the capital because agriculture was still not fully evolved and was still somewhat mixed with pastoralism. Late Shang had a more purely agricultural economy. Because of the ubiquity of omen-casting, the priestshaman's power in some ways was greater than the king's. Priests were the chief repositories of knowledge, and their position the most conspicuous example of the beginning of the complex division of labor characteristic of a high civilization's economy.

During Western Chou the status of agricultural labor was somewhere between that of tenants and slaves. The class struggle between them and the lords which Marxists postulate was somewhat mitigated by ethical norms limiting the degree of their exploitation. The only full slaves were prisoners of war, criminals, certain palace servants, artisans (who held a special position as valuable "property") and certain officials (e.g., minor aristocrats undergoing punishment by being enslaved to particular official roles). But slaves were of minor economic importance.

Though aristocrats did not directly participate in production, they supported it through government, war and religion. The values embodied in these activities, later to be systematized by the Confucians, were the prerequisites for a settled high civilization.

There seems to have actually been a well-field system, but it must have varied considerably by area and time as agriculture progressed, even though the original name for the system was retained. The classics affirm that the original well-field system operated to assure economic justice for the cultivators. Some modern scholars, like Hu Shih, assert that the well-field system was simply an invention after the fact by utopian Confucians. Others, like Hu Han-min, assert that it was in general use during Western Chou. It is most likely that even originally only some of the land was divided to resemble the character for "well" (井 ching), with a commonly-cultivated public field in the middle. Some arrangements lacked the public field. Others simply divided the land according to the logic of irrigation channels.

Han dynasty Confucians' detailed descriptions of the system as the basis for an elaborate social security network are merely exercises in imagination designed to protest against the unsatisfactory systems of tenancy of their own time. Sung and Ming writers of various political persuasions made similar use of the well-field system as a utopian ideal. As such, the concept of the well-field has remained an imperishable part of Chinese economic thought.

Given the fact that oxen were extensively used in sacrifices, Shang probably did not make frequent use of them as agricultural draft animals. Early Shang agriculture was likely based on the use of fire to clear land. Irrigation techniques were probably lacking. Hence, until P'an-keng's time, cultivated lands had to be frequently shifted, as their fertility was quickly exhausted. In Shang times most peasants were still organized within a clan framework. Some captured agricultural peoples may have had a servile status vis-à-vis their conquerors, but probably retained their clan organizational base among themselves. The large numbers of animal sacrifices and oracle records of large-scale hunts show that pastoralism and hunting were still important parts of the Shang economy.

That Western Chou was more exclusively agricultural is shown by surviving documents outlining their ceremonials which followed the seasonal rhythms of agriculture. Specific officials, according to works like the Chou Li, were assigned to supervise specific aspects of agriculture.

In Western Chou times man's domination over nature was more intensive than earlier. More use was made of the loess plain of the middle Yellow River valley which is exceptionally fertile when assured a reliable water supply. Hence, despite its successes, Western Chou agriculture was more vulnerable to drought, as frequent references in the Odes affirm. Initially, Western Chou's impulse was to respond to such disasters by blaming them on human sins and to pray for relief. Eventually, other methods were added to this; it became the ideal goal to attain one year's surplus out of three years' production. Irrigation began to be introduced. It is possible that bronze agricultural tools began to be used, but there were still no draft animals. Insect plagues were met by lighting fires at night, a method still used in north China.

In general, according to such sources as Kuan Tzu, agricultural labor discipline was much tighter than earlier. Common cultivated crops were various kinds of millet, rice, wheat, beans and hemp. Sericulture was highly developed. Herding, fishing and hunting were in decline. Judging from references in the Odes, the peasants' life, though harder than the lords', was still relatively free. Even when taxes in kind were blurred into the traditional labor dues, a portion of the harvest remained with the cultivator, thereby distinquishing him from a slave.

Division of Labor and Scientific Techniques

Division of labor only began to grow fixed in Shang-Chou times. Feudalism tended to make various callings hereditary. Government used and hence supervised a variety of artisans.

According to literary sources, mathematics was one of the subjects in an aristocrat's education in Western Chou times. A mathematical treatise attributed to the Duke of Chou (but probably no earlier than the Warring States), uses an approximate value (three) for pi in calculating a circle's circumference. Iron, of revolutionary import in all phases of life, was (as in other civilizations) a logical outgrowth of the higher stages of bronze technology. There are casual indirect references to iron (implying that it was already common) in the Odes and Tso Chuan, hence it must have appeared during Western Chou.

Eastern Chou recognized seven distinct alloys of bronze, each used for different purposes. Shang and Chou both had carved jade.

The invention of wine is traditionally ascribed to the chief minister of the Hsia's founder. Wine became more common later as the development of agriculture yielded more abundant raw materials for its manufacture. Wine vessels are the most common surviving Shang bronzes. The Shang is traditionally said to have been deposed because of the last emperor's excessive drunkenness. By Chou times many varieties of wine (all grain based) are listed in surviving sources.

Shang was capable of constructing large palaces in cities with an area of ten square li. By Eastern Chou large buildings were found even in the capital cities of local states. Weaving and pottery were well developed by Shang times. Western Chou introduced bricks and tiles for building.

Commerce and Communications

Contrary to popular etymology, the dynasty name Shang 商 is not the source of the word merchant (商 shang), even though the characters are the same. The potential for international trade was, however, present by Shang, given its connections with surrounding peoples. Shang used cowrie shells for money and later carved stone, bone cowries and cast bronze cowries were used to supplement the money supply.

According to the traditional sources, Western Chou had strictly regulated markets under constant official supervision to keep prices honest and quality high. This ethical bent is ascribed to the Duke of Chou's influence. Money was still relatively scarce in what was still a largely natural economy. Cowrie shells continued to be used as money. By at least 524 B.C. cast metal money is reliably reported to have been in existence but not in significant amounts.

Even traditional accounts seem to limit pre-Shang Chinese culture to just southeastern Shansi and northwestern Honan, an area 500 to 600 _li_ from west to east and 300 to 400 _li_ from north to south. Shang's territory was somewhat broader. Its founder was said to have moved some 1,000 _li_ from the east to defeat Hsia. Shang's cowrie shell money came from the coast.

Western Chou's territory was wider still. The Chou conquests extended to the east coast, though not much farther to the north and south than Shang's territory. There were quite a few military campaigns through this territory thereafter and even in peacetime many hunting expeditions and royal progresses through the realm.

There was also regular trade with allied states. Legends exist describing a visit by the ruler of Yüeh in the south to the Duke of Chou and later a visit by King Mu (1001-946) to the "Queen Mother of the West" in Persia. Trade is said to have had a part in the latter expedition. There may after all be something to these stories, though they are unverified by other authorities.

One motive for building the eastern capital near Loyang was to establish a center of political control at a center of communications. The _Odes_ describes Chou's roads as being arrow-straight. There may have been post stations established along them. Chou made more extensive use of chariots than Shang. There were road and war chariots as well as goods carts used by the common people. Road chariots were highly ornamented, much more so than Shang's. The sedan chair was also used. Chou boats were larger than Shang's and a new use was found for them by joining them together to make floating bridges.

Taxation and Fiscal Institutions

According to traditional sources, Shang also used the well-field system, with the produce of the public field, amounting to one-ninth, being given to the government. In addition, a "tribute" in kind of various special products was also levied.

Western Chou's system had five taxes placed on the lands within the king's own territories, with local lords having analogous arrangements:

(1) The field tax was apparently an adaptation of the Shang public field tax to meet a situation where the public field itself no longer actually existed. It was supposed to total 10%. It was linked to a labor tax. There was also a market tax and miscellaneous taxes on non-agricultural activities. All of these were apparently subsumed under the category of field tax. Unlike the Shang system, an attempt was made to collect a nearly constant amount each year, rather than a fixed percentage of a year's production (which was impractical with the disappearance of the public field). Local officials were supposed to strike an average of several years' yield as the base for a constant tax.

(2) Labor service tax. This continued to be levied until Sung. In Chou times this was supposed to be three days per year in good years, less in bad crop years (one man from each family to serve). Except for aristocrats, all able-bodied men were liable from age twenty to sixty (fifteen to sixty-five in rural areas). Not very burdensome in Chou times, it became so when commuted to a capitation tax in Han times and thereafter.

(3) The pass (or gate) and market taxes were levied on merchants. The former varied in rate in different areas. It was a type of transit tax on goods. According to Mencius, the market tax began as a way to finance government supervision of mercantile activities in the market so as to prevent conspiracies in restraint of trade. Market stalls rather than goods were taxed. In addition,

the government's fiscal needs were also served.

(4) The military tax was in addition to the others and was levied at all levels of the feudal hierarchy in chariots, supplies and men. The size of the levy varied by time, locality, and size of state. There were exemptions based on age, size of family, number of dependents, etc. The garrison fields system of later eras descended from this system.

(5) Fines. These were assessed for breaking various rules, e.g., for leaving fields uncultivated, for not sticking to one's hereditarily assigned task, or for failure to pay any of the above taxes.

Tradition ascribes direct supervision of agriculture and trade to specific categories of officials as far back as Hsia. The Chou Li gives detailed lists of central and local officials of this type, including supervisors of currency, tax collectors, etc. Perhaps the most important of these was the ssu-k'ung 司空 , a jack-of-all-trades local official in charge of public works (waterways, roads), whose existence is certified for Eastern Chou by contemporary accounts. The central bureaucracy supervised the collection and storage of tax commodities, and had a corps of accountants to keep track of income and outgo.

Section IV

THE AGE OF METAMORPHOSIS: SPRING-AUTUMN AND WARRING STATES

Outline

Politically this era witnessed the transition from monarchical to imperial organization; economically from feudal to national forms; socially, intensified dominance of Chinese over barbarian culture.

Economic Thought

Economic thought flourished as in no other era, influenced by and influencing economic reality. The Confucians advocated the limitation of desires and hence demand but also called for measures to fulfill legitimate demand. The state should also limit itself, making sure thereby that the people would have enough. No ascetic despising "profit," Confucius (K'ung Tzu) simply subordinated it to the drive for sagehood, at least for the ruling class. Commoners had to seek profit to earn their living. The Sung Neo-Confucians misunderstood this distinction and thereby hindered the further development of economic thought. Nor did Confucius despise merchants, numbering several among his disciples. Denigration of merchants dates only from Han.

Fig. 1 Confucius (Ming illustration)

Confucius argued that the state's wealth was based on assuring wealth for the people. Hence taxes should be low, equitable, and remitted in bad years. Not only should taxes be equitable, but wealth should be equally distributed. This has remained a constant ideal of Chinese economic thought ever since.

According to Confucius' disciple, Tseng Tzu, labor applied to land in accord with each piece of land's nature will yield sufficient wealth for a man to support his parents, if all concerned also practice frugality. This, he judged, was the common man's version of filiality. The early Confucians, like most of their contemporaries (except for the Taoists), affirmed the dignity of labor and hence the basic equality of all the divisions of society. It was only after Han that manual labor was no longer viewed as having dignity.

Fig. 2 Mencius (Ming illustration)

Meng Tzu's (Mencius') economic ideas were more extreme than Confucius' because of the more critical situation of his generation. It was now more necessary than ever to enrich the people so that the state might survive. To do this, merchants should be encouraged, and only conspiracies in restraint of trade should be punished by the state. Contrary to his later reputation, Mencius was actually a strict free-trader. In refuting the agrarian collectivist Hsü Tzu (Hsü Hsing) he also worked out the inner logic of the principle of division of labor. In saying that the ruler is fed by the farmer and the farmer ruled by the ruler he was illustrating this principle and not (as later commentators make it) setting the ruler in a position morally superior to the farmer.

Hsün Tzu's economic ideas differed somewhat from Mencius'. He emphasized that human desires are innate, are not moral and are insatiable. Strife is caused by the fact that goods are scarce and desires many. Strife leads to disorder and poverty. Desires must be tamed and limited by ritual (li) to avoid this. Hence rulers and commoners both seek profit but by different and equally natural routes. It is appropriate for rulers to let commoners follow the division of labor. If farming and trade are encouraged, both state and people will be enriched.

Taoist economic thought was entirely negative, an unqualified laissez-faire based on the doctrine of wu-wei, as opposed to the Confucians' qualified laissez-faire which allowed government intervention to assure popular welfare. Lao Tzu and Chuang Tzu advocated extinction of desire; Yang Chu yielded it free reign. Lao Tzu looked back to the simple societies of extreme antiquity as his ideal. Consequently his and Chuang Tzu's influence has been a negative one, retarding economic growth, as has been Lieh Tzu's fatalism and antipathy to the man-made.

The Mohists resembled the Confucians in their ethical bent their emphasis on economic equality and the division of labor. They differed from the Confucians in their statism and extreme utilitarianism.

Kuan Tzu was the first Legalist and also an economist of great historical influence. A commoner, he spent his youth in trade. As chief minister of Ch'i his policy was to achieve wealth and power (fu ch'iang) for his state. Confucius approved of him.

Kuan Tzu disapproved of taxation because it weakened the wealth of the people and caused them to dislike government. Instead he favored a national monopoly on sale of salt, iron, forest products and ores to meet governmental expenses. In the case of

Fig. 3 Kuan Tzu (Ming illustration.

salt he could take advantage of Ch'i's control of the coastal salt pans to exact monopoly profits from its sale in foreign as well as domestic trade. Since even housewives and farmers had to have a certain amount of iron, a government monopoly on iron and other ores was bound to be profitable, even though its processing and manufacture was left in private hands to disguise the state's monopoly profit and hence obviate popular resentment.

The state should also, according to Kuan Tzu, monopolize the trade in grain whose price would be kept steady by judicious buying and selling by the government. Its profits from this trade would allow lower taxes and also control the prices of other goods which bear an inverse relationship to the price of grain. In addition, the quantity of money in circulation ought to be kept in proportion to the amount of goods for sale so as to keep prices stable.

The mass of the people must be left no alternative to agriculture which is the ultimate basis of the state's wealth and power. Trade is the other pillar of the state's power. If a state attracts the world's merchants, it can control the world's politics. The sumptuary regulations Kuan Tzu had Ch'i establish were not to denigrate merchants (as was the motive of Han and Ming) but to avoid jealousy among the different classes.

The object of foreign trade was to amass cash by exporting goods in short supply elsewhere, in Ch'i's case salt and iron.

Profit from trade could be used to buy abroad goods which are in short supply at home and thereby attract more people to the state by making life there more comfortable. Foreign trade could also be used to trick other states into activities unprofitable to them and their subsequent poverty used to attract their people to one's own state. This was to use knowledge of the laws of supply and demand to achieve political profit. By artificially jacking up prices of grain, all the surplus grain from smaller nearby states could be drawn into Ch'i, thereby causing famine in these countries even in good crop years. Later reformers made profitable use of Kuan Tzu's economic principles, though most later thinkers were blinded to his insights by their own prejudices against commerce.

Li K'uei (470-380 B.C.) was a Wei civil official noted for his economic ideas. He is said to have greatly increased agricultural productivity by discouraging exports and by keeping prices level through government granaries' buying and selling countercyclically according to elaborate calculations of average consumption patterns. He greatly influenced Shang Yang who was born in Wei while Li's methods were in use.

Applied in Ch'in, Shang Yang's methods made it the most powerful of the Warring States. These methods involved encouragement of agriculture by establishing private property in farmland, proportioning taxes to productivity, encouraging migrants from abroad to open new land, and keeping merchants' activities under strict controls so that they could not exploit farmers.

Han Fei had little to say on economics. As a student of Hsün Tzu, he believed that human nature was evil and primarily sought profit and hence he emphasized legal controls over this instinct.

The agrarians, like Hsü Hsing and his disciple Ch'en Hsiang, celebrated the virtue of simple agricultural labor for aristocrat as well as commoner. They would declare all goods of equal value in their homogeneous collective agrarian society. Mencius, their contemporary, criticized them for not recognizing the reality that different goods do in fact have varying values and hence prices. No complicated civilization could avoid chaos in applying their theories. Nevertheless, their emphasis on the dignity of labor was wholesome and it is regrettable they have historically had so little influence.

Yen Tzu of Ch'i, a contemporary of Confucius and representative of the political school, shared his emphasis on ethical controls over the state's economic activities but put even more emphasis on frugality.

Merchants made a great contribution to ancient economic thought, though little of their work has been preserved, except in the economics section of Ssu-ma Ch'ien's history.

Chi Jan lived slightly later than Confucius. He held that wealth was the basis of a state's military and hence political power. Famine should be anticipated and provided against. He foreshadowed modern Western theories of long-range economic cycles with his assertion that famine could be expected every twelfth year. Hence government intervention in the grain market could keep prices from wild fluctuations. Both government and private merchants should sell goods when prices are high and buy them when prices are low. This, he argued, would stabilize prices and maximize the wealth of both government and merchants.

Po Kuei believed in applying the strategic insights of Shang Yang and Sun Wu to business. In a good harvest year grain prices will be low, Po reasoned, but because of high purchasing power goods prices will be high. Hence the good businessman will buy grain and sell goods. He should do the reverse in bad crop years.

The Economy's Metamorphosis

By this time Western Chou's extended family style of political organization had broken down, just as ordinary extended families tend to fragment after the passage of three or four generations. The most successful states now picked advisers for their talent, not their family connections. By Warring States times centrally controlled regional governments began to replace fiefs and sub-fiefs. The 1,700-odd more or less equal fiefs of Western Chou were consolidated into less than a hundred states, with most of the power, economic as well as political, concentrated among some ten of these.

These consolidations also assimilated most of the barbarians within metropolitan China. The nine "provinces" into which most ancient documents divide metropolitan China (all of modern China except Mongolia, the far southwest and Kwangtung-Kwangsi) were not political units but natural economic units with a wide range of climate, terrain and resources. It was this wider China which was now sinified and was to come under centralized imperial rule by the end of the Warring States period.

The Land System and Agricultural Economy

In Spring-Autumn times land was still the most important repository of wealth and measure of political power. As the land had become concentrated in the hands of a few great states, it could only be managed by dividing it into sub-fiefs whose rulers could directly supervise and collect taxes from it. This sub-fief aristocracy came to hold effective sovereignty over the land, and to the peasants remained only usufruct over the land. Without power over the land the people could not be trusted to take interest in cultivating the public fields and hence the well-field system disappeared.

We may view Spring-Autumn's land system as a transitional one between the well-field system of Shang-Western Chou and the Warring States' free private land system. Population increase was pressing against the available supply of land. More sophisticated technology required greater expertise by farmers. The rise of manufacture and trade lowered the status of agriculture and allowed commercial wealth to gain control of land. Hence the trend was toward private property in land. Politically induced mass movement of peasants from place to place broke old customs. The shift from taxes in labor to taxes on land also encouraged private property in land.

This was happening to some degree everywhere and not just in Ch'in where Shang Yang's reforms explicitly called for private property in land. Reformers like Kuan Tzu claimed that private property in land was necessary to assure popular prosperity and hence the popular obedience which was in turn the basis for a state's political and military power.

Though most agricultural techniques in Spring-Autumn times did not much differ from those of Western Chou, the seeds of the much greater changes of Warring States times were present. Iron was beginning to be used, and by the late Warring States era iron plows enabling deep plowing were common. It is not known, however, if they were drawn by animal or man power.

Large scale artificial hydraulic works also became common and were used to avoid both drought and flood. Canals hundreds of miles long connected important rivers and opened much new land to agriculture. Large dikes, built and maintained by farmers under government direction, helped lessen flood dangers.

Human and animal manure was extensively used for fertilizer by Warring States times. The use of different crops on different soils was also understood as was the correct time to plant various crops.

During times of scarcity, grain was lent to the peasants from the granaries of the rulers and aristocrats. Kuan Tzu advocated keeping up prices of grain to keep the peasants from being victimized by merchants and hence assure a strong agriculture. He also advocated strict controls by the government over those who lent to farmers at interest. Kuan Tzu wanted the government to keep track of agriculture at all stages of production so that it could make sure taxes were being paid honestly, have a quantitative basis for estimating relief needs in bad times and could make sure rapacious merchants were not monopolizing the grain supply, a danger to the state should war break out. Kuan Tzu also wanted the government to maintain its own granaries for lending grain to the peasants before harvests were in. These granaries were to buy in the market counter-cyclically so as to maintain steady average prices.

Science and Technology

Pebbles and fingers were used for simple calculations in the earliest times. By Spring-Autumn times all of the simple arithmetical operations could be performed. The casting of the milfoil stalks is an early example of practical arithmetic. Later, bundles of sticks were used, with the sticks laid out to represent the place values in a decimal system, and zero was represented by the absence of a stick.

Military needs stimulated leather making for armor, the development of metallurgy and the design of machinery. Specialization increased the number and precision of the tools in various crafts. By Warring States times workmen were no longer solely dependent on their home states for employment, and this served to greatly stimulate invention.

The coastal areas of Ch'i, Wu and Yen produced enormous amounts of salt. Prospecting for mineral deposits on the basis of the surface soil's nature became a highly developed art. Servile labor was often used in the mines. There were a wide variety of iron and bronze implements. This indicates the existence of a great demand for metals. Large labor forces were involved in smelting, and many private fortunes were made. Dyeing and weaving were also increased in importance by the growth in population. Ch'i earned great profits from its cloth exports.

Commerce and Money

Commerce flourished as the feudal system decayed. In Spring-Autumn times commerce had not yet much penetrated into the villages but concentrated on supplying luxuries for the aristocracy. There were regular markets in the cities and interstate trade took place but largely on a barter basis, though some metal money was in use. Official salaries and taxes were usually paid in grain and cloth.

By Warring States times the use of money became much more prevalent, but even then and for some time thereafter grain was often used to pay official salaries. During the Warring States era lending at high interest was prevalent in urban as well as rural areas and even the state engaged in it. The search for wealth became ubiquitous, and writers like Ssu-ma Ch'ien asserted that the lust for wealth was part of human nature, though he and other moralists deplored this and eventually forced the lust for wealth out of reputable men's overt ambitions.

Ch'i had the most developed commerce of the Warring States era, and this was based on its earlier preeminence in trade. Naturally well endowed with resources and having a large population, it also had benefitted from Kuan Tzu's reforms. Agriculture, weaving, and salt manufacture were its chief activities and the basis for its commerce. Ch'i merchants were numerous and rich enough by Kuan Tzu's time to rival the state in power.

In Ch'u, in addition to agriculture, metal mining was well developed, especially of gold. Ch'u was also famous for its iron swords. Its commerce was based on its gold, iron, copper and tin ores. Commerce in Eastern Ch'u (formerly Wu) became well developed, based on salt and copper. Western Ch'u was well placed to serve as a transit area for commerce. Southern Ch'u's commerce in hides, wood, pearls, and other commodities was funneled up to the middle Yangtze commercial centers of Shouch'un and Hofei in modern Anhui province.

Ch'in originally had a purely agrarian and herding economy which served as the base for its commerce. Its extensive and naturally well defended territory had easy riverine communications with the states to its east and with the barbarians on its other sides. Hence it enjoyed a great transshipment trade in all directions. Though Shang Yang's reforms had placed commerce secondary to agriculture, his third-century B.C. successor, Lü Pu-wei, was himself a rich merchant who encouraged trade and under whose auspices was put together one of the most useful practical compendia of the era. The First Emperor later deposed Lü, lumped merchants with criminals and exiled both to the frontiers.

Small, crowded, and with few natural resources, the state of Lu nevertheless had an extensive commerce based on cottage industry, especially weaving. This was even truer of the Eastern Chou territory centered around Loyang, the greatest commercial center.

The economy of Yen and Chao was centered around agriculture and salt manufacture. Yen traded with Ch'i to the south and with the barbarians of Liaotung to the north. Teng could trade with Ch'i to the east, Chou to the west and Ch'u to the south. Its merchants operated all over metropolitan China.

Commerce remained less important quantitatively than agriculture during Warring States times, but in certain places, as in Ch'i, it was of considerable magnitude.

Although metal money was present in Western Chou, only in Spring-Autumn and later times did a three-tier money system become elaborated. The most valuable objects were precious stones and jade. The next tier was formed of uncoined gold. Rare in Western Chou, it became more common in Spring-Autumn times and was plentiful enough to be used as the accounting unit in interstate trade by the Warring States era. The most numerous money was cast in bronze, most often in the shape of a knife, though other shapes were used in different states at various times. Eventually,

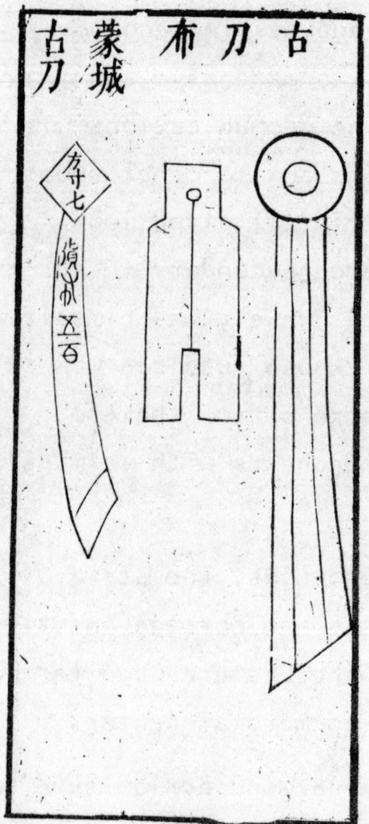

Fig. 4 Warring States Money

pierced round bronze coins became most common, and strung together they remained the dominant small coin all through the succeeding imperial era.

Credit appears along with trade and usually predates money, but it receives its full development only when trade and money are flourishing. The earliest references to credit involved the lending of grain by both state and private creditors. By Warring States there is evidence of credit for both consumption and capital uses.

Communications

The states of Eastern Chou times, though spanning two great river valleys, enjoyed increasingly regular communications. By Warring States times even the states of the Yangtze valley were in ever closer touch with the states to the north. Frontiers with the barbarians to the north and south were pushed out to virtually the points held during most of the succeeding imperial era.

According to the Chou Li, roads and bridges were supposed to be maintained by the officials and trees were to be planted by their sides. The people were supposed to maintain rest houses at intervals along them. With some exceptions these regulations were observed during this time. Armies required supply routes to remain in the field for any length of time. The Golden Ox Road (chin niu tao) between Shensi and Szechwan was built by Ch'in as part of its conquest of Shu. It is said but not proven to have been a covered road, a new type of road with a kind of wooden roof over it for protection against landslides and erosion in mountain country.

Privately operated hotels appeared by Warring States times for the convenience of traveling merchants. Postal rest houses for official couriers (on foot, riding chariots or later on horseback) existed and by Warring States times accommodated travelers as well. There were several canals big enough to carry boats and hence to serve transportation needs in several places along both major river valleys. They were also used for irrigation.

Horseback riding was the most significant improvement in transportation methods. According to Han Fei, it was present in Spring-Autumn times. By Warring States times the adoption of barbarian costume greatly increased the efficacy of cavalry which became numerous, much reducing the importance of war chariots. But civilian wheeled traffic became much denser. Grain was being shipped by boat from Ch'in to Chin. During the Warring States era, on one occasion Ch'in sent large boats down the Yangtze from Szechwan, each carrying fifty men and three months' provisions. They traveled 300 li per day. The overseas voyages of the Ch'in dynasty were made possible by Warring States era connections with Southeast China and Vietnam developed during Ch'u's earlier expansion to the South.

Tax Systems

Tax rates were increased over the 10% which the traditional sources say was constant from Hsia through Western Chou. In Spring-Autumn times rates varied, and reached as much as two-thirds of the crop in some states at some times. Mencius accused the Warring States rulers of imposing taxes like brigands. The rulers themselves recognized that taxes were getting out of hand. With the spread of trade and money it became possible to begin to collect land taxes in cash. In the *Kuan Tzu*, tax receipts were already calculated in cash and later on in Wei were actually collected in cash.

Mercantile taxes were already a significant part of Ch'i's revenues in Kuan Tzu's time. Frontier taxes were important enough for Mencius to also complain about them. The number of tax collectors increased significantly as did the percentage of taxes which they kept for their own enrichment. Hence it was possible for both the people and the state treasuries to be simultaneously impoverished.

Section V

THE FLOURISHING PERIOD: CH'IN-HAN

Outline

The 438 years from Ch'in through Eastern Han represents the culmination of the trends of the Warring States era as first crystallized by the Ch'in empire. The new national economy established by Ch'in might have progressed indefinitely but for the excessive burdens Ch'in placed on the people and which led to its overthrow. The economy remained in confusion for five decades after Ch'in's fall, but by Emperor Wu's time the new forms of a national economy had been restored under Han auspices. Wang Mang's reforms, rational though they were, were too badly executed to succeed. Eastern Han's economy was patterned on that of Western Han, but ultimately was hampered by its narrower sphere of control.

Fig. 5 Han Wu-ti (Ming illustration)

The Economic Successes and Failures of Ch'in Unification

Even in Warring States times the competing powers realized the inefficiency resulting from their political and military quarrels and the resulting lack of standardization of weights, measures, and written languages, and they made tentative attempts at unity in such matters. Hence the unity the Ch'in conquest imposed completed a natural process already under way. By formally abolishing the old states and ordering mass migrations, Ch'in undermined both local patriotism and the basis for the old aristocratic system. It separated political from economic power whereas feudalism had conjoined them. Private property in land and capital were now clearly distinguished from public administration. Regional impediments to the road, waterway and monetary systems were removed. Gold was established as the standard of value and round bronze cash was settled on as the standard ordinary currency.

Although its changes proved to be irreversible over the long run, over the short run Ch'in placed itself in the position of enemy of its own people. Aside from the enormous casualties of the wars of unification and then the wars on the frontiers, there were many lives lost in the great building projects of the new dynasty. Taxes rose precipitously to pay for these projects and to support the large number of government servants who were not directly engaged in production. Ssu-ma Ch'ien estimated that half the population was ready for rebellion by the last years of Ch'in. Hence even the uninfluential commoner Ch'en She was able to set off a local rebellion which quickly engulfed the entire empire.

The Unification and Extent of the Ch'in-Han Economic Realm

In size Ch'in was midway between Shang-Chou and Sui-Ch'ing China. Its 40 chün and 800 hsien were the local and regional economic centers. Han was of comparable size, but its administrative units were more various to accommodate the quasi-feudal restoration which accompanied Western Han, and they were also more numerous at the most local level.

Thirty of Ch'in's forty chün were conquered from its rivals. Han's boundaries extended past Tunhuang to the northwest and into northern Korea in the northeast. The forcing of the Hsiungnu out of the northwest in Wu-ti's time was expensive in both blood and treasure and had to be repeated with varying degrees of success several times during the next few centuries. The southern branch of the Hsiungnu was eventually assimilated. Sinkiang was held during the latter part of Western Han but lost during Eastern Han.

The Policy of Emphasizing Agriculture After Han's Unification

A number of writers all through Western Han advocated concentration on agriculture. Farming had been disrupted during Ch'in's unification wars and the disorder which accompanied its fall. Some Western Han writers advocated the forcible return of vagabonds to the land. Some called for more indirect measures, such as accepting grain as payment for government grants of perquisites to the rich and as fines to avoid punishments. This would allow the government to reduce the land tax in kind, leaving more grain in the hands of the farmers.

Early Western Han saw many imperial exhortations to encourage agriculture, and special officials were appointed in each prefecture for this purpose. For a time taxes were reduced to 1/15 and later to 1/30 of the crop. Population growth was encouraged by calling for earlier marriages and fining spinsters thirty years or older. Rural security was encouraged by urging people to sell weapons and buy oxen. Five years of free rent on government land was offered to those without land, with the option of then returning to their native place without penalty.

A number of new types of specialized iron tools came into general use with government encouragement. Notable among them was the ox-drawn plow which greatly increased productivity but also rendered agriculture vulnerable to plagues affecting cattle. Poor families and regions were still dependent on hand-drawn plows.

New planting methods came into use. One was planting in straight lines in the depressions between furrows and pushing the furrows into the depressions as the plants grew so as to reenforce their roots against wind and drought. Another was planting in regularly spaced square depressions so as to facilitate irrigation. The latter technique appeared in Eastern Han.

Several great irrigation canals were built under state auspices, including one near the capital over 300 li long which took several tens of thousands of men three years to build. The amount of irrigated land and hence productivity increased significantly.

In addition to measures to encourage population growth in general, Han moved large numbers of people, especially workmen and rich merchants to the capital so as to build up its population base for defense purposes. In addition, criminals and paupers were transported to the frontiers to help guard against barbarian incursions. But periods like Wu-ti's thirty years of war drastically reduced the population, as did Wang Mang's usurpation. Eastern Han's population never quote rose to the level of Western Han.

After Wu-ti's time, the proportion of land which fell into the hands of rich men and officials greatly and steadily increased and so did the number of poor landless peasants. Through grants of public and uncultivated land as well as by encouraging migration the government tried to alleviate this problem but without significant success. Scholars like Tung Chung-shu advocated limiting private estates and the number of their tenants and dependents, but the disapproval of estate owners was too great for such policies to be carried out. Wang Mang's attempt to restore a pure well-field system ended in disaster. Some later scholars, admitting the impracticality of the well-field system, called for restricting right over land to usufruct, abolishing the right to buy and sell land. During Eastern Han the garrison fields system was extensively used within the country as well as on the frontiers, partly to curb rebellion and partly as a system of rural relief.

Farmers incurred short-term loans in seed, implements, oxen, foodstuffs and money from the state. The latter engaged in countercyclical trade, but less (so said the critical Confucians) to stabilize prices than to assure adequate supplies for its frontier outposts, thereby reducing supplies for the interior of the country. Hence countercyclical trade was abolished soon after its introduction in the first century B.C. Some local officials illegally lent government funds at interest. Long-term loans were more indirect, usually involving the grant of public lands to the impoverished with a term of tax exemption. Grants of forest and marsh lands to villages were also made to encourage a wider range of crafts.

Han Science, Technology and Management of Manufacturing

Mathematics flourished. The use of fractions was understood. More exact values of *pi* were calculated. Earlier works on mathematics were collated, and several new ones embodying some new methods of calculation were composed. Chang Heng invented a device which could detect the presence and direction of earthquakes. He is also said to have invented a mechanical bird which could fly. But the society of that period gave no particular encouragement to inventors. A hand-operated waterwheel for irrigation was invented. Doctors practiced surgery using wine as an anaesthetic. Damask silk and paper were invented. Wall and palace building was done on a great scale, beginning with Ch'in and continued by Han. Imperial tombs were so large and so richly furnished that construction of an emperor's tomb had to begin upon his ascent to the throne. Decorated and inscribed tiles and bricks were extensively used. True porcelain probably appeared by Han, based on techniques which had been evolving since Shang, now supplemented by glassmaking techniques for adding the glaze which probably came from West Asia. The word for porcelain did not, however, appear until Wei and Chin times.

Industry was not as well developed during Han as in late Warring States times. This was especially true of the salt and iron industries which became state monopolies in Wu-ti's time. Dynastic precedent limited the land tax. Hence military expenses to fight the Hsiungnu could only be raised through the profits from these monopolies. Adminstrative abuses limited the state's profit and jacked up prices, but these abuses do not prove the principle of state monopoly was wrong. The state also maintained large establishments of artisans in both the capital and provinces to supply the palace with luxury goods. For a time the state even maintained a monopoly over the manufacture and sale of wine but eventually settled for a sales tax instead.

Han Commerce and Money

Commerce soon recovered from the bad effects of the decade of civil war which followed Ch'in's fall. Han unity opened a national market. Salt and iron dealers became as wealthy as the nobility and, according to Ssu-ma Ch'ien, grievously exploited the people, in part through manipulation of currency which was privately coined without state control. Private trade reached its peak in Wu-ti's time and then inexorably declined as Wu-ti conscripted merchants and their capital into service of his military campaigns rather than let the merchants make great profits out of such activities as was earlier done. Wu-ti's successors favored agriculture over commerce, as did Wang Mang and his Eastern Han successors. Merchants were now compared to robbers and were blamed for rural poverty, though in fact they were not powerful enough to cause such mischief. One writer went so far as to advocate the abolition of money. Western Han's overt repression of merchants was less effective in limiting commercial growth than the pervasive contempt of Eastern Han which became the norm thereafter and had much to do with China's eventual failure to continue to progress economically into the industrial age.

Sang Hung-yang, a high fiscal official of Wu-ti's court, was responsible for the state monopolies in salt, iron, and alcoholic beverages, and a scheme for a centrally administered wholesaling operation which bought and sold countercyclically. It replaced the former merchant-dominated system for forwarding tribute to the capital. But the state's needs for funds and collusion between officials and merchants sabotaged the system's countercyclical aims and hence obliged most of the people to sell cheap and buy dear.

In the famous debate on salt and iron in 81 B.C. Sang argued that frontier defense against the Hsiungnu required the revenues from these monopolies. Internally, the monopoly system supported such aids to agriculture as hydraulic improvements. It also made possible necessary imports. The resulting increase in commerce made all goods more generally available and hence raised the level of life of farmers as well. Sang's Confucian opponents in the debate argued that his policies actually undermined agriculture, the fundamental occupation, which ought to be directly supported. Merchants can only profit by buying cheap and selling dear. This means, the Confucians argued, that the people must sell cheap and buy dear. Hence the merchants' interest runs counter to that of the people. The state monopolies obliged the state to adopt the merchants' methods and hence exploit the people. Indeed, they argued, private merchants would still profit excessively as government purchases would tend to drive up prices. They also opposed government controlled coinage as more harmful to the masses than free private coinage. Buying off the Hsiungnu would be cheaper and less harmful to the domestic economy than expensive attempts to conquer them. The virtues of a true king, they concluded, would ultimately evoke a virtuous response even from barbarians. Conversely, if the state seeks profit so will the people who will be drawn into nonfundamental activities.

And yet Sang's policies must be judged a success. They supported the frontier wars and made possible domestic relief. Wang An-shih approved of them and so did Sun Yat-sen. Unfortunately, when Wu-ti died, Sang lost his chief protection. The opposition of the Confucians and his own family's speculations brought about his execution and that of his family.

Commerce took place in political centers, centers of production, communications junctions, and foreign trade centers. Emperors encouraged the natural tendency for men of wealth to settle in the capital, Ch'angan, lest they get into mischief in the provinces. Ch'angan lost its earlier commercial predominance when the capital was moved to Loyang. Ch'engtu was Szechwan's commercial center and an important foreign trade entrepot. An official of Wu-ti's reign said that his greatest regret was not ever having seen Ch'engtu, ample testimoney to that city's great development. Its merchants lived and were buried like aristocrats. Lintzu in Shantung was noted for its wealthy salt manufacturing houses. Its population was over 300,000 even in Warring States times. Loyang was a great communications junction even before it became Eastern Han's capital.

When Chang Ch'ien visited Ta Hsia in West Asia he found Chinese goods already present there, but the policies of Wu-ti and his successors greatly increased China's foreign trade in the course of the many wars against the Hsiungnu. New plants, like the grape, came from Central Asia. China was in indirect touch with Rome through Persian merchants. Marcus Aurelius Antoninus sent a mission to China via Annam and attacked Persia in an attempt to open direct links to China. There was also trade with India, Korea and Japan.

Han nominal feudalism (su feng) gave the revenue of a territory to its nominal ruler but political power to a centrally appointed official. Because such rulers were more interested in profit than wholesome government, they allowed merchants to become powerful enough to make high profits from trade within these fiefs and by charging high interest to poor farmers within them. Up until Wu-ti's reign Han permitted free private coinage in the fiefs which was dominated by merchants and officials. Wu-ti banned such coinage, though it continued illegally for some time.

Ch'in's dual monetary system (gold and bronze) was modified by early Han to allow free coinage because the excessive weight of

Ch'in money proved inconvenient. But the new coins were too various and usually too light to maintain their face value. Initial government attempts to replace these coins with standard government issue were not successful. Finally, after experiments with coins of various weights of metal, Wu-ti managed to issue a coin of sufficient value and convenience to stay in circulation and was able to ban local coinage and collect and melt down all unofficial coins. Aside from a period of monetary confusion during Wang Mang's usurpation, this coin remained standard all through the Han.

Han Communications

Wen-ti had abolished the requirement for travelers to show passes at boundaries, thereby freeing communications on the network of official roads which had been begun in Ch'in times. There were guard stations on these roads every ten *li*, each with a five-man garrison. In all there were 29,635 such stations by the end of Western Han. Rest houses with spare horses were placed every thirty *li*. Private parties could use these facilities by payment of a fee.

The Yangtze was navigable downstream from Szechwan east, and from its middle sections east easily navigable in both directions. There were transport canals in the lower Yangtze region and others connecting Ch'angan with the Yellow River. By Wu-ti's time shipping was using the Gulf of Chihli to Korea and the northern frontier. The coast route from Chekiang to Fukien was also in use.

Overland, indirect communication with Rome was possible, and direct links with Japan and with India via Southeast Asia were opened. Wu-ti had fleets of tower boats in the northeast and off the coast of Chekiang. He annexed the areas of modern Canton and Hanoi as trading outposts, and Chinese were trading as far as Madras in India, though apparently not in Chinese vessels. The throne closely supervised this trade through eunuch overseers. Traders came from as far away as the Red Sea and by late Eastern

Han an envoy from the Roman empire came to Loyang. Contact with Japan brought that country out of the Stone Age by Eastern Han times, and migration of Chinese from Korea in the Three Kingdoms period gave the Japanese a genetic connection with the Chinese race.

The Han Tax System

There were four kinds of tax: land, artisan-merchant, capitation, and miscellaneous. Kao-tsu reduced the land tax to 1/15, but this was an idle gesture as the central government was not yet powerful enough to get local authorities to forward much of the tax they collected. Hui-ti reduced it to 1/30, at which level it remained for the rest of the dynasty, except for a short time at the beginning of Eastern Han.

All men from age fifteen to fifty-six were liable to pay the capitation tax in cash. Some rulers reduced or waived it, but others increased it from its standard rate of 120 cash. Hui-ti ordered merchants and slaves to pay at double the normal rate. Wang Mang put a head tax of 3,600 cash on slaves. Originally males from age seven to fourteen were to pay twenty cash which Wu-ti increased to twenty-three. In addition there was a tax in lieu of labor and military service of 300 cash paid by males from the age of twenty (later twenty-three) to fifty-six.

Prior to Ch'in-Han times commerce was insufficiently developed to require a very complex tax structure. During Han commerce was heavily taxed, particularly the salt and iron trades but also wine, commercial carts and boats, and commercial capital. Han did not lower the high Ch'in tax rates. Wu-ti placed the salt and iron trades under state management where they intermittently remained thereafter. For a short time Wu-ti collected twenty cash as tax for each 1,000-cash string issued by government in payment for goods so as to put some of the tax load onto profiteering merchants, but this proved too difficult to collect. There is little evidence on the short-lived liquor tax. Taxes were also levied on market stalls and on goods crossing local government boundaries, the latter designed to pay the maintenance of border guards.

Miscellaneous taxes were of little importance. The tax on capital was 120 cash per 10,000 cash of capital. Wang Mang increased it to 10%. There was also a tax of twenty cash per thousand on the value of livestock, a tax on money lent at interest, one on fish caught, and one on official property lent to the people.

Contrast of the Good and Bad Aspects of the People's Livelihood in Han Society

The Ch'in oppression was followed by a decade of chaotic civil war which disrupted agriculture and the crafts and reduced city populations by 70%. After Liu Pang won out, he proclaimed a general amnesty and encouraged refugees to return to their homes by urging local officials to treat them leniently. Hence by Wen-ti's reign, Han's golden age had begun, aided by the court's frugality. Officials practiced magnanimity. Abundant harvests kept grain prices low and life in the villages peaceful. This early Han prosperity continued up to Wu-ti's ascent to the throne, a period of some seventy years. The eighty years after Kuang-wu's restoration of the dynasty, though good, were not as perfect as the earlier era of prosperity. Hence of Han's 400 years, only seventy can be considered truly prosperous.

Fig. 6 Han Kuang-wu (Ming illustration)

Wu-ti had to fight the Hsiungnu for thirty years. Eastern Han was never free of wars against the Hsiungnu, Hsien-pi, or the Yi rebels in the Southwest.

The nomadic Hsiungnu had inherent military advantages over the agricultural Chinese. Hsiungnu raids devastated agriculture, requiring expensive relief operations and expensive support for defense armies sent to the north. In some parts of North China, where draft animals and horses had been plentiful, horses were now conscripted and fields left to waste as the population declined. Eastern Han saw barbarians settle in Chihli and Shansi. An Eastern Han writer describes harvesting being carried out by women and girls, the horses and men all having gone west to fight the barbarians.

The subtropical climate and difficult terrain of the South were alone sufficient to cause high casualties among the unacclimatized northern troops. Men died of poisonous plants and insects before they ever saw the enemy. Ssu-ma Ch'ien judged that all the taxes of Szechwan were insufficient to finance a successful campaign against the Southwestern Yi. But such sacrifices were necessary to keep these and the northern barbarians from overwhelming Chinese culture. They made possible sinification of the South and maintenance of contact with Central Asia, Korea and Japan.

Wu-ti's desperate attempts to raise revenues for these foreign wars encouraged official corruption. By Eastern Han official positions were as a matter of course being sold to raise money. Unscrupulous rich men bought offices as a way to make still more money. In the process they diverted money and talent from legitimate commerce, thereby helping delay China's evolution of an industrial economy. This noxious custom began under Wu-ti as did the practice of allowing the well-off to buy absolution from crimes by contributing grain to the state. These abuses greatly undermined public morality. By late Eastern Han office buying had become so ubiquitous that even able men who had demonstrated their talents had to buy their positions. Many of the best men left public life or committed suicide. A contemporary aphorism went: "Straight as a sage, die in a ditch; crooked as a hook, enfeoffed as a duke." The gap between rich and poor grew wider and more obvious. We know that such a society must be on the brink of revolution.

From Wu-ti's time on luxury grew ever more conspicuous from the Court on down. If the emperor kept a thousand women in his harem, an aristocrat would keep several hundred and a rich commoner several dozen. By Eastern Han moralists were complaining about there being 5,000 to 6,000 women in the imperial harem and the burden they placed on taxpayers. One Eastern Han ruler placed a surtax of ten cash on each <u>mou</u> of land to finance palace building. Imperial tombs required tens of thousands of laborers, used up much valuable agricultural land, and took years to build. Rich merchants lived and died with a scale of expenditure commensurate with that of the great aristocrats.

For commoners, the time of peace and plenty ended with Wu-ti's thirty years of war and the accompanying rise in taxes, conscription and exploitation by the great merchants. The pressure of foreign wars let up for a time under Wu-ti's immediate successors, but before long the consequences of domestic corruption were impoverishing the masses as much as before. Within a century after Eastern Han's inauguration famine and banditry were rife.

The official Han histories abound with references to slaves of various types. Government slaves were usually criminals or war prisoners or palace eunuchs and servants. They could have their freedom restored by the state. Private slaves were usually sold into bondage during hard times and worked as servants for rich households. They usually remained servile. The sources allude to tens of thousands of slaves in Court service and great families holding hundreds or even thousands of servile retainers. Since most did not take part in production, the loss to the people's livelihood was significant.*

*It is nevertheless likely that only a small proportion of the total Han population was of servile status (EHK).

The Economic Disaster of Wang Mang's Hsin Dynasty

The ideological and political ferment which led to Wang Mang's usurpation had its roots in the increasingly unsatisfactory economic situation since Wu-ti's time even though the outward forms this ferment took in Wang's hands were expressed in terms of yin-yang and five-elements superstition. Born in 45 B.C. the nephew of an empress, Wang and his family dominated the court during the reign of his cousin, Emperor Ch'eng, and he was brought up in the palace by his aunt. He stood out as a scholarly and modest exception to his family's otherwise licentious behavior. In 8 B.C. he became head of his family and the dominant power at Court. From 9 to 23 A.D. he ruled as emperor of his own Hsin dynasty. Pretending to rule as a sage in imitation of Shun, Yü and the Duke of Chou, his power actually rested on the women of his family, and he was prepared to use bad means to achieve his ostensibly noble ends. His superstitious practices eventually alienated the Court, and he was without effective support when the Liu clan challenged him militarily. He was particularly condemned for his lack of a constant policy. He not only frequently changed officials and their titles but also the money system, impoverishing thereby the merchants and artisans. He was also accused of excessive taxation and encouraging official corruption as well as of engaging in ruinous and unsuccessful foreign wars.

Wang's military adventures flowed from his egomaniacal refusal to acknowledge that any border people could remain outside his sovereignty. He stirred up the enmity of the Hsiungnu after they had been quiescent for more than a generation and had allowed peace to return to the northern frontiers. His ten years of war in the north and his campaigns against the southwestern barbarians were both unsuccessful and economically ruinous.

Wang's monetary policy was the most conspicuous example of his economically disastrous policies. His frequent changes in the value and style of the currency were designed to fit his own abstruse theories and not the actual needs of the people. Hence despite strict punishments, his coins did not circulate and were replaced in practice with illegal private coinage. His twenty-eight different denominations of money eventually evoked contempt, the more so as his attempts to coerce their use were impossible to enforce.

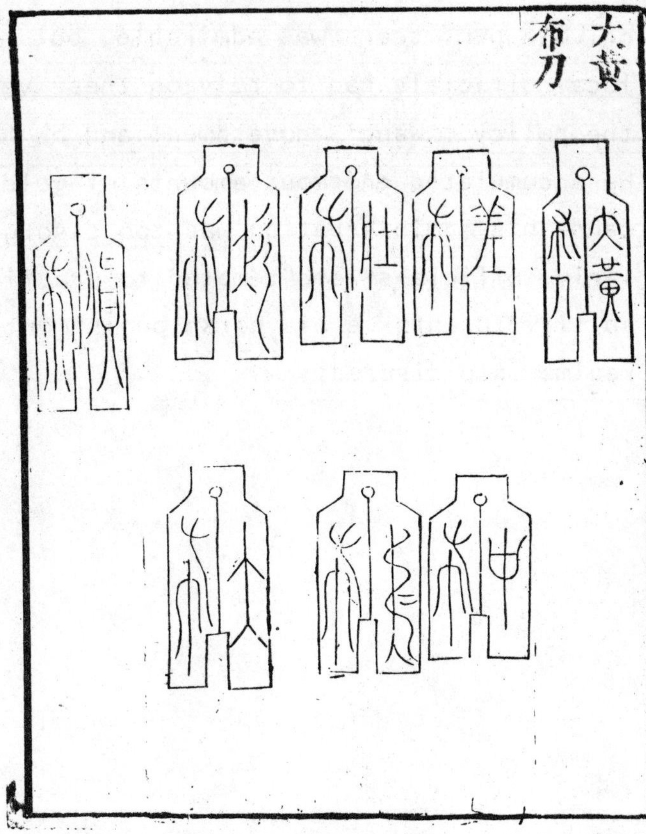

Fig. 7 Money during Wang Mang's reign

Wang's land reform went well beyond what had been called for by earlier reformers, a simple limitation of the size of private holdings, and by fiat he nationalized all land with the aim of restoring the ancient well-field system. Private sale of land was forbidden. No family with eight or fewer men could hold more than 900 mou. Surplus land along with government land would be distributed so that each family (one man and one woman) would get 100 mou. Slaves, relabeled "private dependents," (ssu shu) could no longer be bought and sold. Violators of these edicts were to be exiled to the farthest frontiers. But violations were numerous from the first. His critics objected that private landownership was now too deeply established to be overturned even by a Yao or Shun. Within three years Wang was obliged to back down.

Wang also imposed excise taxes on salt, iron goods, liquor and a variety of other goods. For grain lent to the people, 3% per month interest was to be charged. Wang's aim to displace private profiteers was admirable, but he failed because he and his local officials had to rely on these very profiteers to administer the policy. Wang's government and he himself were also covetous. He accumulated enormous amounts of gold in his treasury. But because his administration was too disorganized to pay salaries regularly, officials were tempted to practice corruption. Wang's inability to enforce his harsh punishments only brought his whole regime into discredit.

Section VI

THE AGE OF TROUBLES: LATE HAN, WEI, CHIN, SOUTHERN AND NORTHERN DYNASTIES

Outline

This period of over three centuries was largely one of disorder and disunity. Agriculture and commerce suffered. Landlordism increased and became still more unjust. In the southern dynasties, the politically powerful great landed families dominated commerce and manufacture as well as agriculture. The barbarian invasions of the north threw that region's economy into disorder, left many agricultural areas desolate and ultimately evoked the Hsienpi's response of instituting the equal-fields system.

The Late Han Military Disorders and Socio-economic Vicissitudes

Refugees fleeing the barbarian attacks in the north were caught up in the consequences of the Yellow Turban revolt and the various local uprisings linked to it. Communications were blocked and agricultural areas devastated. The political battles in the capital involving the eunuchs and then Tung Cho's usurpation devastated the entire region surrounding Loyang. To cope with local disorder, the great landed families organized private armies and the empire was divided into warlord satrapies, with all loyalty to the central authority soon dissipated. Even nominally loyalist local armies were privatized in the course of these local wars.

Enormous numbers of refugees fled the Yellow and Huai River valleys into the lower Yangtze, Szechwan and southeastern Manchuria. Many came as dependents, virtual serfs, of great landlords. Others went into hitherto unsettled frontier areas and remained out of the control of the southern dynasties for a considerable time. In 157 A.D. the population was 56,500,000. By 280 it was only 16,000,000, though this did not include refugees, bandits, local armies and others. Registered agricultural land had been reduced to one-fourth of the peak Han level. Whole regions in the Huai valley were totally depopulated. The destruction and emptying of cities, cutting of roads, and Tung Cho's unsuccessful recoinage all helped paralyze trade and manufacture. Soldiers in the local armies were recruited from among ex-bandits, barbarians and ordinary commoners. They became professionals, hereditarily limited to the military life and hence unavailable for productive labor or taxation. The number of those of servile status grew enormously, and they were now used largely for agricultural work. This continued to be the case until the T'ang.

The Three Kingdoms' Economy

The late Han famines had driven up the price of grain. Hence each of the three kingdoms which succeeded Han placed great emphasis on economic policy as the base for securing their rule. In the north, Ts'ao Ts'ao successfully used the military colony system. Commoners either volunteered or were conscripted to work public fields under the supervision of army officers. The chief agricultural official in each locality reported directly to the Ministry of Agriculture, by-passing the local officials. The numerous refugees of the north were easily recruited for these military colonies. Government funds were used to purchase draft animals and finance irrigation works. The soldiers used in these military colonies gradually merged with the civilians and good order and a slowly increasing population resulted.

Shu-Han and Wu lacked this system. Shu-Han was sufficiently prosperous and its government received enough revenues from the salt and iron trades, so that it did not require the military colony system. Wu constituted a natural economic unit. Politically it was dominated by a few great landowning clans at whose sufferance the Sun clan ruled. Hence its government lacked the power to institute military colonies.

The lines of commerce between the three states remained open as each lacked products the others could provide. Shu traded across its southwestern boundaries, and its silk reached as far as the Roman empire. Though Wei's commerce was the least extensive of the three it did trade with the Hsienpi and the Japanese. Wu had an extensive domestic and foreign trade. On at least one occasion a Roman merchant came to its shores. There were complaints that luxury goods were so numerous in Wu as to interfere with the production of necessities. Wu's fleet was large and had a greater variety of vessels than Han. Unable to match Wei's land power to the north, Wu used its fleet to expand its commerce and territory to the south. Vietnam, a part of China since Han, contributed a variety of products. Sun Ch'üan, Wu's ruler, probably learned much about Southeast Asia from the Roman merchant whose name was transliterated as Ch'in Lun, though unfortunately the emissary who accompanied the Roman back home died on the way. Nevertheless, after putting down a Vietnamese rebellion, Sun used Vietnam as a base for a ten-year-long naval expedition which used vessels capable of holding one hundred men each and which may have reached as far as India. An expedition numbering 10,000 armored men was also sent to Taiwan in 230 A.D. This is the earliest mention of Taiwan in Chinese records. Another, but unsuccessful expedition was sent to the Philippines.

The severe decline in population in Wei made it impossible to collect the traditional 1/30 land tax, even though it was official policy to base the state's revenues on agriculture rather than commerce. The tendency was to shift from a field to a household tax, a system perfected by Western Chin. Wu also reduced the land tax so as to stimulate production. Like the other two, Shu also had a special class of officials to collect the tax in grain.

Metal money, debased by the several political authorities,

no longer circulated effectively and was replaced by grain and cloth. Wei attempted to make grain and cloth official money, but when insiders monopolized these commodities, it was obliged to reissue Tung Cho's unsatisfactory coins. Shu issued a similar coin and Wu one twice as heavy which was recalled because it failed to gain circulation.

Liu Hui, who lived either in Wei or Chin times, calculated the circumference of a circle by inscribing ever more many-sided polyhedrons within a circle. He also developed a method for indirect measurement of height and distance. Liu-Sung's Tsu Chung-chih improved on Liu Hui's calculation of pi as 3.14, to arrive at the accurate figure of 3.1415926, a degree of accuracy not matched in the West until Valentinus in 1563.

The Chin Economy

Chin relaxed Wei's legalist controls and allowed free rein to the great clans who monopolized land and servile labor and also much of the commerce, including the lucrative trade with Southeast Asia. Their wasteful style of life, epitomized by the "Pure Talk" group, established a pernicious model for gentlemanly behavior for the next millenium and more. The military colony system was taken out of military hands and placed under local officials who took over 70% to 80% of the crop and thereby became great landlords. Members of other influential and rich clans could use their political power to control the scarce supply of labor and their wealth to buy up land the price of which had been driven down by the shortage of labor. Each commoner family was supposed to be allotted 100 mou of land in lifetime usufruct.

Field and household taxes were combined on the assumption that each household of equivalent size had the same amount of land. But as there is no evidence that Chin ever so distributed land, one may assume that this system was followed because it was easier to count households than to measure land. Though there is no hard evidence on the weight of taxation, Ma Tuan-lin is likely right in judging such a system to be harder on taxpayers than a tax directly on the land. This system also encouraged keeping large households together and hence gave a tax advantage to great clan estates over small peasant holdings. Partly to compensate for this, Eastern Chin collected a higher tax, a larger proportion of which was placed directly on the land, but the great landowners could still dodge most of their tax load.

Though commerce revived with the Chin unification, it again slumped in the north with the renewed barbarian invasions. The south's commerce continued to thrive, and with Eastern Chin the political center moved to coincide with this new southern economic center. Trade relations were maintained with Central Asia and Japan. An anonymous late third-century ironic "Paean to the God of Money" (<u>ch'ien shen lun</u>) whose product, cash, substitutes for all the moral virtues, testifies to the spirit of the times when the lust for wealth dominated even the court. Such selfishness was a natural reaction to the decades of chaos since late Han.

The Southern Dynasties' Economy

Eastern Chin's successors, Sung, Ch'i, Liang, and Ch'en, all had their capitals in Chienk'ang [Nanking]. Men rather than land were taxed. Hence household registers were very important. Aristocratic tax avoidance heavily burdened the masses. In one ten-year period during Ch'i, the number of those on the tax registers dropped by nearly half. Yellow (bamboo) registers were kept for those who had migrated from the north in Eastern Chin times. White (paper) registers were for southerners. Southern aristocrats eventually got themselves transferred to the yellow registers which carried more privileges, while commoners were shunted to the white ones. Ch'i and Liang continued to collect taxes according to the population. Ch'en (557-89) shows evidence of basing its taxes on land. This was the source of the tax system of T'ang.

From Eastern Chin through Ch'en, transactions made by contract had to pay 400 cash tax for each 10,000 cash worth of business done, with 300 paid by the seller and 100 by the buyer. Transactions without contract paid a 4% tax. Sung had a tax of 10% on fish, firewood, and other items which was very burdensome. Ch'en had a wine tax and Sung a liquor tax.

The imperial clans of these dynasties took a direct role in the commerce of the major cities. Their officials followed suit, as did the great landed clans in their home areas. Yangchou, to become the chief economic center of T'ang times, was already very important. Canton was a rich entrepot for foreign trade. Szechwan's Yichou was also very prosperous. Trade with Southern and Western Asia was more extensive than in Han times and could regularly use the southern sea route as could the continental Southeast Asian trade.

Pawnbroking, based on precedents going back to the Spring-Autumn era, appeared in Ch'i times. Ch'i used monasteries as its agents for refugee relief in times of famine and flood. Such relief work also got monasteries involved in pawnbroking, though not initially for profit (as was the case in T'ang-Sung secularized pawnbroking) but rather as a service to poor commoners.

Sung issued the first dated coins but was unable to come up with a coin of appropriate weight to forestall private coinage. For a time private coinage was legalized, but this only led to still more debased coins. In early Liang only a few cities used coins. Liang's official coinage started in 502, was unsuccessful and was replaced by a still more unsuccessful iron coinage in 523. By 556 the state legalized the circulation of old coins as well as its new bronze issue. Early Ch'en continued this practice, but its coins were rapidly melted to make private coins of lighter weight which circulated at the same face value. Commodity currency continued in use, especially in the south.

The Northern Dynasties' Economy

Han Kuang-wu, the founder of Eastern Han, had invited the southern branch of the Hsiungnu within the frontiers. Their northern branch was later driven west into Europe by the Hsienpi. Eventually the Southern Hsiungnu became the dominant force in the northern frontier provinces, though they were increasingly sinicized. During the fourth and fifth centuries they and four other barbarian groups succeeded one another in an irregular series of sixteen kingdoms holding various parts of the north. Their incursions completely upset the agricultural land system, especially during the first generation of invasions. Great migrations to the south were set off. The period from 383 to 439 was the time of darkest confusion. Not only was agriculture thrown into chaos, but all the major cities were destroyed and their merchant inhabitants fled south. Trade virtually disappeared from the north for over a century, as did the use of money. Money was not coined again until Northern Wei and did not come into general use until late in that dynasty.

The old Han clan structure was also destroyed and hence the social structure imposed by the Toba peoples of Northern Wei differed greatly from that of southern China.

The Buddhist church became a great social force, strong enough to avoid taxes, for the first time during the Sixteen Kingdoms era. Where Southern Liang had 2,846 temples, Wei and Northern Ch'i had 40,000. The number of monks and temple fields grew inordinately. Northern temples became as privileged and profit seeking as southern landed families. By the time of Northern Ch'i's Wen-ti, monks were said to be more numerous than laymen. Their numbers did not begin to lessen until Sui. Many monks took the tonsure as a way to avoid taxes. Aristocrats also used this device.

The equal-fields system was the basis for Northern Wei's ability to reunify the north, just as the military colonies enabled

Ts'ao Ts'ao to so do earlier. The equal-fields system was the most successful version of the kind of reforms Confucians had been urging since late Han. The ultimate Confucian aim, however, had been to restore the ancient well-field system, whereas the Northern Wei system appears never to have had such pretensions. Unlike the other barbarians, Northern Wei had earlier established its own version of the military-colony or garrison-fields system. This later served as the base for the equal fields, first established in 485. Every adult male, free or unfree, was to receive forty mou, every woman twenty mou. A family would also receive thirty mou for each ox it possessed, up to four oxen. These figures refer to prime quality land. Less desirable land would be distributed in greater amounts. Additional land was to be distributed for growing mulberry, hemp and for home sites, though less of the latter was to be given to unfree people. Only these latter types of land could be kept in perpetuity. The rest was to be returned to the state for redistribution at age seventy. Mulberry land was to be sold should it come to exceed a family's quota.

Ma Tuan-lin believed this system was designed less to cut down the power of great landed families than to attract farmers to depopulated areas. Northern Ch'i and Northern Chou used variants of the Wei system. Northern Ch'i limited the number of unfree persons each officially ranked aristocrat could enroll for land distribution. Northern Chou distributed more land per person and had no regulations for unfree persons.

During the 150 years from Northern Wei through Northern Chou, the equal-fields system revived agriculture and enabled the northern dynasties to exceed the southern dynasties in wealth and power. Northern Wei continued to use the garrison-fields system as well. Aristocrats could maintain and even expand their holdings through grants of equal fields to their unfree dependents and animals. Officials also got land grants, and larger ones than commoners. The pao-chia system of local government was linked to the equal-fields land arrangements.

Before the equal-fields system, taxes may have risen as high as 80% on occasion. Aristocrats avoided taxes which were assessed by household rather than by field. Under the equal-fields system taxes were also assessed by head, using the population registers of the pao-chia system, but these were difficult to keep accurately. To meet government crises, taxes were often collected in advance. From Northern Chou on the trend was toward assessing the taxes on land. By late Northern Chou those without land were not to be taxed. The northern dynasties' market taxes were light. Salt and iron were intermittently left free of regulation during Wei but in the end made a significant contribution to state revenues.

Commerce not only failed to develop but actually regressed after Han. Many areas were reduced to barter as only the old Han coins remained to circulate. After 298, as north and south came into closer contact and life in the north became more secure, commerce revived. During Northern Wei Loyang revived as a great economic center, comparable to Chienk'ang in the south. A contemporary wrote of Loyang's marketplaces: "Whatever the central lands lack is all brought from the western frontiers." This foreshadowed the great international trade of Sui and T'ang. Official coinage first began again in the north in 495 but had great difficulty competing with private coinage. Northern Chou fell before it could fully replace Northern Ch'i's coins with its own still not fully accepted coinage.

Section VII

THE AGE OF REESTABLISHMENT: SUI, T'ANG, AND FIVE DYNASTIES

Outline

The period from 580 to 755 witnessed the economic equivalent of a dynastic revival. The following period, from 756 to 960, was one of renewed warfare and consequent reversion to economic depression. The preceding Six Dynasties era had been a period of regression, the localized economies of the great landed estates somewhat resembling the manorial economy of late antiquity in Europe.

The Sui-T'ang restoration was worthy to be called a golden age. Nevertheless, though quantitatively greater, it did not, economically, represent a qualitative advance over the centralized agrarian empire of Han. During Sui-T'ang times a reinvigorating mixture of Chinese with northern barbarian blood and customs occurred. Sui's enormous expenditures on public works give evidence of the size of the treasury available to it. These public works made possible T'ang's economic revival.

The An Lu-shan rebellion was the economic watershed of T'ang. The period prior to this was one of prosperity and cultural efflorescence. After the rebellion, despite a new tax system, the former prosperity was never quite recovered. T'ang's tenure was extended for a century, but it was succeeded by the disorder of the Five Dynasties and Ten Kingdoms.

The Influence of Taxation Methods on the Chinese Economy

Sui did not last long enough to evolve a distinctive tax system. T'ang, in its first generation under T'ai-tsung and again after 755, made notable changes.

T'ang reestablished the equal-fields system. Northern Wei's version had disintegrated by Sui times. Under the T'ang system 20% of the land allotments were permanent; the rest reverted to the allotment pool at death. Taxes were assessed by head rather than directly on the land and paid in kind in grain, cloth, and labor (twenty days per year, twenty-two days in years with intercalary months), and the latter could be partially or totally commuted into an additional tax in cloth. If twenty-five days of service were required, other taxes were partially remitted; if thirty days, all other taxes were remitted. Service was never to exceed fifty days annually.

But this system presupposed the success of the equal-fields system. The elite undermined this system by amassing too much land through imperial grants to officials and favorites, buying up the alienable 20% of allotments, and having land allotted to aristocratic dependents and, consequently, the tax system had eventually to be changed. The tax load on the fewer people who remained outside the tax-avoiding great manors became inordinately high even before An Lu-shan's rebellion added its burden to rural life.

Yang Yen, the creator of the double-tax method, came from an old scholarly family in Shensi. In addition to instituting the double tax, he kept revenues from going into the emperor's private treasury and clearly separated the imperial household expenditures from the state's fiscal administration. Talented but inhumane, he persecuted his rivals in office and was himself driven from office and then killed on his way to exile.

Under the double-tax system, instead of collecting taxes during the eighth or ninth month, they were now to be collected in two installments, in the sixth and eleventh months, and local and capitation taxes were to be subsumed in these two installments. These taxes were not assessed on households because census registers had been too greatly disordered by the An Lu-shan rebellion, but rather in proportion to the amount of cultivated land in each district. Despite opposition from those used to the centuries-old former system, the new arrangement succeeded in returning fiscal power from the regions to the Court, though it required periodic modification, including a sharp rise in the quantity of commodities to be paid as taxes in kind so as to make up for a fall in commodity prices.

Lu Chih, the new system's leading critic, argued that the old system had much clearer criteria: possession of fields by a clearly defined household having men of the proper age. Capital, the basis for the new system, was much harder to measure precisely because it could be more easily hidden. As the tax was calculated in cash but paid in kind, the actual rate could vary with prices and the honesty of officials at various levels. Lu did not advocate abolition of the reform but its modification, particularly the calculation as well as the assessment of taxes in kind, not cash, and broader time limits for its collection.

Most later writers approved of the reform, Ma Tuan-lin observing that it was the only alternative to reestablishment of the equal-fields system. According to the principles of fiscal theory, the double-tax system was simpler than the one it replaced, and it was progressive because the amount collected varied in proportion to the amount of capital an individual possessed. It also treated farmers and merchants equally, introduced the practice of taxation in cash, and introduced something akin to modern budgetary controls on the state.

Yang Yen was the first in our nation's history to call for a precise accounting of government income and outgo. He got Emperor Teh-tsung to return to the early T'ang practice of putting tax receipts in the Left Treasury, where they were accessible to bureaucratic audit, rather than in the imperial treasury which was not accessible to the bureaucracy. Unfortunately, Yang's idea of a budget was never put into actual practice. The old assessment rates were kept under the new tax system and were not regularly adjusted to accord with actual expenditures.

The Sui-T'ang Land System and Agricultural Economy

Until late T'ang, a somewhat modified version of the Northern Dynasties' equal-fields system continued to be used, but the system was undermined by increasing dominance of the economy by the great families and the monasteries. Initially Sui had no difficulty extending the equal-fields system to the south as the registered population was at first small compared to the amount of state-controlled and formally ownerless land.

T'ang restored the equal-fields system in 624. Its version differed from earlier systems in that minors, unfree persons and livestock were not granted land. The amount of land distributed was the same regardless of the size of the household, and a flat 20% could be retained as private property regardless of the use to which it was put. In 713 monks and unfree persons were included in the system. Men of rank were allowed to keep as private property three to five hundred times more land than commoners. In addition, officials received large amounts of office land. By mid-T'ang over 14,000 official families qualified for such land and their number was still growing. Commercial, artisan families, and unfree households qualified for half the amount of land granted ordinary households. Unfree households appear to have been regarded as mere human capital, their lands actually belonging to their masters.

The system broke down well before the An Lu-shan rebellion, mainly because the long peace had allowed the population to grow beyond the limited amount of land available for redistribution. The amount of allotment land was reduced still further by aristocratic preemption. Various forms of the garrison-fields system were tried to restore a measure of equity in the use of those fields still nominally under public control, but these lands tended to be preempted by military officers by means analogous to those used by aristocratic civilians.

The T'ang manors resembled the Roman campagna or the estates created by the sixteenth-century English enclosure movement, except that management of the Chinese manors was more decentralized than the latter. The manorial system had originally developed out of the old feudal economy, and though a portion of the peasantry was now free, the great manors were so nearly self-sufficient entities that the system still resembled an offshoot of a feudal economy.

The structure of the system was exceedingly complex. Nominally there were public and private manors, but many of the former were actually the private property of the imperial family, though managed by public officials. Cultivators were either full slaves or tenants referred to by a number of labels incorporating the word "guest" (k'o). Absentee owners were represented by resident managers, references to whom are still found in Five Dynasties and Sung times.

Private estates were owned by officials, the relatives of the imperial family, and military men as well as by great aristocratic clans, all of whom used their politically privileged positions to amass more and more land. Rents on these estates were as much as ten times the tax rate on non-manorial land. Private estates were in part worked by slaves who could be bought and sold with the land.

Buddhist and Taoist temple estates fell midway between the status of private and public manors. They enjoyed political privileges, like tax exemptions, and were used as tax-avoidance institutions by aristocrats and hence flourished despite periodic attempts by the state to limit their growth. It was only after the persecution of the 840's that temple manors went into decline.

Like feudal serfs, tenants on private manors owed labor service as well as rent in kind to the lords of the manors. Local place names were often derived from the names of the owners of the local manor.

As rural prosperity returned during the early seventh century, cooperative societies appeared as early as Sui. The first of these was the Hsin-an Association in Anhui. There is no evidence that, as one theory holds, such organizations originated in T'ang-Sung times as a result of commercial and religious contact with India. Sui Wen-ti also set up Righteous Granaries to receive contributions of extra taxes from the rich to be used to relieve the poor during bad times. The system gradually lost its voluntary character and by Sung-Yüan times became just another head tax. Its level of administration rose from the village to the prefecture and hence became more remote from the people, more subject to corruption, and less likely to actually carry out relief when needed.

The great development of commerce during T'ang resulted in the spread of usury into the villages. Peasants could lose their liberty as well as their land and moveable property to usurers. By manipulation of the rent of official lands, local officials also participated in this usury. From the late eighth-century attempts were made to anticipate bad years and lend grain from government granaries to the people. Attempts were also made to limit the interest charged by private lenders, to remit debts after a given time and/or a given amount over the original principle had been paid, and to prohibit private lending.

Government-run Ever Normal and Righteous Granaries were used to mitigate usury, a network of the former being set up early in the eighth century to attempt to keep grain prices level. The T'ang Righteous Granaries were financed solely by taxes and lent grain at interest rather than merely providing relief as was done during Sui. These two institutions were all but ruined by the An Lu-shan rebellion and never reached their potential because of corrupt administration.

Sui-T'ang Communications

It was an improvement in communications, the construction of the Grand Canal, that made possible the new epoch of Sui and T'ang. This new epoch is analogous to sixteenth-century Europe's new era of commercial capitalism which was a consequence of the new communications links with America. In addition to international trade routes, the Sui-T'ang economy drew great strength from the opening of the Grand Canal. The canal changed the context of the south's economy.

In Han times still a region of much land and few people, the south had developed greatly during the Age of Disunion, and the Grand Canal further stimulated its commerce to make it the dominant commercial region by T'ang-Sung times. Running north to south, the canal linked the great natural waterways flowing from west to east.

The two Sui emperors connected the Yellow and Yangtze Rivers, and early in the ninth century the canal was extended south to the Hangchou region. The canal made possible adequate supplies for Yang-ti's invasion of Korea.

The canal made possible use of the south's resources to support the capital in the northwest. The amount transported increased from 200,000 tan to over 7 million tan every three years by the eighth century.

Road building was also energetically pushed, notably an eighth-century road linking Canton with Yangchou to facilitate foreign trade. A network of eight major trunk roads fanned out from Ch'angan to each major region, with post stations at regular intervals. As the roads were originally designed to transmit military news, these post stations were administered by the Board of War. These stations were equipped with spare horses, or boats along waterways, and could house and feed messengers and officials in transit. There were 1,639 stations, placed every thirty li. Private travelers were not supposed to use the system. There were seven major routes leading across the frontiers to the northeast, northwest and southwest.

Sui-T'ang Commerce

Sui Yang-ti greatly valued the products imported along the land routes from Central and Northern Asia. Three major routes branched off from Tunhuang reaching by land and sea to the Mediterranean. The diplomatic preliminaries to trade with Japan were initiated.

By the end of the seventh century T'ang had reduced much of Central Asia and Korea to tributary status. Traders and goods from these areas filled the great city markets. Unfortunately, at the local level, the anti-commercial practices of the great manors hindered the full commercialization of the countryside. Canton, filled with Arab and Persian vessels from the Persian Gulf, was the great foreign trade entrepot. Much of the trade with Japan originated in Yangchou and proceeded by way of the coast to Liaotung and Korea.

The south played a more important role than the north in foreign trade. In the south, Chinese silk was exchanged for precious stones, ivory, and other commodities; in the north tea was exchanged for animal products. Since the first century foreign vessels had given up the coastal routes for direct runs across the open sea, taking advantage of the seasonal monsoons. Chinese vessels had been trading with the Persian Gulf at least since the fifth century and dominated the trade as far west as Ceylon. Chinese settlers were beginning to appear in Southeast Asia.

Politics and economics mutually influence each other. Up until mid-T'ang a laissez-faire policy was followed; thereafter policy turned anti-commercial and economic development was hindered.

The early T'ang military victories helped secure commerce, particularly with Central Asia. Commercial law became more formalized, with penalties prescribed for not using standard measures and attempts to set up monopolies. Contracts were required for the sale of slaves and livestock. These laws, far more detailed than those of earlier periods, were retained in later eras.

T'ang entered a period of decline after the An Lu-shan rebellion, with the central government losing much of its power to regional warlords who often passed their power on to their children. Such local particularism hindered communications and hence commerce. The wealth of south China could no longer be funneled into the north.

The weakened central government resorted to confiscatory taxation of commercial capital. Merchants viewed the tax collectors as bandits and trade was stifled. Forced sales to palace officials at arbitrarily low prices ruined even small merchants and artisans in the capital. The limited excise taxes associated with Ever Normal Granary operations were replaced by excessive direct excise taxes after the rebellions ruined the old system.

The state supervised only the larger markets serving areas with 3,000 or more households, but many smaller markets at river fords and other natural trade junctions flourished. The structure of commerce grew more complex, with warehouses and shops now more formally organized under private auspices.

The major cities were the capitals, Ch'angan and Loyang, Pienchou (K'aifeng) at the confluence of the Yellow River and Grand Canal, Yangchou at the confluence of the Yangtze and Grand Canal, and the great seaports Canton, Chiaochou, Ch'üanchou and Mingchou.

As the capital, Ch'angan was the communications hub, and Sui Wen-ti restored to it the glories of Ch'in-Han times. Though virtually barbarized during mid-T'ang by the large number of foreign merchants residing there, the city recovered by late T'ang from the wounds of An Lu-shan's rebellion.

Loyang was rebuilt by Sui Yang-ti, using two million corvée laborers each month. He moved several tens of thousands of merchants there from all over the empire. It was the secondary capital in T'ang and Sung times.

Yangchou was the most flourishing city, the entrepôt of the seacoast salt trade, the communications link between north China and Canton's foreign trade, and hence the residence of many foreign merchants. The city suffered much during the late T'ang troubles, and though it remained important during Sung it never recovered the primary position it held during T'ang. It was also an important manufacturing city, noted for its bronze, cloth, hats, wood implements and cane sugar, the latter product first imported from India in T'ai-tsung's time. In addition to being the chief junction between the Yangtze and Grand Canal, it was the temporary capital in Sui Yang-ti's time and was much celebrated for its beauty and thriving urban life.

Canton was the main port for foreign trade. Its foreign residents were more numerous than those of Yangchou. Over 100,000 foreigners were said to have been killed there during the late T'ang disturbances which greatly affected foreign trade. Its commercial wealth made it a magnet for grasping local officials.

Sui-T'ang Science and Technology

Sui had bureaus specializing in such sciences as astronomy and calculation of the calendar, and T'ang expanded them. Mathematics was one of the six subjects taught in the T'ang National Academy. Mathematics reached its greatest degree of importance during T'ang. Definitive editions of the earlier mathematical classics were compiled under state auspices. A mathematics examination was instituted in Sui times and continued by T'ang.

From India came the concept of zero (indicated by a dot) to give place value to numbers, and the use of sand-boards to write out calculations. Scholarly pilgrims from Japan introduced Chinese mathematics into their new schools. The long forms of Chinese numerals for use in commerce first appeared in Sui-T'ang times, not during Sung as was long believed.

A water-powered armillary sphere was invented. It revolved once a day and indicated the passage of fractions of a day by mechanical wooden men who beat on drums and bells. This served the same function as later Western clockwork mechanisms.

In addition to the great fleet of canal barges used in the imperial progress along the Grand Canal, Sui technology was able to build a great five-storied warship capable of carrying 800 soldiers. The technique of carving words on boards was begun in Sui times for imperial orders, and this represented the beginning of printing technology which was applied directly to printing by late T'ang and Five Dynasties times. The great palaces built in Loyang were of a size and complexity unknown since antiquity.

The scale of operations of individual workshops was no greater than during Han. In the cities, workshops of the same trade were clumped together in particular districts known as _hang_, with the workshops often both making and selling their products. The name _hang_ or _t'ung-hang_ became a synonym for street. Ch'angan had twelve such _hang_. Within a _hang_ each establishment had its master, with apprentices and hired laborers working under him. Each _hang_ had a head who led its members in religious worship and was its representative before the government.

There were some large government and private business establishments engaged in trades like weaving, dyeing and wine making to meet imperial household needs. Mints and armories were also large-scale state enterprises. Some of their skilled workmen were conscripted for twenty-day annual terms from artisan families as their share of the labor service tax. Others were hired. Some of the less skilled workers were official dependents owing the state fixed periods of service during a portion of each year.

The center of silk production tended to shift from the Yellow River valley to the lower Yangtze during late T'ang as a consequence of the disturbances in the north. Cotton, originally from

Central Asia and South Asia, was becoming rather common. The technique of printing on cloth began during T'ang, and a variety of special weaving and dyeing techniques were practiced.

Porcelain manufacture developed greatly in both north and south China from its pre-T'ang roots. Printing, of which an example from Tunhuang in 868 A.D. is still extant, was well developed in the two capitals, in Szechwan, Yangchou and Hangchou.

Sui-T'ang Money

Sui Wen-ti's initial recoinage was successful. The coins were of appropriate weight and honestly labeled. Systematic recovery of old and private coins was made at all excise tax stations. But bad regional coinages, Yang-ti's devalued coins and a renewed upsurge of private coining ruined the currency system by the end of the dynasty.

T'ang's recoinage in 621 was initially successful, but the dynasty was later plagued by competition from private coinage and, from the ninth century, by a coin shortage. Government edicts prohibited coin exports from the country and from individual prefectures. It was also ordered that one string equal 850 cash rather than the black market rate of 800. None of these measures alleviated the ills of the monetary system.

"Flying money" was a system of mercantile notes of exchange which evolved to get around the inconvenience of sending direct cash payments over long distances and the prohibition against sending cash across even regional boundaries. Issued by large-scale private interests and government treasuries, this flying money was also known as "convenient exchange."

As these certificates gradually circulated more widely as a substitute for ready cash, hard money disappeared from circulation. When government edicts forbidding the use of this paper for money were ignored, the state determined to monopolize its issuance, but the state paper could not command sufficient popular confidence to effectively displace the private paper. This practice was the origin of later banking institutions and "flying money" the equivalent of modern checks.

The Economy During the Age of Disunion of the Five Dynasties

The land tax was increased and collected ruthlessly to meet the demands of military expenditures. Despite periodic attempts at reduction, taxes on salt and the raw materials for brewing wine were also kept high and the death penalty exacted for black market sales of more than a certain minimum of these items.

The political dislocations did not destroy trade opportunities. Overseas trade continued from places like Fukien. North-south trade within China was also maintained, with southern tea being sold in the north and used to finance southern military preparations. Hostilities, however, periodically blocked communications within China.

Four of the five dynasties of the north had their capital in Pienliang (K'aifeng), already a densely populated commercial center, and its walls were extended outward to accommodate its commercial growth. Its riverine communications with the east and south were also perfected.

Trade with northern barbarians like the Khitan and the Koreans flourished. There were formal horse markets on the former's borders and trade missions to Korea to barter cloth for bronze.

The Nine Classics were printed under government auspices during the Latter T'ang. Porcelain came into wider use.

As during late T'ang, bad coins continued to circulate illicitly in the south. In other areas, T'ang's old official coinage still circulated, but private melting of these coins because of the value of their metal content reduced their quantity sufficiently to hinder their circulation. Melting of coins flourished despite government edicts forbidding the practice.

Society and People's Livelihood

Sui Wen-ti eased the burden of taxation on land, wine and salt, and labor service. Ma Tuan-lin praises the frugality of his administration. Yang-ti completely reversed his father's policies. His Korean invasions, palace building, and construction of a great fleet of enormous canal boats to transport the court so burdened the nation that he was overthrown.

The casualty rate among his corvée laborers often approached 50%, and the agriculture of whole districts was in consequence ruined for want of timely labor. Yang-ti alienated even his courtiers, who were mostly northerners with families and estates remaining in the north, when he moved the capital to Yangchou and abandoned the north to the numerous rebels who had sprung up. Sui's fall was entirely due to Yang-ti's profligacy with the people's wealth.

T'ang T'ai-tsung's humane administration established the basis for the dynasty's prosperity. Hsuan-tsung's reign up until the An Lu-shan rebellion was the most prosperous era of T'ang, looked back upon with nostalgia by both poets and historians. The poet Tu Fu described the K'ai-yüan era (713-42) as one in which both public and private granaries were overflowing. There were networks of inns for the convenience of commercial travelers.

All this prosperity ended with An Lu-shan's rebellion and the succeeding nine years of related uprisings. Production dropped drastically and communications were blocked. The dominance of the manorial system increased and the ruin of the equal-fields intensified. The registered population dropped from 49,000,000 to 17,000,000. The state sold increasing numbers of ordination certificates for monks, gaining revenue over the short run but cutting its tax base over the long run.

Though after 780 the reforms of Liu Yen partially restored the state's finances, the earlier glories of T'ang were never fully restored.

In the midst of a great drought in eastern China, an ex-salt seller named Huang Ch'ao raised a great rebellion in 875. It soon encompassed Shantung, Honan, Anhui and Hupei. Eventually Huang raided south to Fukien and Canton and then back up to the Ch'angsha area. Huang alternately fought and feigned negotiating his surrender. Failing to push north of the middle reaches of the Yangtze, Huang moved downstream to Hangchow. By 880 he had renewed his strength and struck north again across the Huai to Loyang and, a month later, to Ch'angan itself. There he proclaimed a new dynasty.

Huang had acquired a spurious reputation for humaneness, but once in the capital his bandits showed their true nature. They looted and filled the streets with corpses. The T'ang emperor had fled to Ch'engtu, but loyalist forces rallied, drove the discredited Huang from the capital, but then began looting themselves. This allowed Huang to successfully reoccupy the city and impose a renewed bloodbath on its inhabitants for initially welcoming the T'ang forces. By 883 Huang's own depredations had ruined his base for supply, and a loyalist force led by Li K'o-yung again drove him from the capital. Huang escaped into Honan while the loyalists once again delayed pursuit to carry on looting, but by 885 he was finally run down after causing a decade of chaos and the death of some eight million persons. Accounts of Huang's conquest of Canton and murder of foreign merchants there even made their way into the Arab histories.

The life of the people continued to be bitter during the Five Dynasties. According to one contemporary story, it would not rain within a hundred _li_ of the capital because even the rain feared taxes and would not approach so close to the city. Though no accurate figures are available, the evidence indicates that the population continued to shrink as a consequence of the ongoing disorder.

Section VIII

THE AGE OF RENEWAL: THE TWO SUNG DYNASTIES

Outline

The period from 755 to the fall of Northern Han in 978 was one in which China was divided among numerous warlord states whose economies varied widely. The degree of economic development enjoyed by any area depended on the degree of peace and good order imposed by its government as well as on its previous level of development.

Hence Fukien, Canton, Szechwan, and the Ch'ien-t'ang region (that southern part of the lower Yangtze centering on Hangchou) recovered and prospered while Yangchou, which suffered repeated disorders after Huang Ch'ao's rebellion, continued in a depressed state. Much of the Yellow River valley also quickly recovered from the late T'ang troubles. The southeastern states were particularly well insulated from the northern military disorders and their trade flourished.

Pienliang (K'aifeng) became the great entrepôt of north-south trade. For this reason the Sung founder was obliged to use it as his capital, as adequate supplies for the centrally controlled army he created to end the Five Dynasties' cycle of military usurpations could not be adequately accumulated at Loyang or Ch'angan.

Because of winter freezing, the main waterways were only open half the year, and the Sung state carefully organized the transport system to compensate for this, sending salt from the north to the south on what would otherwise have been the empty barges which had been rushed north with the year's supply of southern grain. Chenchou replaced Yangchou as the southern entrepôt of the canal network.

Northern Chou had melted down over a third of the Buddhist

images, imported copper from Korea and forbidden the manufacture of copper implements so as to gain enough bronze for its coinage. Silver was also in extensive use as money.

The rulers of several of the states preceding Sung were closely connected with trade and the protection of trade. The townsmen of the Yangtze valley were demanding peace and unity even before Sung reunited the north and realized it needed the supplies of the south even to maintain itself in power in the north. Hence Sung was able to rapidly unify north and south.

Thereafter a monetary economy spread rapidly throughout the empire. Even the state's fiscal operations were soon monetized. Both army and bureaucracy thenceforth were paid salaries directly by the central government. No longer, therefore, could locally supported armies serve as the privileged base for warlord power. The pre-T'ang decentralized bureaucratic powers were replaced by a centralized fiscal, military and sovereign power and the bureaucracy was professionalized. All this was the consequence of the economy's monetization. Sung's centralization may be said to have been based on popular demand for reform and for progress on the basis of peace and good order.

The Current of Economic Thought of the Two Sung Dynasties and Wang An-shih

The heart of Wang An-shih's famous reforms was his aim to enrich state and people. The twelve items in his reform encompassed reform of the state structure, the state's taxation and social controls over society, the military and educational systems. To understand why more than half of these items involved economic and fiscal matters it is necessary to examine the background of the age.

Sung's founder had accepted a weaker position on the frontiers as the price for preserving central control over the armies and thereby preventing the sort of coup which had originally given the throne to him and his predecessors during the Five Dynasties. If Khitan suzerainty over the Yen-Yün territories of the north had not been conceded, the dynasty might have had to flee south much earlier than the second quarter of the twelfth century.

Emperor Shen-tsung (r. 1068-86), who smarted under the humiliation of paying tribute to the Khitan, viewed fiscal reform chiefly as a means of amassing military power to avenge this shame. The fiscal demands on the Sung state were large and rapidly growing. By Ying-tsung's time (r. 1064-67) there were over 24,000 officials in the bureaucracy. Military expenses in the north ate up two-thirds of the budget which was chronically and drastically out of balance. The main reason for such chronic deficits was the inequality in the application of the land tax and the consequent reduction of the amount collected in taxes.

Edicts were unable to halt the trend toward concentration of land in the hands of the elite, its avoidance of taxes, and what some contemporaries described as the reduction of tenants to the status of slaves, subject to whipping and private corvée. Wang An-shih took it as his task to reform this desperate situation.

Born in 1021 into an official family in Kiangsi, at the age of nineteen Wang was orphaned and he, his mother and elder brother were impoverished. After his period of mourning, he passed his chin-shih examinations, entered local office and won the patronage of Ou-yang Hsiu. Thereafter Wang rose steadily in office, continuing to win the admiration and support of influential men like Ou-yang and Ssu-ma Kuang. By 1060 he was advocating better pay for minor local officials as the basis for reforming fiscal policy. Ying-tsung's short reign (1064-67) largely overlapped Wang's period of mourning for his mother.

The new emperor, Shen-tsung, called him to Court in 1068 and the next year, at age forty-nine, Wang became chief minister. He had the emperor's full support for the fundamental reforms he now proposed. Wang's reorganization of the central fiscal agencies, his equal tax and "green shoots" plans were begun that year.

By the following year massive opposition, led by such former supporters of Wang as Ssu-ma Kuang and Han Ch'i, had begun, but Wang forced these men into retirement and kept the now fearful emperor on his side to begin the pao-chia and voluntary labor service reforms. In 1071 he converted the Broad Grace Granary fields into capital for the Ever Normal Granaries and the following year reformed the examination system and the national university. The next year he instituted the market exchange reform, horse-breeding system and equal-fields tax reform, thereby completing the bulk of his reforms.

In 1074 Wang temporarily left office as drought intensified opposition to his reforms. But his protegés maintained the reforms and the next year he returned to power. Within another year, however, dispirited by the death of his son, Wang again left office after over seven years in power and at age fifty-six was not again to hold office.

Though in retirement, he retained the emperor's favor. Nevertheless, Wang lived a simple life visiting monastaries, writing poetry and editing the San Ching (Three Classics). In 1086, anguished at the death of Shen-tsung and at Ssu-ma Kuang's abolition of the reforms, he took sick and died. It may be said that he never acted selfishly but rather for the public good, though he did harbor resentment of his opponents to the very end of his life. The nobility of his character and thought have always been venerated by posterity.

His goals were twofold: first to enrich the state and strengthen its armies, and second to encourage increased production. Each goal was to interact with the other. The base for all his reforms was a new office he set up directly under the premier's control to unify the hitherto separate three offices (revenue and population, budget, and salt and iron) which controlled fiscal policy. His aim was to make sure taxes were collected fairly, thereby removing state-imposed obstacles to popular prosperity.

Within fifteen months, however, this fiscal coordinating responsibility was returned to the secretariat (chung-shu-men-hsia, the chief political authority of the central government) because of the criticism of men like Han Ch'i. Nevertheless, in this short period it reduced waste by some 40%, something Ssu-ma Kuang had been unable to do when in power at the beginning of Shen-tsung's reign.

The market exchange law was designed to remove the abuses committed by the great shops established in the capital by rich merchants and aristocratic officials. First established in K'aifeng and then in five other major cities, the market exchange offices organized merchants into hang or guilds through which alone government purchases would be made. Interest rates on commercial loans were to be limited. Though edicts had to be issued against excessive interest charged under the system, the fact that the rich merchants opposed it indicates that it was of benefit to the poor ones.

Wang's equal contributions law was similar to the reforms of Han's Sang Hung-yang and T'ang's Yang Yen. It attempted to modify the requirement that regions send in the same tribute (i.e. tax in kind) whether the year was good or bad. It would do so by giving a sum of cash and grain to the transport officials to use as capital in buying and selling tribute goods within and among the six major regions. This would minimize transport costs and maximize government receipts of taxes in kind. This scheme was criticized for encouraging official corruption which merchants could take advantage of for profit, just as happened in Han Wu-ti's time when the state attempted to buy cheap and sell dear. But these were not criticisms of the law, rather of the men who enforced it.

The "green shoots" law was designed to lend cash to the

peasants in the spring and collect it back with interest in the fall, using capital from the Ever Normal and Broad Grace granaries. Borrowing was to be done by groups of ten households, with landlords as the guarantors for their tenants. No household was to be forced to borrow and limits were set to the amount each category of household could borrow. Urban households could borrow on analogous terms. Five years after the system was begun the number of officials supervising it in each circuit was increased from 200 to 500 so as to provide sufficient supervision and to minimize official corruption. The system lasted sixteen years in all. It was designed to end the usury which had always been the chief inhibitor of rural growth and prosperity.

Its critics argued that the interest rate charged amounted to 40% annually in practice if not in law, and that such easy loans constituted an unwarranted temptation to ignorant peasants to live beyond their means. Nevertheless, its early critics later called for its reinstitution, proof of this reform's essential merit.

The field survey and equal tax law attempted to alleviate a problem going back to the founding of the dynasty. Ou-yang Hsiu had asked for such a reform as far back as 1042 and had actually carried it out in a few localities. The twelve years during which Wang and his successors carried out half of this land survey compares favorably with the eighteen years taken for a land survey in Napoleonic France.

Sung, like the many dynasties before it, called on the people for a bewildering variety of labor service taxes. These were for both civilian and military tasks at the _hsien_ and _chou_ levels. But the exemption of official, military and monk households encouraged abuses and great hardship for those households unable to obtain exemptions. The better-off households which were responsible for such tasks were encouraged to split up or even turn to banditry when ruined by the expenses of carrying them out.

Wang's Avoidance of Labor Service law divided households of property into five grades based on their wealth, and it imposed a tax proportioned to their wealth in lieu of labor service. Monasteries and official families were not exempted from this tax. Men were hired to carry out the services with the revenues generated by the tax. An additional surtax could be collected to anticipate flood or drought relief expenses. In the greater K'aifeng metropolitan area, where the system was first tried, several thousand men were hired to substitute for the former labor service.

Critics objected that well-off non-gentry households did not benefit as much as the poorer non-gentry households by the indirect subsidy the latter obtained when official and monastic households were added to the tax rolls. It was also argued that the men hired were not as reliable as those formerly impressed into service, and that the tax tended to not be effectively collected in bad years whereas the old system had been enforceable even in bad years. In its favor, it may be argued that this was a progressive tax, capable of increasing in proportion to the growth of the economy.

Wang also appointed officials to spread knowledge of irrigation and drainage techniques in each circuit. Because he rewarded these officials for concrete accomplishments, over 360,000 ch'ing of fields were newly irrigated during his administration.

A guild exemption tax was also instituted in lieu of compulsory contributions in kind to the Court by the various trades, thereby ending, it was hoped, extortion of kickbacks by palace servants. The tea and salt trades were not much affected by the reforms, having earlier been freed from government monopoly licensing.

In general, Wang favored free trade. He increased the amount of coinage by more than threefold and ended the prohibition on manufacture of bronze implements and export of bronze cash. That these measures were opposed indicates the strength of reactionary forces.

Though Wang was unable to accomplish all his aims, his unquestioned loyalty was reciprocated by Shen-tsung to the end. Though he was not able to much improve the lot of the people, the state's resources were increased and these new resources were used along the northern and southern frontiers more successfully than ever previously. That the reforms were basically in accord with the need of the times is evidenced by their partial restoration even by such opponents as Ssu-ma Kuang.

The reforms did run up against the interests of the great families. When Shen-tsung once observed that though the reforms displeased the elite, they were of use to the masses, it was pointed out to him that the elite were those used to govern the empire, not the masses. If before the reforms were instituted Wang had been able to train cadres to propagandize them among the masses, he would surely have been able to overcome the reactionaries. Nevertheless, his was a noble failure and his career a glorious page in our history.

Land Distribution and Agricultural Credit Policies

Farming techniques did not differ from those of earlier times, but credit and land measure methods did. The first two Sung emperors followed policies of tax abatement and agricultural relief and thereby successfully raised the level of agricultural production.

Later emperors placed restrictions on the amount of land the elite could own, but these laws proved unenforceable. By mid-Northern Sung tax-free elite estates comprised 70% of all arable land. The situation in Southern Sung was comparable and worsened late in the dynasty. There were official and imperial manors in addition to privately held ones. In late Sung many official manors were sold to raise revenue for the state.

The agricultural population was divided into "master" and "guest" households, the former being landed cultivators with a measure of capital, the latter being landless and often of servile status. In 1021 there were 6,039,331 master households and 2,638,346 guest households. By 1080 there were 10,109,542 master and 4,734,144 guest households, showing the increased degree of land concentration in the hands of the rich and well-born.*

The average household appears to have cultivated around 100 mou in mid-thirteenth century and to have shouldered a heavy tax burden. Guest households had to pay capitation taxes in addition to their rent, and though they avoided corvée to the state they often had to do various equivalent tasks for their landlords.

Wang An-shih's land survey was designed to measure all land, grading it into five degrees of fertility. Local residents were to check the records, copies of which would then be filed locally as the basis for levying taxes. Ts'ai Ching, Wang's early twelfth-century successor, claimed that these land records made it more difficult for large landowners and local officials to cheat the peasants in land sales and tax assessments. The obsolescence of these records by late Southern Sung contributed greatly to the decay of agriculture then and the consequent fall of the dynasty.

Official fields had been accumulated from time to time by confiscation of the lands of disgraced officials. In 1263 lands in the lower Yangtze region held by private owners above the legal

---

*Chou's figures, though they indicate an increase of 3% (from 43% to 46%) in the percentage of guest households, may not necessarily support the point he wishes to make. The total number of households in 1080 is so much greater than that of 1021 that it must to some considerable degree reflect better reporting in 1080, probably in part because of Wang An-shih's cadastral survey. Hence the figures for the two dates are likely not sufficiently commensurable to permit comparison of their component parts. Even for the latter date evasion of population registration must have been considerable. Cf. Ho Ping-ti, Studies in the Population of China, 1368-1953 (Cambridge: Harvard University Press, 1959), pp. 264-65, which notes that in 1102 20,000,000 households were registered (a suspiciously large increase of more than five million over the figures for 1080), and that even this figure must be corrected for "rampant" evasion of population registration. (EHK)

limits were purchased to serve as public fields. Chia Ssu-tao has always been accused of corrupt practices in buying this land. The administration of the system does appear to have allowed confiscation of smaller peasant holdings despite its original aim of reducing large estates. Hence though it aimed to increase state revenues from the rents received and thereby bolster military preparedness, its actual effect was to accelerate the dynasty's decay during the years just before the Mongol conquest.

The long-term bad effects of rural usury obliged the state to devise policies dealing with rural credit. Most of Sung's fiscal resources were based on taxation of commerce. Tax receipts from overseas trade increased drastically during the dynasty, especially during early Southern Sung.

In early Northern Sung there were complaints that only 20% to 30% of the arable land was being cultivated and that tax receipts were consequently barely half of what they should be. Interest rates charged by the rich were extortionate. One <u>tan</u> of grain borrowed in the spring had to be repaid with two <u>tan</u> in the fall. Labor service was so heavy as to drive many farmers from their homes either actually or through forging of official documents.

The consequent rural poverty stimulated government attempts at reform even early in the dynasty. Attempts were made to use the various civilian and military government granaries for seasonal relief, but these schemes were all ruined by the corruption of local officials. Wang An-shih's "green shoots" law and, during Southern Sung, Chu Hsi's attempts to set up local cooperative granaries to remedy this situation were the forerunners of modern agricultural banks and constituted a glorious page in the history of our country's agriculture.

All the various schemes for state credit emphasized lending seed grain or oxen which would directly contribute to increases in productivity. Attempts were also made to mobilize local private capital for relief through various kinds of government guarantees. Attempts were made to limit or eliminate interest on loans to succor disaster victims.

Wang An-shih's and Chu Hsi's plans were designed to eliminate the official corruption which had ruined all earlier attempts at agricultural credit reform. The latter was an attempt by Chu to transcend the urban limits of earlier official granaries (like the Ever Normal and Righteous granaries) by placing cooperative granaries right in the villages and to correct the major flaw of the "green shoots" scheme, its administration by remote officials, by having these granaries administered by the local gentry.

Under the general supervision of the hsien, Chu's system grouped households into units of ten and fifty, with a granary for each fifty households. The local gentry was encouraged to contribute a granary's initial capital. Loans were to be made carefully and only to those who actually needed help. Interest was to be limited or abolished during bad years. When capital had been increased tenfold, the surplus was to be applied to public use. Ultimately, interest would be limited to three sheng per tan of grain, or 3%.

Chu himself tried this scheme in one area for a decade and a half. He advocated its use nationally on a voluntary basis, with no compulsion exerted on the part of peasant households to join a cooperative granary. Chu's model was widely imitated during Southern Sung, but with the passage of time this system too fell into disuse.

Science and Technology

Sung was China's golden age of mathematics. The earlier mathematical classics were printed by the late eleventh century and reprinted during Southern Sung. There were several mathematicians whose treatises were also published. The eleventh-century mathematician Liu Yi worked out the equivalent of "Horner's Method" which was not achieved in the West until 1819. The Northern Sung mathematician Chia Hsien did work similar to the trigonometry of the seventeenth-century Frenchman Pascal. Ch'in Chiu-shao of late Southern Sung was the first to use the symbol for zero and the simplified forms of the numerals now used in commerce. He also improved on the formulas of his predecessors for extracting roots of numbers.

Gunpowder, known by Sui-T'ang times, was used for military purposes in early Southern Sung to make smokescreens. A late twelfth-century device used true gun powder to fling projectiles more than two hundred paces.

Fig. 8 A south-pointing carriage.

A "south-pointing carriage" was used in Han-Wei times, but a true magnetic compass was first used for navigation during Sung and was then transmitted to Europe by the Arabs. Pi Sheng invented movable-type printing in the mid-eleventh century. Foot-powered paddle-wheeled boats had been in use since T'ang, and though they played a notable role in several early Southern military campaigns, they were not, unfortunately, taken seriously by contemporaries.

The rocket, now being used to explore the universe, was invented in early Northern Sung and used for military purposes. It was likely transmitted to the West by the Arabs in the thirteenth century. The term "fire arrow" goes back to Three Kingdoms times but must have then referred to arrows shot from a bow. Fire arrows as true rockets could not have preceded the late T'ang-Five Dynasties invention of gunpowder. The fire arrows described in an early Sung and a Ming treatise on military technology are unquestionably true rockets.

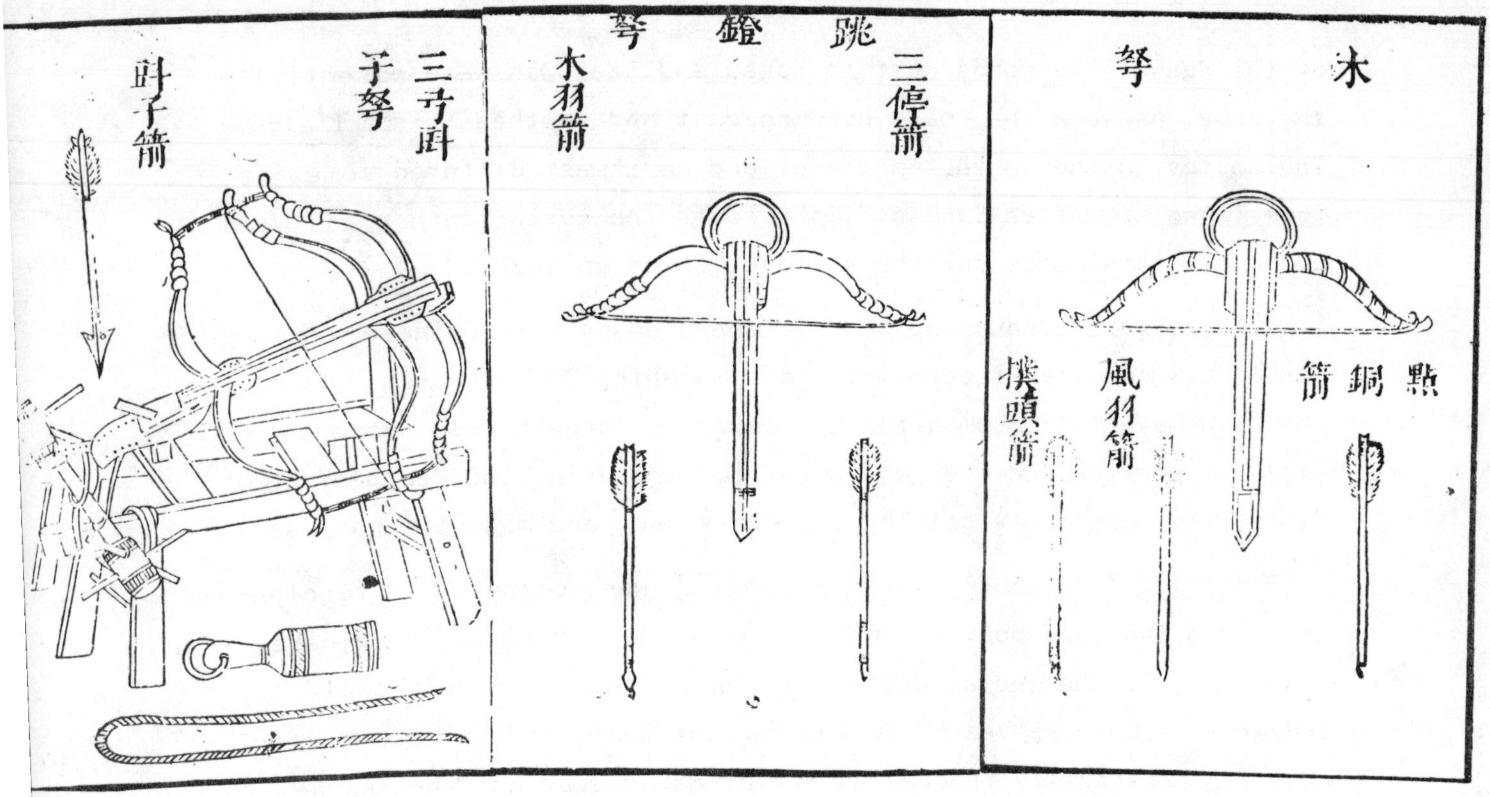

Fig. 9 Crossbows

Porcelain manufacture flourished in several famous kilns, such as the Chün in Honan, the Lungch'üan of Chekiang, the Ko of Hangchou, the Ju of Honan, the Ting of Hopei and the various Kuan (or official) potteries in Fukien and Hangchou.

The amount of tea drunk had increased prodigiously since the introduction of the practice during T'ang. There were now many varieties produced, some very expensive. The state taxed and monopolized the marketing of tea through several regional offices. Relatively free trade in the commodity was not permitted until after the middle of the eleventh century.

There were several centers specializing in the production of various types of silk cloth.

<u>Communications</u>

Sung's area was more constricted than Sui-T'ang's, but its communications network was highly developed. The main difference was that Ch'angan was the hub of the T'ang road system and K'aifeng of the Sung. The roads west to Kansu and Szechwan were essentially the same, as were the roads heading east and southeast from K'aifeng. The routes to the north, northeast and northwest differed somewhat from T'ang's. After Sung's flight south the north-south roads were cut until later eras saw the restoration of unity.

There were oceangoing vessels operated by both Chinese and foreigners capable of carrying loads weighing 300,000 chin. Equipped with watertight compartments, carrying large crews, weapons to ward off pirates and even equipment for measuring the depth of the water, they could navigate by the stars, sun and magnetic compass.

Unlike T'ang whose overseas commerce was dominated by foreigners, Sung overseas commerce was increasingly dominated by Chinese, especially in the Indian Ocean. By Yüan times Marco Polo could travel in a Chinese vessel to the Persian Gulf, and Chinese merchant vessels occasionally reached as far as Madagascar and the Red Sea.

Commerce

The early Sung emperors were sympathetic to commerce, allowing no tax increase on it and occasionally reducing taxes as well as removing taxes altogether on minor items. During Northern Sung certain valuable imported goods (different categories at various times) had to be sold initially to special government bureaus which then wholesaled them onto the private market.

Temple markets were highly developed. In K'aifeng, one temple's market ground could hold ten thousand people and markets were held there five times each month. The markets of K'aifeng were numerous, large, and in certain trades witnessed very large transactions. Tea and wine houses were numerous and many people ate all their meals in such places, never eating at home. Markets remained open well into the night. Goods, including bulk products like grain, came by water from most areas of the country to the capital's markets. Dishes cooked in the styles of all regions of the country were available in the restaurants of the city.

Foreign trade flourished more than in any previous dynasty. To Canton as an officially sanctioned port of entry for foreign trade were added Ch'üanchou, Hangchou, Mingchou, and Michou. Trade was engaged in with Korea, Japan, continental and insular Southeast Asia, and Arabia. Exports included gold, silver, strings of cash, lead, tin, various kinds of cloth, and porcelain. Imports included spices, ivory, coral, various precious stones, and tropical hardwoods.

Both foreign and Chinese merchants engaged in foreign trade were closely regulated. Exports of armaments or goods capable of being manufactured into arms were forbidden to places like Korea.

Though Northern Sung frequently fought with Liao and Western Hsia, trade with these states nevertheless flourished during peaceful intervals. Each state established tax offices on their mutual frontiers and these served as marketplaces where spices, ivory, and tea were traded by China for precious metals, wool and horses. Liao attempted to bar trade with Sung in commodities in short supply domestically, such as horses and sheep. Trade with Western Hsia also flourished, so much so that Sung had difficulty limiting illegal private trade by managers of the official markets.

Though the early Southern Sung emperors frequently reduced or remitted commercial taxes to ease the burden on northern refugees reestablishing themselves in the south, local and transit taxes continued to be collected illegally by local officials to an extortionate extent, putting a great burden on the poor and contributing to the ultimate demise of the dynasty.

The capital, Linan (Hangchou), became as great a commercial center as K'aifeng had ever been, its avenues and lanes crowded with shops. Both official and private trade, involving export of grain and manufactured goods in exchange for horses and tropical products, flourished with the barbarian states of the southwest.

The Monetary System

Bronze money continued to be used, supplemented by silver and paper. After banning inferior coinage, the Sung founder in 971 circulated a bronze one-cash coin similar to the eighth-century T'ang issue. From T'ai-tsung's time on dated coins were issued for each new year period (nien hao).

Early in the dynasty, because of localized bronze shortages, large iron coins were issued in Szechwan and Fukien. To support this currency for a time it was forbidden to import bronze coins into Szechwan. The Fukien iron issue was soon withdrawn.

A mid-eleventh century attempt to debase the coinage by adding a large bronze coin worth ten cash and a small iron coin worth one-third of a cash to the issue stimulated forgery and inflation. The amount of bronze cash continued to decline during Southern Sung, causing broader use of iron cash.

Gold was scarce during Sung and silver gradually replaced it as a monetary metal, with taxes frequently being collected in silver. The silver "shoe" of fifty ounces and worth one hundred strings of bronze cash became standard nationwide.

As a "shoe" was often split up in actual use, by 1197 a new standard was devised with each ounce of silver being worth about two strings of bronze cash, but by 1200 the practice of alloying baser metals with the silver ruined attempts to use it as a standard of value. Nevertheless, the use of silver as a monetary metal continued to become more popular during the thirteenth century.

Sung's use of paper money represented a great advance in the history of Chinese currency. In Szechwan paper certificates initially called chiao-tzu (but known by other names at various times) replaced the heavy and inconvenient iron money. Each certificate expired three years from the date of issue. Initially they were issued by sixteen rich mercantile houses, but disorder caused by occasional failure to honor the certificates by their sponsors led to takeover of their issue by the state early in the eleventh century. Thereafter their use gradually spread.

In early Southern Sung such notes were issued extensively (initially to the amount of 500,000 strings) under the label hui-tzu and then kuan-tzu. But overissue and the ease with which they could be forged greatly reduced their value despite imposition of the death penalty for forgery and high rewards offered informers. Ultimately even local governments would not accept the notes even in payment for taxes.

There were also various kinds of local note issues, but these were not permitted to circulate nationally. Government manipulation of the monetary system impeded circulation of the money and caused much popular resentment against the dynasty.

Taxation

During its first two decades Sung was distracted from tax reform by the need to complete the unification of the empire. It accumulated official fields from the holdings of the various states it conquered and from their ruling families. The rental it got from these holdings, amounting to 50% of the crops they produced, made a larger contribution to early Sung state revenues than the tax on private land which amounted to only 10% of the crops. Prior to Wang An-shih's land survey, records were so inadequate that only a fraction of the taxes actually owed were ever collected. T'ai-tsung's policy of allowing renters to keep official fields as their private property and giving them a three-year tax holiday followed by a two-thirds reduction in taxes thereafter was insufficient even to fully repopulate the region around the capital.

In addition to rent on official land and tax on private land, there were taxes on buildings, a head tax and miscellaneous taxes on livestock, silkworms, and salt. Taxes were paid in grain, cloth, cash and commodities, with the quantity of commodities varying each year according to their market prices.

No fundamental changes were made in the tax system until Wang An-shih's land survey system was instituted in 1072 to record the quantity and quality of all land as the basis for an equitable tax. Unfortunately, when the reform was ended after twelve years, only half the land had been surveyed. Though reinstituted between 1104 and 1120 when the system was then again abolished, the old methods of allocating taxes were reverted to.

By early Southern Sung all the old abuses had returned, exacerbated by the destruction of war. Official corruption remained, as always, and was one of the main causes for the failure of Wang's reforms.

One of the main reasons for Sung's ability to unify the realm was its policy of remitting commercial taxes. These had reached extortionate levels during late T'ang and Five Dynasties times. Sung's goods in transit tax was only 2%, its tax of fixed businesses' transactions only 3%.

Though the dynasty continued to limit commercial taxation into the eleventh century, surtaxes for military needs and on goods for palace consumption constituted important exceptions. Such abuses were especially prevalent during the times Southern Sung was under military pressure.

Sung's salt laws were revised several times. Originally salt transport was handled officially, and _hsien_ officials wholesaled it to merchants. But this placed a great transport burden on corvée labor and in 1030, in exchange for payment of a fee at the capital, private merchants took over transportation of salt. This reform not only cut down on the burden of corvée but reduced state expenses and allowed for more efficient market allocation of transportation resources.

In 1042 the old system was restored because state revenues, which had originally gone up under the new system, had then declined. In 1048 the system was again changed to allow merchants to buy salt certificates regionally. Abuses soon crept into this system as well.

Wang An-shih moved from a state monopoly to a free enterprise position, and Ts'ai Ching ultimately returned to the certificate system though it soon suffered from the old abuses. The monopoly-sales system failed in part because it controlled only a portion of salt production and hence could not effectively eliminate a black market, and in part because political conflict within the central government led to frequent changes in policy before any one policy could establish itself.

Early Sung used the latter Chou system of state control of the production of wine at the capital and provincial centers. Private production was permitted locally but subject to government supervision and taxation. By T'ai-tsung's reign abuses appeared. High prices charged by state wineries and high taxes imposed on private production led to tax dodging which the imposition of stiff punishments, including execution for violators, could not eliminate.

Several regional state offices were founded to buy up and tax tea production. Free trade in tea was permitted in Szechwan, Shensi and Canton, though their tea could not be sold outside these three regions. Elsewhere the state bought tea cheaply and sold it in the producing areas to private retailers who had previously purchased tea certificates at the capital. By the 1070's this policy, which both tempted the official tea plantation managers to sell on the black market and threatened them with heavy punishment if they did so, was tending to drive tea-producing areas out of production. There was a saying: "The land produced not tea but misfortune."

At the beginning of Sung local ferry taxes were abolished, and the preceding era's tax on those who wished to hold high office was restored. The tax on the raising of aquatic products like fish and ducks was removed, but these were taxed once they entered the market. A certificate had to be bought to validate sales of land

and livestock.

Several excise taxes were collected as surtaxes, especially during Southern Sung. These surtaxes were first imposed to meet extraordinary military expenses, but most were continued even after military threats had abated. The state also made a good profit through its monopoly of the wholesale trade in incense. Almost all incense was imported and had to be initially sold by importers to the state.

Sung's corvée system was based on its predecessor's. Initially officials and the military were exempt. It was administered at the chou and hsien levels. Only men between the ages of twenty and sixty were subject to it.

In 971 in the north corvée was limited to river conservancy work during spring. In the south the old practice of commuting corvée to a tax in cash and grain was continued, and though the cash tax was ended in 1011, the grain tax was continued. In parts of the southeast a cash tax was retained and, as it was linked to the salt laws, was increased when the salt certificate system was instituted.

Sung also conscripted commoner families for various civil and military tasks at the local level. This proved extremely burdensome as monks and elite households were exempted from service. Wang An-shih's labor service avoidance law was designed to end these abuses. It was, however, abolished in 1086.

Society and People's Livelihood

So as to avoid the chaos of the preceding era of disunion, Sung T'ai-tsu instituted a policy of centralizing power, in particular he placed the main army under direct imperial control at the capital. Garrisons on the frontiers along with their officers were regularly rotated back to the center.

This policy and the long period of peace led ultimately to a slackening of military efficiency. To restore the army's effectiveness, Wang An-shih instituted a militia system to substitute for mercenaries at the local level. But after 1086 the end of the reform led to a weakening of this militia, and Sung was no longer able to match the power of Liao and Western Hsia on the frontiers. Hence it eventually fell to Chin. The responsibility for the loss of the north must be shared by both the centralized state, which could not guarantee security despite all the taxes it collected, and by Ssu-ma Kuang and his faction who took too narrow a view of their responsibilities.

It is evident that economic development and the political system are intertwined. The Sung Shih (Sung History) concludes that the central government was not in fact truly centralized. The constant rotation of its personnel made it certain that 80% to 90% of the high officials never really knew their jobs. Sung attempted to centralize power and at the same time avoid the corruption which centralization encouraged. In practice, this meant that those with responsibility were so constricted by regulations designed to avoid corruption that they lacked power and those with power lacked responsibility, a system certain to bring disaster to both state and people.

Sung factionalism set the gentlemen against each other, leaving room for lesser men to take over. This was the fate of Wang An-shih's reforms. If the great men who led the opposing factions had been able to work together, the dynasty could have been saved and there would have been hope for raising the level of the people's livelihood.

The estrangement of Sung Neo-Confucianism from social needs is also one of the reasons for the failure to maintain the people's livelihood. The quarrel between the war and peace factions at the time of Northern Sung's fall ended with the latter traitorously selling out both state and people.

Conflict with Liao continued from early in the dynasty until the treaty of 1004 which made Sung the subordinate power. In 1074 additional territory was ceded to Liao. Peace was made with Western Hsia in 1044 after six years of war. Renewed war in Shen-tsung's time only increased the tribute Sung had to pay to Western Hsia.

The deal with Chin in 1122 gave Sung only empty cities and merely transferred its tribute payments from Liao to Chin. The two attacks by Chin in 1125 and 1126 beggared the capital and set the stage for the loss of the entire northern half of the country and a humiliating peace a decade and a half later. The peace with Chin in 1207 increased the annual tribute which had to be paid.

These successive defeats and indemnities had all to be paid for by the people. Military expenses also were a heavy burden on the people, the south alone paying taxes of 70,000,000 strings through a tax system which left hardly any items untaxed.

Even before the foreign disasters at the end of Northern Sung, two great popular rebellions, led by Sung Chiang and Fang La, had taken place largely because of bad social conditions. Such popular rebellions continued during early Southern Sung, led by men like Li Ch'eng and Yang Yao.

Section IX

THE AGE OF DESTITUTION: LIAO, CHIN, AND YÜAN

Outline

The nine rulers of Liao reigned from 918 to 1125 over much of Manchuria and the northern parts of Shansi and Hopei. The Jurched who founded the Chin rose in northeast Manchuria and eventually controlled all of Manchuria, the Yellow River valley and part of the Huai valley. Their nine rulers reigned from 1115 to 1234.

Yüan's founder Temuchin ascended the throne in Mongolia in 1206 with the appellation of Chingis Khan. He conquered Western Liao, Western Hsia and joined with Sung to attack Chin. His grandson Kubilai ascended the throne in 1260, established his capital in Yenching and adopted the dynastic name Yüan. Sixteen years later he conquered Sung and united China. He then attacked Japan, Korea, and various states in Southeast Asia, many of which sent him tribute. His territory extended across Asia to Eastern Europe, to an extent unprecedented in all antiquity. Though he reduced this great area to peace and good order with the aid of able officials, his armies were constantly in action and the people much burdened.

Because it was compiled during Yüan, long after the fall of the dynasty, the economics section of the Liao Shih (Liao History) is rather incomplete. The economics section of the Chin Shih (Chin History) is rather more complete, but as it put so much emphasis on warfare, the Chin was not much interested in economic issues and hence left few records on the subject.

By contrast, the Mongols who founded the Yüan dynasty, although a barbarian people without a recorded history before they entered China, once in control of China used Yeh-lü Ch'u-ts'ai's aid and hence had much in their economic system worthy to record. Because of the Mongols' great military successes their contributions were especially numerous in the realm of economic connections between China and foreign civilizations.

The Special Features of the Economy

Yeh-lü Chu-ts'ai (1190-1243) belonged to the Liao royal Yeh-lü clan. Since his grandfather's time his family had served the Chin court. His father held high office and was learned in both Confucianism and mystical studies. Ch'u-ts'ai was born when his father was already old, and hence he was lovingly brought up in his father's scholarly tradition. His greatness is measured by the fact that though by blood a Khitan, he was in the mainstream of Chinese culture.

A man of peace and good order, he could only bide his time with scholarship during the decadent and corrupt last years of the Chin dynasty. When Yenching fell to the Mongols he was granted an interview with Chingis because as a Khitan he was expected to be thirsting for vengeance against their Chin conquerors. His unwillingness to denouce Chin because his family had loyally served them impressed Chingis and the khan kept him in his entourage.

With his talents as an astronomer, physician, and diviner Ch'u-ts'ai gradually won Chingis' confidence and hence on his deathbed Chingis recommended him to his successor, Ögödei, who made Ch'u-ts'ai chief minister.

Ch'u-ts'ai was deeply learned in Buddhism as well as secular studies. He was also the most important political figure of early Yüan, the man who completed the process of assimilating northern China into the Mongol empire begun by Chingis.

His career is documented in the writings of contemporaries, his own collected works and in the Yüan Shih (Yüan History). He has also been much studied by modern Western and Chinese scholars, beginning in detail with Bretschneider's work in the nineteenth century. He is first mentioned in the West in de Mailla's

Histoire generale de la Chine in the eighteenth century.

Ch'u-ts'ai's most notable accomplishment was to establish the principle that China had to be governed according to Chinese principles, the principles of the Confucian tradition. As a consequence, the Mongols were slowly sinicized. To begin with, during the completion of the conquest of Chin, he had the Mongol policy of annihilating resisting cities' populations rescinded. He also rescued and subsidized the numerous Confucian scholars whose work helped sinicize the Mongol administration. In the realm of fiscal policy he persuaded Ögödei not to enforce the jokingly put forward scheme of reducing China to pastureland and instead established ten regional tax offices to collect the usual land and excise taxes. So pleased was Ögödei at the revenues thereby produced that he placed fiscal policy entirely under Ch'u-ts'ai's control.

He established a budget and ordered that the amount and type of taxes had to be first approved by him before being levied. Though some were still hurt, so honestly did he run his system that he was universally hailed as a loyal and public spirited prime minister. His measures increased the strength of the dynasty while curbing the Mongol impulse to loot.

After his death he was slanderously accused of amassing private wealth while in office, but these accusations were unjustified. Like Sun Yat-sen, with whom he is comparable in honor, he did leave a large private library.

Unfortunately not only did his successors fail to build on the foundations he had established but let these fall into ruin, thereby allowing Yüan to fall into decadence.

Though China had had sea navigation since Warring States times, the sea routes were never of crucial importance for internal communications until Yüan times, when there was an enormous increase in the use of coastal shipping to transport southern grain to the north so as to avoid the expense and labor needed to maintain the inland waterways. The sea transit route was eventually reduced to a ten-day run to the north by going far enough out to avoid shoal waters and take advantage of the prevailing winds. The route was not as safe as in recent times. The wind and waves were not dependable and ships and cargoes could be lost. Specially constructed grain freighters of two thousand _tan_ capacity came into use.

Special attention was also paid to river conservancy. Central and regional bureaus were used to supervise such work. The Yellow River shifted its mouth to the north in 1344. In 1351 a seven-month project using 150,000 corvée laborers restored it to its former course, flowing into the Huai and then into the sea. This project was, however, blamed for the rise in popular discontent which preceded the fall of the dynasty. The methods used by its manager Chia Lu, constructing embankments of earth, stone, metal, wood and straw, continued to be used by later generations.

Yüan's postal system was highly developed. There were land and water postal stations which supplied means of transport, food and lodging for their users. This network stretched from Korea south to Annam, with 115 stations along the route from Annam north to Yenching. To the northwest there were stations strung out into Sinkiang and southern Siberia. The greatest number of stations were in the lower Yangtze transportation centers.

Somewhat later a separate network of express courier stations was established. Traveling night and day, these couriers automatically had the right of way on all highways. Ming and Ch'ing used postal systems similar to Yüan's.

Hsien officials were responsible for bridge maintenance under the supervision of the Board of Works. A set annual schedule of road and bridge maintenance was enforced, and interference with the trees planted along rights of way was punished.

The Mongol military campaigns extended from Korea and Japan

in the east to Eastern Europe in the west, from the Arctic Ocean in the north to the Indian Ocean in the south. This unprecedented scope of activity led to numerous contacts between Chinese and foreign civilizations.

In addition to the famous official missions there were numerous merchants, craftsmen and adventurers from all over Europe who spent all or part of their lives among the Mongols. Many eastern techniques were brought back to Europe by these anonymous travelers. Silk and porcelain became familiar objects in Western Europe, and these and other innovations served to stimulate progress there. Chinese navigation techniques and gunpowder were also transmitted to Europe by the Mongols as were the techniques of carved-board and movable-type printing. Eastern Europe received the Chinese abacus.

Though Korea was reduced to tributary status, two seaborne invasions of Japan failed, and no political relationship with Japan was established. Nevertheless mercantile relations between Japan and Yüan China were not broken and pilgraimages by monks from both sides continued. Many of the states of Southeast Asia paid tribute to China. According to Ibn Battuta, Chinese vessels dominated the trade between China and India during the Yüan period.

The Liao Economy

Liao's acquisition of northernmost China gave it a base for commercial growth under its state's supervision. Its southern capital (modern Peking) had three markets to serve its 300,000 inhabitants. The main capital in Inner Mongolia had foreign merchants in residence, and cloth rather than cash was used for money. All the other main cities had markets as well.

In addition to markets on the border with Sung, there were markets adjoining the states in the northeast. Imports included gold, cloth, furs and livestock. Salt and wine were state monopolies.

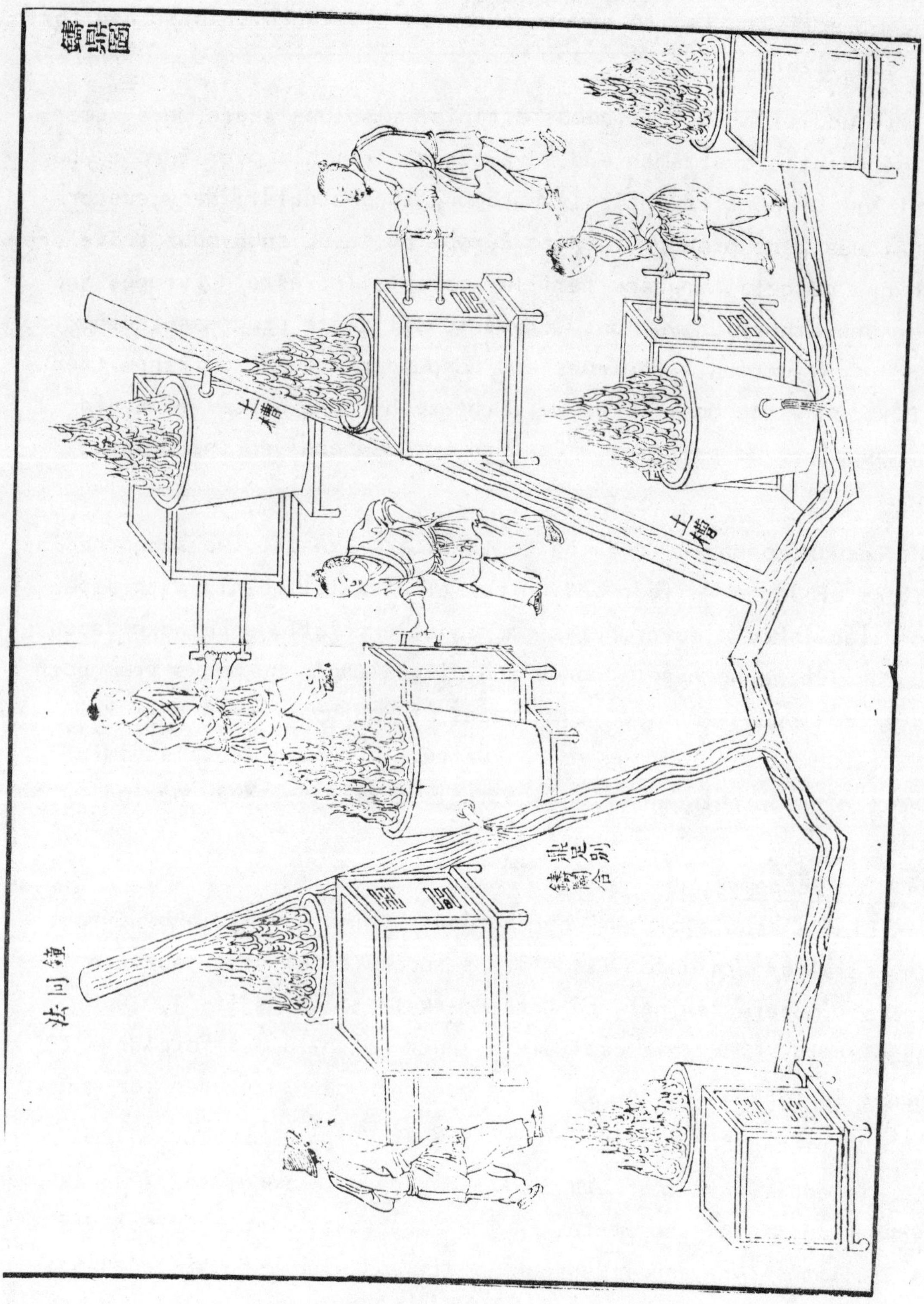

Fig. 10 Bronze casting

An abundance of locally produced copper permitted coinage from 922 on. To avoid private coinage, in 1063 the people were forbidden to sell copper cash, and sale of copper cash to foreign merchants was strictly prohibited.

A land tax was instituted by T'ai-tsu and a census by T'ai-tsung. After 1027 several types of partially or totally tax-exempt public fields were established and coexisted thereafter with tax paying private land. The corvée became especially burdensome for the maintenance of the postal stations and was replaced by a tax-supported hired service system.

The Chin Economy

The Jurched had no commerce to speak of when they were still a nomadic herding people of the north. After conquering half of China, however, their people engaged in some commerce.

As late as the 1160's most of Chin's coinage was engrossed by the officials. This obliged the population at large to resort to barter or paper vouchers.

Ten items were state monopolies, including salt, wine, tea and iron. All tea was imported from Sung either as part of the annual tribute or via the frontier official markets which were set up after 1142.

After the capital was moved south in 1154 a more elaborate paper money system was set up, with large denomination bills worth from one to fifteen strings and small denomination bills worth from 100 to 750 cash. These were to circulate for seven years and be used interchangeably with cash.

Overissue and an end to the use of expiration dates devalued this currency and drove good cash into hiding. An early thirteenth-century reissue failed to solve the problem of devaluation, and the practice grew of quoting all prices in terms of silver rather than in terms of this increasingly valueless paper.

Rent was paid to the state by the cultivators of official lands. Tax on private lands was calculated in terms of ox units, with three oxen per unit. Every unit of twenty-five individuals was to have four *ch'ing* four *mou* of land and pay no more than one *tan* of grain per year. Using a variant on the *pao-chia* system, the tax and corvée burden was to be proportioned to the size and wealth of a household.

The Yüan Economy

Though Chingis had to be dissuaded from turning China into pastureland, Kubilai put great emphasis on the encouragement of agriculture through both state supervision and the encouragement of local Righteous and Ever Normal granaries.

Fig. 11 Kubilai (Ming illustration)

The official fields acquired by the state during late Southern Sung were used during Yüan to reward officials. The Mongols also adopted the Chin practice of confiscating peasant land and reducing its cultivators to the status of agricultural slaves. Estates containing as many as 80,000 households were in this way given to court favorites. Officials were given smaller estates. Taxes on these did not need to be forwarded to the central authorities. Monastic estates, also tax exempt, expanded greatly. Though in 1327 monasteries were forbidden to buy additional land from the people, this rule was widely broken.

Two attempts at a land survey so as to increase tax receipts failed, largely owing to the interference of the Mongol aristocracy. The unequal burden of taxation created many tax absconders from north China and ultimately contributed to the downfall of the dynasty.

The Mongols ultimately came to use commerce as their initial weapon of conquest and their military power only secondarily. For example, prior to the conquest of Southern Sung, the Mongols cut off all trade across the border, but after a while they pardoned a number of Sung merchants who had violated the prohibition, thereby earning their gratitude and easing the task of their armies during the subsequent military campaigns.

Yüan's international trade policy was to encourage the establishment of tributary and hence trade relations with even remote countries of the south seas. The dynasty also received substantial tax revenues from internal commercial taxes. There was a sales tax of 1/30 (later 1/20) and a surtax on that as well as a tax on shipbuilding materials. Tax farming by rich merchants was the method used for collecting these taxes.

During the early years after the conquest of the south, foreign trade was taxed at 1/10 (coarser goods at 1/15). Eventually shipping offices were set up in seven major ports and the only foreign trade permitted was placed under government auspices, with the state taking 70% of the profit from each voyage.

Severe restrictions were placed on the hours of business in the south. All travelers had to have official documents without which they were not to be accepted into inns. Coastal residents were not allowed to trade for cash with foreign merchants. Private foreign trade was forbidden. Violators were to be whipped and their ships and goods confiscated. All vessels had to be registered. Southern iron products were not permitted to be sold in the north.

Numbered among the merchants were Mongols, North Chinese (including Khitan and Jurched), South Chinese, and, most influential of all, foreigners from Central and West Asia and Europe. Though among merchants there were adherents of all the major religions of Eurasia, Muslims were most numerous. Most of those Muslims who had settled within China had gone into trade to make a living. In addition to priests like Friar Odoric, European merchants like Marco Polo came to China. The accounts of Chinese life written by some of these men whetted a European interest in China which was to become more manifest in Ming times.

Yüan had state monopolies over salt, tea, wine and vinegar. Ch'üanchou was the chief entrepot of foreign trade. Marco Polo considered it one of the world's two greatest ports. For a time the tax rate there was lower than in the other six major ports.

The state occasionally used its monopoly right to finance foreign trade to earn revenues specifically for such needs as financing the empress' palace establishment. The new capital city became the focus of foreign and domestic trade and the center of industry producing solely for palace consumption. Its suburban population was as great as that of the city itself. The other major cities of the two river valleys and Canton also flourished. Ibn Battuta wrote that Ch'üanchou harbor held a hundred large vessels and countless smaller ones and that its Muslim merchants constituted a separate market.

Kubilai issued Yüan's first paper currency, one version backed by silk and another in various denominations calculated in terms of copper cash and strings of cash. Later smaller denomination notes proved impractical and were withdrawn. Different forms of the other notes were periodically reissued as they depreciated in value. Despite this depreciation such notes continued to circulate to the end of the dynasty.

In addition to the local and national academies, Yüan

established a network of local medical schools with standardized examinations of their graduates. Kubilai established a network of regional astronomical observatories. Mathematics also continued to advance, with the invention of quadratic equations and a new technique for performing long division. In the realm of military technology, a cannon built by a Muslim technologist was used in the siege of Hsiangyang in 1273.

State-owned workshops staffed by salaried artisans conscripted by the authorities produced a variety of specialized goods, such as multilayered lacquerware inset with precious metals, and clay and cast-metal statues.

Artisans were conscripted for service with the armies recruited locally during the conquest of North China, and later of South China. Most of these were skilled in making arrows, armor and catapults.

Yüan's Board of Works was responsible for all engineering tasks, gathering materials and recruiting skilled workmen for these tasks. It controlled various subordinate institutions, most of them in the north, which carried out a variety of specialized tasks from smelting silver to dyeing silk. The various segments of the palace establishment also controlled enterprises, often with local subdivisions, producing goods for their use.

At heart the Yüan treated China as conquered territory, to be parcelled out in feudal fashion among the conquerors. This was the source of great popular suffering. The Yüan institutions for managing the various crafts greatly influenced Ming and Ch'ing practice.

The Mongols always gave great weight to technical expertise, at first for warfare and later, as they grew more sophisticated, for the adornment of their women and for their personal luxuries. Even in his early conquests Chingis spared captured artisans to satisfy his and his aristocracy's love for ornate trappings.

Originally prisoners of war and then a part of the armies, organized groups of craftsmen eventually became a distinct caste within society. Craftsmen were divided into thirty-two subdivisions, all paid by and working for the state. There are records of many such artisan families who did exceedingly well in the Mongols' service. Unfortunately the traditional Chinese distaste for technical ability did not allow this high position for artisans to continue. Otherwise our industrialization might have occurred two or three centuries earlier.

The early Yüan land tax resembled the T'ang system. At first it was a simple head tax, but when that produced insufficient revenue, a dual system was instituted. A family was to pay a tax either on its property or by head count, whichever was larger.

There were also taxes in kind collected in cloth and silver which were destined for use of the court establishment. These were collected by the central government at different rates from various categories of households.

Though its adoption of Confucian goals was vitiated by its racism, Yüan was not without its accomplishments in such departments as encouragement of agriculture, water conservancy and the restoration of a measure of peace to the north. But its racism and harsh taxation caused much popular resentment.

Southerners especially suffered from discrimination. Chinese were forbidden to possess weapons. The population was divided into ten classes: officials, minor officials, Buddhist monks, Taoist monks, physicians, artisans, hunters, commoners, Confucians, and beggars. Local officials were often foreigners, and they frequently extorted excessive taxes from the people and offended opinion by, for example, robbing the graves of the Sung imperial family and its high officials. Kubilai himself used several venal and incompetent high officials, and his successors showed even poorer judgment in their choice of men.

Rents on the estates of the south were several times higher than taxes, and tenants were treated like slaves. Three-year tax holidays for newly opened land were more than made up for by extortionate surtaxes levied by local officials. Agriculture was also much harmed by the conscription of horses. In the north these had been used for both transportation and as draft animals. The Mongols wanted these animals for their own use and as a precautionary measure wished to deny their use to the Chinese. Approximately 700,000 horses were conscripted between 1286 and 1328.

Many southerners were reduced to serf-like status on estates extorted by officials. Many northerners fled south as refugees. Institutions like the Righteous Granaries existed more in name than in fact.

So close to the margin of existence did the people live that when natural disasters struck many were obliged to abandon their families and join movements of resistance. By the 1330's popular rebellions began in several places in the south and central regions, and the Yangtze valley was soon totally out of control. These rebellions were led by men of all classes, salt-smugglers, impoverished peasants and priests. So ended the Yüan hegemony.

Section X

THE AGE OF REVIVAL: THE MING DYNASTY

Outline

The 275-year long Ming, with its first capitals in Nanking and K'aifeng and its move of the capital to Peking during the reign of the third emperor, was the first native Chinese dynasty to rule all of the country since the fall of the T'ang. Ming's founder, observing the lessons of history, took the road of centralization. The economy was progressive compared to that of earlier times. Taxes were collected in silver rather than goods, and the aristocracy was paid in rice rather than land, and in mid-dynasty in part in paper money. The manorial system gradually fell into decay. The Ming Single Whip tax system remained the basis for the tax system into Ch'ing times.

Ming centralization much increased the power of the eunuchs, who greatly oppressed commerce. Their heavy punishment of the gentry was a fundamental reason for the fall of the dynasty. The seven voyages to the western oceans of Cheng Ho during the Yung-lo era represented an important development in Chinese economic history. In addition, the fiscal policies of Chang Chü-cheng wrote a new page in the economic history of Ming which was long discussed by posterity.

The Contribution of Chang Chü-cheng to Ming National Planning for the People's Livelihood

Chang was one of the great statesmen of the sixteenth century, an age when internal and external problems reenforced each other. The Ming manorial economy was more developed than during Yüan. Many manors were tax exempt and peasant land was being encroached upon, often voluntarily as peasants sought to avoid taxes. As a consequence land was becoming less equally distributed, land records were losing accuracy and government revenues were declining. From the beginning inequities were built into the land tax. The founder's home area, among others, was very lightly taxed. Several areas in Chiangnan associated with the rebellion of Chang Shih-ch'eng were very heavily taxed. The tax on confiscated and official fields was higher than that on private land.

Compilation of a land register was undertaken early in Ming. The more than 8,570,000 <u>ch'ing</u> then registered had declined by 1529 by half, but a new land census could only be carried out in a few places. In 1578 Chang's recommendation to carry out a land survey was accepted. This increased the amount of registered land from over 4.5 million to over 11.5 million <u>ch'ing</u>. In addition to the Single Whip system, Chang instituted several other reforms in the collection system to end cheating by the elite. His policy of forgiving delinquent back taxes by the peasantry evoked great approval among the people.

Before the Single Whip system, there were so many taxes and their types were so complex as to lead to abuses. The new system was a response to the objective needs of the times. The relative simplicity of the calculations involved in the system drastically limited opportunities for tax avoidance by the rich and corruption by local officials. From the modern viewpoint it represented a progressive tax system. It was both simpler and cheaper to collect than earlier systems, and constituted less of a burden on the people.

Even before taking office Chang advocated frugal government, arguing that this was the only way to assure a prosperous people and hence the only true basis for warding off foreign threats. When he took office the treasury held only enough revenue for three months' worth of expenditures. The assured revenues from the numerous central and local state-controlled weaving establishments had in turn stimulated growth in state expenditures and led consequently to extraordinary levies on their production, even in bad times. Chang sought to reduce these levies during times of depression. He also drastically limited the use of the state post system and thereby reduced expenditures and the burden on taxpayers.

Though the official histories have an ambiguous attitude toward Chang as an individual, they could not but approve of his fiscal policies. He was praised for increasing the state's grain reserves while lessening the burden on the people. This enabled successful pacification of tribal peoples in the north and southwest. He is also criticized for having obstructed debate within the Court and for arousing thereby much resentment within government during his eighteen years in power. But though there is disagreement about him, given the conditions during mid-Ming and thereafter, a man of his strength of character was needed.

The Accomplishments of Cheng Ho's Voyages to the Western Seas

Though the south and east have a coastline, including islands, of over 20,000 kilometers, our mentality has traditionally been that of a continental power, with little emphasis on maritime development. Only by Sung and Yuan did maritime trade become significant. The Yunglo emperor changed his traditional landlocked policy for one which emphasized expansion both by land and sea.

Cheng Ho's seven voyages constituted a new and glorious page in Chinese history. Though not a new development, his voyages were unprecedented in scale, distance covered and duration. They occurred nearly a century before the voyages of the great Westerners, Columbus and Vasco da Gama. He carried an average of 27,000 men on each voyage, 400 men on each of some sixty large vessels. The length of the voyages varied from a year and a half to two and a half years, and a supply station had to be set up on the Malay peninsula to meet the needs of such long expeditions.

The first three and the sixth voyage were limited to the coast of the Indian Ocean. The fourth and fifth went to the Persian Gulf, Red Sea, Arabian coast and East Africa. The seventh also went to the Persian Gulf with side expeditions to the Red Sea. Cheng was thirty-five when his first expedition departed in 1405 and fifty-two when the sixth returned. He was an old man of sixty-three by the end of the seventh expedition of 1432 which departed after Yung-lo's death. Estimates of the number of countries he visited vary from seventeen to fifty-nine, largely because of the political fragmentation of South Asia at that time.

One motive for these voyages was to search for the Emperor Hui whom Yung-lo had deposed and who was rumored to have fled overseas. Yung-lo is reported to have still been worried over this near the end of his reign. Another motive was linked to the traditional impulse of a Chinese dynasty to have all peoples acknowledge its suzerainty. Naturally as a usurper Yung-lo wanted such symbolic acknowledgments even more than had the founder. Cheng Ho's seventh voyage was to hasten tribute missions which had lagged in the five years since the Hsüan-te emperor had taken the throne. An economic motive is reflected in the label given to Cheng Ho's fleet--"treasure ships." Yung-lo, who had set up tax offices for overseas commerce in Canton, Ch'üanchou and Ningpo, wanted to go beyond merely receiving the profits from foreign merchants who came to China.

Yung-lo hoped to gain great profits from the official expeditions to defray the expenses of the campaigns against the Mongols. The tribute missions stimulated by the expeditions often, however, required great expenditures by the Court in return. Private trade was also stimulated. Unintended by the government, migration to the South Seas was also stimulated to the point that by the sixteenth century the area had become linked genetically to the Chinese empire.

The tens of thousands of men who accompanied Cheng returned with a taste for the foreign which they spread among the Chinese of the coastal areas, thereby changing the nature of the Chinese to accommodate a taste for the seagoing life and its profits. From 1405 to 1435 some fifty states came to China to offer tribute, and the experiences in China of the hundreds of tribute bearers, some of exalted rank, sowed the seeds of increased international trade later.

The Han Race's Basic Position and the Establishment of Agricultural Policy After the Economic Revival

The life of the peasantry was hard in late Yuan and early Ming. Much land had been abandoned in the Yellow River valley. Despite attempts by the Ming founder to use the army for rural reconstruction, 90% of the peasants of Kiangsu were hardpressed tenants. The situation was gradually improved by the detailed land survey ordered by the founder, the "fish-scale register" and by the "golden register," so called because of the color of the paper of the copy sent up to the Census Board, which organized all farmers into groups of 110 households, with ten groups of ten families each led by the leading ten grain-producing families. The latter were revised each decade in accord with the production record of the unit over the previous ten years.

The land was divided between official and private fields. The former included manors for the imperial family, office lands for the bureaucrats and garrison fields for the army. The founder ordered that private fields be divided equitably according to population, and that they be taxed equally. Cooperative fields owned by the state in each village were to be collectively cultivated. The founder also ordered extensive use of garrison fields to reduce the burden of military support on the civilian population. Eventually, however, these garrison fields tended to be taken over by the elite, throwing on the treasury the burden of supporting the armies. Anyone who opened hitherto uncultivated land was allowed to make it his private property.

The founder sponsored hydraulic works in over 40,000 locations. Those opening new land were granted draft animals, tools, seed and capital. The Ming local granary system represented a reform of the T'ang-Sung institutions. The founder ordered Preparation

Fig. 12 Water-powered mill.

Granaries, managed by local dignitaries, established in all major towns. These were similar to the old Ever-Normal granaries. There were Righteous granaries as well, one for each twenty or thirty families, headed by local gentlemen, and with the families belonging to it giving contributions to it proportioned to their wealth. There were also cooperative granaries, entirely under control of the thirty families constituting the membership of each. These, a contemporary argued, were superior to government granaries as they were more likely to be efficiently managed and give loans to those who most needed them because of their superior knowledge of local conditions. Rewards, up to official rank, were given to those who gave generous contributions to the government-sponsored granaries. The laws held officials strictly accountable for operations of the granaries. Eventually _chou_ and _hsien_ officials were made responsible for the Preparedness granaries rather than local managers.

The manorial economy had developed out of the feudal economy. It had originated in T'ang, continued in Sung and flourished during Yüan, using the official fields as manors for the elite. The Ming founder originally enfieffed his family with land but eventually shifted to paying them in rice instead. Such salaries originally ranged from 200 to 50,000 _tan_. By mid-Ming a part of these salaries was paid with silver certificate paper money. But manors for the highest ranks continued nevertheless to be very extensive. Official fields continued to be augmented by lands confiscated from disgraced officials and from land without heirs. In early Ming official fields constituted one-tenth the amount of private land.

Manors continued to develop for three reasons: imperial grants to the imperial family and others (in 1601 a proposed 40,000 _ch'ing_ grant to the emperor's three sons would have brought one-half the land of Honan into such manors), the opening of new land by manor holders (similar to the T'ang and Sung practice), and the obtaining of private land by various means (fraudulently getting title to new land opened by the people, taking advantage of unclear land titles). Buddhist and Muslim temples also received many manors. Taoist lands were confiscated during a late Ming persecution.

The extent of manorial holdings is not clear, but in the late fifteenth century in the imperial domain alone, all kinds of manorial land totaled around 46,000 _ch'ing_. Manors were managed by a hierarchy of officials either selected from local households or from among various men without fixed sources of income. One _hsien_ in fifteenth-century Anhui had 279 households in manors out of a total population of 17,145 households. The holders of these manors paid no taxes and governed their holdings independently of local authorities.

Commerce

Though a farmer by origin and hence inclined to favor agriculture over commerce, the founder reduced the market tax from 1/10 to 1/30 and even had a reading primer, unfortunately no longer extant, composed to teach illiterate farmers, craftsmen and merchants how to read. He forbade the practice of having officials advance the money for goods before delivery to the state. This custom had led to exploitation of merchants because officials discounted prices. Prices were to be publicly posted by local officials and weights and measures were to be periodically checked by them as well. Official warehouses were set up just outside the capital, but aside from the payment of the 1/30 tax, free trade was permitted and small dealers were exempt from the tax. Though, as in previous dynasties since Han, there were such anti-commercial edicts as sumptuary regulations, in early Ming real repression of commerce was rarely encountered.

Each of the many crafts had its own district in Nanking. Most of the commercial men were not natives of the Nanking area. When the capital moved to Peking, southern merchants and goods accompanied the government in large numbers. There were large numbers of specialized and periodic markets. One great merchant for a time became the country's richest man through his connection with the founder. Another founded a great emporium in Soochow which kept his family rich for centuries.

Initially, all official trade with Japan had to pass through Ningpo, Ryukyuan trade through Ch'üanchou and southern seas trade through Canton. Pirate raids on the east coast caused the founder to ban all foreign merchants except Ryukyuan and some South Asian ones, though these limits were somewhat liberalized during the

Yung-lo reign. Tribute missions were limited, for example, the Ryukyuan to once each two years and the Japanese to once each decade, with the average for all missions being once each three years. The strict rules allowed a measure of private trading by tribute missions, but these rules were often stretched or broken.

The South Asian trade was eventually shifted to Macao when the Portuguese appeared. The Portuguese, referred to in the Ming Shih (Ming History) as the Folangchi (Franks), were permitted their own city at Macao as a device to wean them away from their earlier freebooting tactics with which the local authorities could not cope. Sovereign power over Macao was nevertheless retained in Chinese hands.

Taiwan was not explored in ancient times, but in his voyages Cheng Ho often visited it and it was first described in a travel book subsequent to his voyages.* It was first settled by the Dutch with the aid of several illicit Chinese merchants. At the end of Ming the Dutch were ousted by Cheng Chih-lung and his son, Cheng Ch'eng-kung. The Cheng family remained loyal to Ming during the Manchu invasions and mobilized its 200,000-man army and several thousand ship fleet. Though he had only a foothold on the Fukien coast, Cheng Ch'eng-kung's fleet and his commercial relations with Japan and Southeast Asia gave him a base which the Manchus could not break. Taiwan was to be his main base for the restoration of the Ming, and in the process he made Taiwan Chinese.

When the Europeans came to the South Seas, Fukien and Canton merchants were already active there, and if the dynasty had understood the methods of imperialism, the Europeans could have been forestalled. Tens of thousands of merchants from nearby Fukien settled in Luzon, but were persecuted by the Spanish conquerors of the area. Chinese merchants also traded profitably with other

---

*This statement is not quite correct; Taiwan was reached by an expedition in 230 A.D. See Section VI. (EHK)

parts of the Philippines, Borneo (which also served as a refuge for Chinese pirates), and other parts of the Indonesian archipelago. At that time the power of the Chinese people greatly exceeded that of the Europeans. That subsequently their power waxed and ours waned is truly regrettable.

Manufacturing and Mathematicians

The Ming founder had a parsimonious palace building policy so as to avoid burdening the masses during the early years of the dynasty while their loyalty still had to be won. Yung-lo, however, built extensively in Peking. The new capital resembled Nanking but on a larger scale. The palace complex on the southeast of the imperial city had 8,350 rooms. Extensive building and rebuilding was also done by later emperors. Among other notable accomplishments of Ming building were temples, city walls and imperial tombs.

The Yung-lo reign was the most developed period of Chinese shipbuilding. During its first seven years 1,632 seagoing vessels were ordered built. These vessels required a high degree of scientific and technological knowledge in the places where they were built: Fukien, Nanking, Chekiang, Canton, Kiangsi, Soochow, and Yangchou. The shipyards were very large. The Nanking shipyard, begun by the dynastic founder, was supervised by an official of the fifth rank, had a complex division of labor and a permanent staff of around two hundred, augmented by hired workers during busy times. Little is recorded of the methods used for fitting out and supplying these enormous vessels, each holding 450 men, but they must have been elaborate.

The mid-Ming plague of Japanese pirates was met by the building of a variety of large and small military vessels for coastal work. There were large and small tower ships with wooden armor along their sides; there were patrol vessels and attack vessels with a variety of shapes, one type of which could use both sails and oars.

Fig. 13 Pottery Wheel

The Ming is notable in the history of porcelain in our country. The imperial kilns at Ching-te-chen were established during the founder's reign, and several new types of porcelain were manufactured. The first three reigns of Ch'ing continued these developments, the progress of the kilns resting on the power and prosperity of the state. When national power decayed from the Chia-ch'ing reign on, the porcelain trade also decayed. Even everyday ware was often elaborately painted.

There had been kilns in the Ching-te-chen area since the Northern and Southern Dynasties and by T'ang its product was fine enough to be called "false jade ware." An officially supervised kiln was established there in Sung during the ching-te year period (1004-7) and this ultimately led to the name of the place and product being changed. Even in Sung it was famous as one of the four most notable kilns. Ming porcelain tended to be thinner than that of earlier periods and colored glazing techniques such as five-color glaze and cloisonné were perfected at Ching-te-chen.

The rise of a craft is not an accident. The rise of Ming-Ch'ing porcelain is partly ascribable to objective needs of the environment, partly to the state's leadership as well as to the contributions of technical specialists. Ching-te-chen reached its peak during the more than twenty years it was led by a man named T'ang Ying during the Yung-cheng and Ch'ien-lung eras of the Ching. T'ang shared the life of the potters and wrote a still indispensible book on the trade. The division of labor was as complex as under modern scientific management techniques. Since the late eighteenth century there has been no further progress in techniques even though as late as the early republican period there were still over a hundred kilns and several tens of thousands of craftsmen in Ching-te-chen.

Ming produced three notable mathematicians, Wu Ching, Wang Wen-su and Ch'eng Ta-wei. When a book by the latter appeared in 1592 it was immediately transmitted to Japan where it became the theoretical basis for Japanese use of the abacus. The earliest abacus-like device appeared in Greece around 500 B.C. But this device received its fullest development in China, while even as late as the fifteenth century Europe did not make much use of it. Not long after the second world war a contest held in Japan for speed and accuracy between electrical calculators and the abacus was won by the abacus. Western mathematics was introduced in late Ming by several Chinese collaborators of the Jesuit missionary Matteo Ricci who translated his works into Chinese.

The Monetary and Postal Systems

The founder established bronze cash as the general-use currency, but the scarcity of copper evoked so much counterfeiting that in 1375 a paper money was issued to circulate in parallel with bronze cash. It was issued in six denominations, from one string (equal to 1000 cash or one ounce of silver) down to 100 cash. Four strings were equated with one ounce of gold. Commercial taxes were

Fig. 14 Casting bronze coins

to be paid three parts in cash, seven parts in paper. Private use of gold and silver for money was forbidden, but specie could be exchanged for paper. Local treasuries were established to exchange worn notes for new ones. The exchange rules, however, had to be loosened before the system would work since worn notes not acceptable for exchange would not be voluntarily circulated by the public.

The founder commuted office-rice to notes at the rate of two strings 500 cash to one _tan_ of grain. Lower denomination notes (from 10 to 50 cash) were issued, but overissue depreciated them relative to higher denomination notes at different rates in various areas. Inflation hindered their circulation.

In 1394 all cash was called in to be exchanged for new style paper notes within a period of half a month. Circulation or hoarding of cash was forbidden. The prohibition was repeated in 1403 in more severe terms, forbidding gold and silver to circulate. But increasing quantity depreciated the value of the paper. An ounce of silver would get eighty strings worth of paper, an ounce of gold 400 strings of paper. Specie and cloth became media of circulation among the people. Further measures proved ineffective. By 1426 paper had depreciated by a factor of twenty in terms of grain compared to its value in the early years of the dynasty.

In 1428 printing of the new currency was halted and all treasury stocks burned. The next year taxes were increased and made payable in paper money so as to increase faith in the currency. The circulation of paper increased somewhat. In 1448 circulation of copper cash was again forbidden but relaxed again a decade later. In 1452 officials in the capital were allowed to exchange their salary paper for silver at the current rate of 500 strings of paper for one ounce of silver. In 1466 their salary rice was discounted from twenty-five to ten strings of paper for one _tan_ of grain. The new paper had depreciated to only ten cash for one string; the old paper to only one or two cash for a string. Copper and especially

Fig. 15 A 50-cash Ming dynasty paper money note

silver were increasingly used for exchange. During the next century even the government steadily went over to collecting its monetary taxes in silver.

In 1429 commercial taxes were raised by a factor of five on all business establishments and all means of commercial transport. In most places vessels were taxed according to their carrying capacity rather than on the value of their cargo. A vessel might be taxed a hundred times for a total of 100 strings in paper on a given voyage. Though the rates were later reduced, the network of tax offices was maintained.

The postal system resembled that of the Yüan, with water and horse stations and express courier posts. There were also official hostels in Peking and Nanking for the reception of tribute missions, the former having a 300-man and the latter a 100-man staff. Horse stations were forty or eighty li apart and each stocked from five to eighty horses, depending on its importance. Water stations, established at important junctions had from five to twenty boats, each with a crew of ten men. Transport offices had large and small carts or freight vessels of varying numbers.

Express stations were placed every ten li and staffed with ten or fifteen soldiers recruited locally. A letter was to travel at least 300 li a day. Official messages were to be immediately forwarded whether received day or night. Official credentials were necessary to use the system. These credentials could only be issued to those carrying official messages, those carrying out tasks for members of the imperial family, foreign diplomats on tributary missions, civil and military officials going to take up their duties at least 1,500 li away and for transport of sick or dead officials and their families back to their native place.

The Tax System

The founder initially abolished all Mongol customs and restored Chinese ways of doing things. He tightened administrative efficiency and lightened taxes to win back popular confidence in government. Various miscellaneous non-agricultural taxes were abolished and the surtax on the land tax was removed. The land tax resembled the T'ang two-tax system. The founder's aim was to make payment easier and to make certain that additional illegal taxes would not be collected by officials. The Yellow Register of 1381 and Fish Scale Register of 1387 provided the basis for the land tax in Ch'ing as well as Ming times.

After the north had been conquered, merchants were induced to transport grain for its garrisons by grants of salt certificates. Government offices on the frontier traded the surplus tea of Szechwan for barbarian horses.

In later reigns,the people suffered as expenses were increased to maintain the imperial clan and, in the sixteenth century, to finance renewed military expenses on the northern frontier and against south coast pirates. The Japanese invasion of Korea was an especially heavy fiscal burden. Taxes were increased and their scope broadened. Particularly obnoxious methods were used to collect the new mine tax which had evoked clandestine mining. Evaders of this tax even had their hands chopped off and were thrown into rivers.

Internally there were new market, crafts, and paper money taxes. Externally, though the Ming customs houses were initially not supposed to tax but merely supervise foreign goods, it became necessary for foreign merchants to pay over 60% of their goods to officials to gain permission to land them.

In 1581 the Single Whip land tax system was instituted, consolidating the head and corvée tax with the land tax. It was levied solely according to acreage. After the land tax, the excise taxes on salt, tea, fish, wine and on various commercial activities represented the largest source of revenue.

The land was divided into official and private fields, in the proportion of one to seven by 1502. Official land included various imperial manors, office lands and garrison fields, among others. Initially the tax on private fields was about 3/5 that on official fields, except in that part of the lower Yangtze which had the heaviest taxes since pre-Sung times and was additionally punished because it was the seat of one of the Ming founder's chief rivals. The founder's home area was lightly taxed. Such favoritism is regrettable.

The Fish Scale Registers recorded the size and productivity of all fields and were so called because they resembled a picture of fish scales. The earlier Yellow Registers had taken household numbers as their basis. All land sales had to be officially registered. This system was rightly believed to be a reliable basis for honest taxation because "though men move, land remains fixed." So long as land was viewed as the "mother" and men as "sons," meaning taxes were based on land rather than households, abuses could be checked. But by the late sixteenth century the Fish Scale Registers of early Ming had become obsolete. In 1577, on Chang Chü-cheng's advice, a resurvey was undertaken.

In early Ming the land tax was collected by the wealthiest landowners in each neighborhood, each responsible for a ten-family unit, the chia. Collection of taxes in advance tended to increase and thereby raise the actual tax rate. The Single Whip system, by consolidating corvée (which the elite had been exempt from) with the land tax, spread the burden more evenly. Like the earlier Sung corvée-avoidance tax it allowed local government to hire its workers with the proceeds of taxation, which reduced the service burden on taxpayers.

In early Ming men from sixteen to sixty were subject to corvée. According to a 1375 edict, every ch'ing of land had to contribute the labor of one man for thirty days annually at the capital. A man could be hired as a substitute, with the landlord paying one tan to defray his expenses. Though the landless were legally not subject to this corvée, they were the ones usually hired by landlords to carry it out. Using the Yellow Register of households as its basis, corvée hit each _chia_ once every ten years as it was rotated among the ten _chia_ constituting one _li_. There was also a corvée levied on individuals once every five years, with families divided into three classes and an extraordinary corvée levied at irregular intervals. Attempts to equalize the burden of these labor taxes were undone by gentry exemptions.

Before completion of the reunification the founder levied a tax of 1/20 on salt. Afterward he sold exclusive rights to purvey salt to merchants who supplied the frontier armies. Each salt producing area had to meet a set annual quota to forward to the officials. Initially 400 _chin_ of salt was exchanged for one _tan_ of grain. Later paper money was substituted for grain. In its early years this arrangement yielded high profits, but by mid-Ming low-priced smuggled salt undercut sales of the government product. Various schemes to increase the tax only led to worse corruption in its administration. All salt had to be transported in government vessels and be accounted for by official tallies. Heavy punishments were decreed for private smugglers and corrupt officials within the salt administration. In addition to receiving exclusive marketing areas for salt, merchants could receive salt in exchange for grain, horses, paper money, iron or cloth deliveries to various places at various times depending on the state's needs. On several occasions the populace was ordered to buy set amounts of salt and pay for it with paper money.

In the tea producing districts any merchants buying tea had to report the amount bought to local authorities and buy a proportionate number of tea certificates from them. In some areas various other commodities had to be exchanged for tea. This system was used successfully throughout the dynasty.

The _Ming Hui Tien_ (_Ming Statutes_) and the economics section of the Ming Shih record nothing of a wine tax, which at times must have been subsumed within other commercial taxes. At times prohibition was enforced. This was the case in early Ming because of fears of a grain shortage should liquor grains be planted. Though this prohibition was kept up, wine was occasionally taxed directly, but never became an important segment of the tax system.

In early Ming all goods were taxed at 1/30. Goods not marked were not taxed. There were 382 tax offices distributed through the country, each with several sub-stations under it. The lack of a detailed list of taxable items initially led to burdensome taxation of anything and everything by these local tax stations until in 1403 all personal property and ordinary household and agricultural tools and objects for religious use were declared exempt. In the 1450's the old system was restored, but detailed lists of taxable items and their value had to be kept by the authorities. From the late sixteenth century on, private tax offices were set up at roads, bridges, passes, ferries, and other locations, levying a variety of increasingly burdensome taxes.

Late in the fourteenth century private mining was allowed but always thereafter under government license only and for payment of a tax of 2/30. Tax was levied on silver, iron, copper, mercury, alum, and other raw materials. The mines of Chekiang and Fukien were from the mid-fifteenth century on supplemented by those of Szechwan and Yünnan. Silver mines had to pay a set annual amount in tax regardless of changes in production. Receipts from this tax increased by a factor of twenty-three during the Yung-lo period and by a factor of twenty-seven during the Hsüan-te period, not because of a correspondingly great increase in production but rather entirely because of changes in government policy. In 1596, because the state needed more revenue, new mines were ordered opened, especially in Honan, Shantung, Chekiang, Shansi, Shensi, Szechwan, Liaotung, Kwangsi, Kiangsi, Fukien and Yünnan. The officials in charge proved villains who confiscated private

Fig. 16 Coal mining using bamboo pipes for ventilation.

property in the guise of opening these mines. Posterity recognized this as one of the reasons for Ming's fall.

Society and People's Livelihood

Sensitive to his humble origins as a monk, the founder feared and hence persecuted gentry intellectuals, even executing many of them for writing phrases which might be construed as puns on his origins as a monk and bandit. From the mid-fifteenth century the power of the eunuchs rose. They became supervisors of the army, the markets and of taxation, the unstoppable masters of the central administration. Factionalism became chaotic. The eunuchs were responsible for the cruel rise in commercial taxation, both licit and illicit, after 1573. Great merchants were hounded out of business and even petty transactions in the villages were taxed.

Though taxes were nominally reduced in 1620 during the brief reign of Kuang-tsung, under his son capital merchants were ruthlessly exploited and in 1625, after several loyal officials were executed, a market tax of 10% was imposed at important communications junctions. Conditions worsened thereafter, evoking the bandit uprising of men like Li Tzu-ch'eng and ultimately the Manchu invasions. The last emperor and most of his clan proved selfish to the end, refusing to contribute their wealth to the defense of the major cities from the rebels. The corrupt central bureaucrats were capable only of buying off the rebels to save their own skins.

It is certain that had there been brave leadership, the crisis could have been surmounted. But the last emperor was a cowardly leader and the moral of people, military and gentry was ruined. If the emperor had executed his evil civilian and military officials and undertaken a fundamental reform, the dynasty's recovery would have been possible, as this would have restored popular morale.

The system of tax exemptions had reached the point where those who had the strength to pay taxes and who ought to have paid them did not and those who ought not to have paid and lacked the strength to do so had their burden increased. Contemporaries had warned that such inequality was more dangerous to the state's tranquility than inadequate production. The great clans had walled themselves off in isolation from the people. True leadership would have, by establishing equality, brought the people back to unity.

The pervasive selfishness of the gentry had led to a *fin de siècle* spirit among the people. The merchants dissipated their wealth in riotous living, thinking only of the day and not of their future fate, prepared to invite the bandits in once they reached the gates. If the ruler had been able to make the people his primary interest, wiping selfishness from his own heart, he could have brought men's hearts together and warded off the bandits to save the dynasty.

The exploits of the "rushing bandit" Li Tzu-ch'eng are the bloodiest in the annals of Chinese history. Originating in Shensi, he affected the entire empire for nearly two decades. Li began as a postal runner in a part of Shensi suffering from the depradations of one of chief eunuch Wei Chung-hsien's henchmen and then joined the ranks of rebellious soldiers who had turned to banditry. Born in the Yenan area, he moved to Ninghsia after his widowed mother's remarriage to a soldier. After his stepfather's death he drifted into a lower-class life of violent crime and thence to banditry.

In 1641 Loyang fell to him, but K'aifeng successfully resisted his siege. In the course of his career Li besieged K'aifeng three times. Though never successful, the last siege was so tight and evoked such Draconian defensive measures that human flesh was selling for two ounces of silver per chin and barely 20,000 people remained alive in the city when the siege was lifted.

Having devastated Honan, Li moved into Hupei where his power waxed and he began to consolidate his power over other roving bandits. He set up his capital in Hsiangyang and began to plan for the seizure of the north and Peking. He soon occupied most of Shensi, with Sian as his new western capital and began to receive the surrender of Ming generals, even including the former defender of K'aifeng.

He then sent men across the Yellow River into Shansi and proclaimed a new dynasty with himself as its head. His army now totaled 400,000 infantry and 600,000 cavalry. Having broken Ming military power in Shansi he advanced on Peking. Earlier, cavalry raids had given him excellent intelligence while simultaneously cutting off all sources of information to the Ming Court.

The last Ming emperor committed suicide as Li's forces broke into the capital. Li drained the capital of its wealth, renamed all the bureaucratic institutions and decreed that each five families be responsible for the maintenance of one of his men. But the looting and murdering by his men cost Li the loyalty of the people of the capital, and though Honan and Shantung nominally recognized his suzerainty, General Wu San-kuei ultimately invited the Manchus to his aid at Shanhaikuan rather than come over to Li's side.

The Ming-Manchu force defeated Li at the pass and he fled Peking, carrying his loot back with him toward Sian. In defeat the bandits turned on each other. The Manchus forced Li from Sian back to Hsiangyang and then Wu-ch'ang. Li was finally forced into the hills with only a remnant of his old force where he was killed while raiding a village.

Almost as spectacular was the violent career of Li's contemporary, the roving bandit Chang Hsien-chung who ravaged Shensi, Honan, Hupei and Szechwan, for a time in concert with Li Tzu-ch'eng until jealousy drove them apart. After feigning return to loyalty to the dynasty, Chang took the first opportunity to again rebel and set himself up in Szechwan until repeated defeats forced him to save himself by joining Li Tzu-ch'eng's now more successful movement. A series of bloody campaigns put Chang in control of Wu-ch'ang, but fearing Li's jealousy he fled into Hunan, taking Ch'ang-sha and moving far enough east into Kiangsi to alarm the Kwangtung border before deciding to pull back into Szechwan to evade his pursuers. With his capital at Ch'eng-tu, he soon reduced virtually all of Szechwan to submission.

Chang's twin passions were murder and drink. He regretted letting a day pass without killing a man, and his policy toward the gentry in his service in Szechwan was predictable only in its violence. After being driven out of Peking Li Tzu-ch'eng tried unsuccessfully to force his way into Szechwan. By this time Chang's cruelties had left Szechwan ripe for a comeback by the authorities. Chang tried to hold on to power by intensifying his terrorism and changing his own abode every night to avoid assassination. He finally evacuated Ch'engtu, leaving it in flames and the territory around it for a thousand _li_ a desert. Intending to kill off his own Szechwanese troops before taking off for Hupei, Chang was instead betrayed to the Manchus by one of them and killed by the Manchus. Just before his death Chang ordered his most trusted subordinate to return his loyalties to the Ming. At the last even this bestial bandit uttered this expression of renewed loyalty.

History is the melancholy record of mankind's struggle for existence. In this struggle, error and obstacles and disasters are unavoidable. Much blood and tears must be shed before history's lessons are learned. There are many earlier precedents for the depradations of roving bandits like Li Tzu-ch'eng and Chang Hsien-chung, going back to the Yellow Turbans. In spite of earlier successes, they have all been ultimately destroyed. Their Taoist religious basis was not enough to save the Yellow Turbans. Huang Ch'ao, Li Tzu-ch'eng and Chang Hsien-chung all relied on terror as well as the pretense of setting up a new dynasty. But none of their acts could ultimately save them. Indeed, their terror was what ruined them for, as Mencius said, the world will only be united by one who does not kill men.

Fig. 17 Water-powered chain pump

Fig. 18 Foot-powered chain pump

Fig. 19 Water-powered pounding machine

Fig. 20 Ox-powered chain pump with differential gears

Fig. 21 Silk thread spinning machine

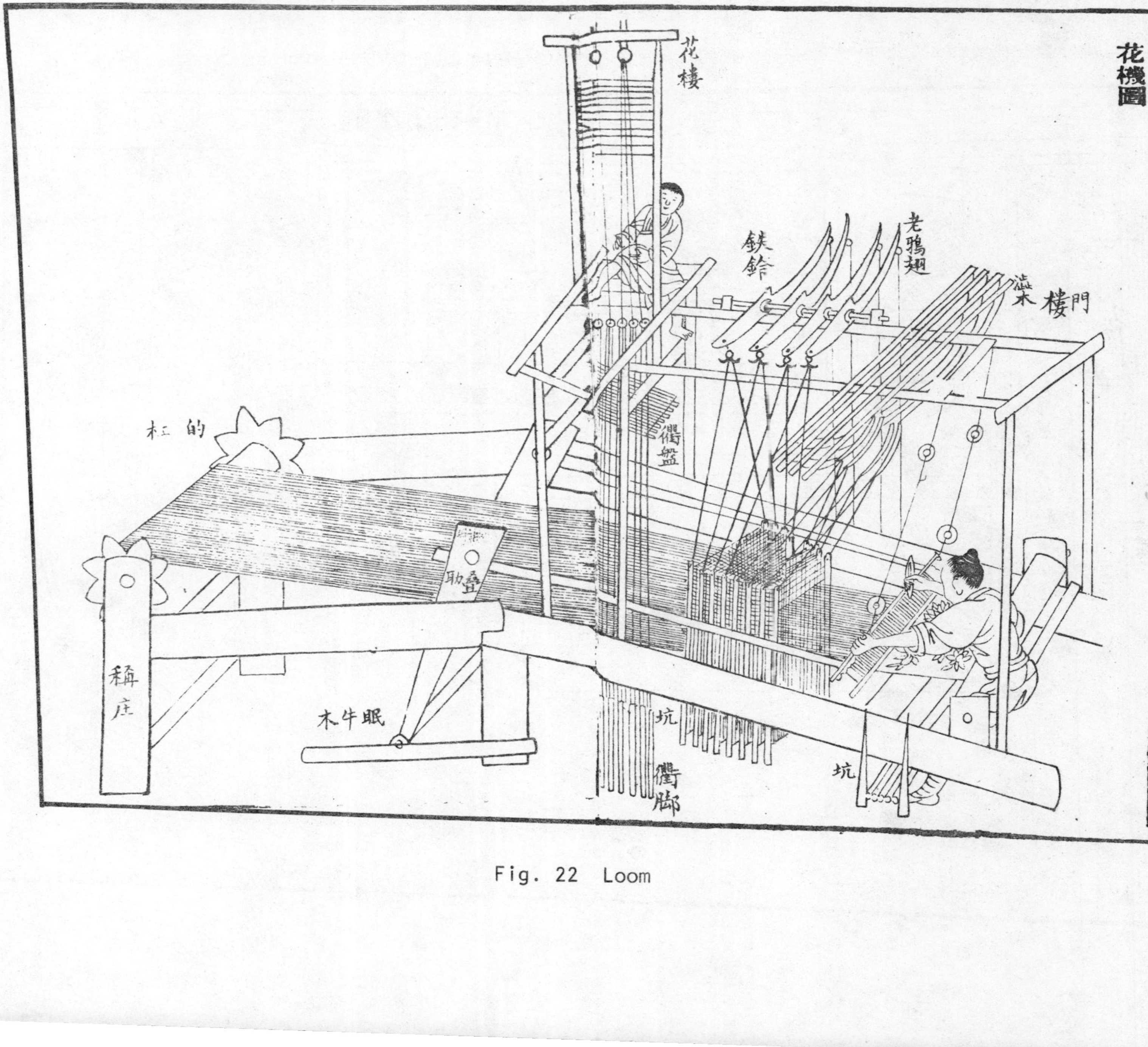

Fig. 22 Loom

Fig. 23 Lining a salt well with bamboo pipes

Fig. 24 Pin making

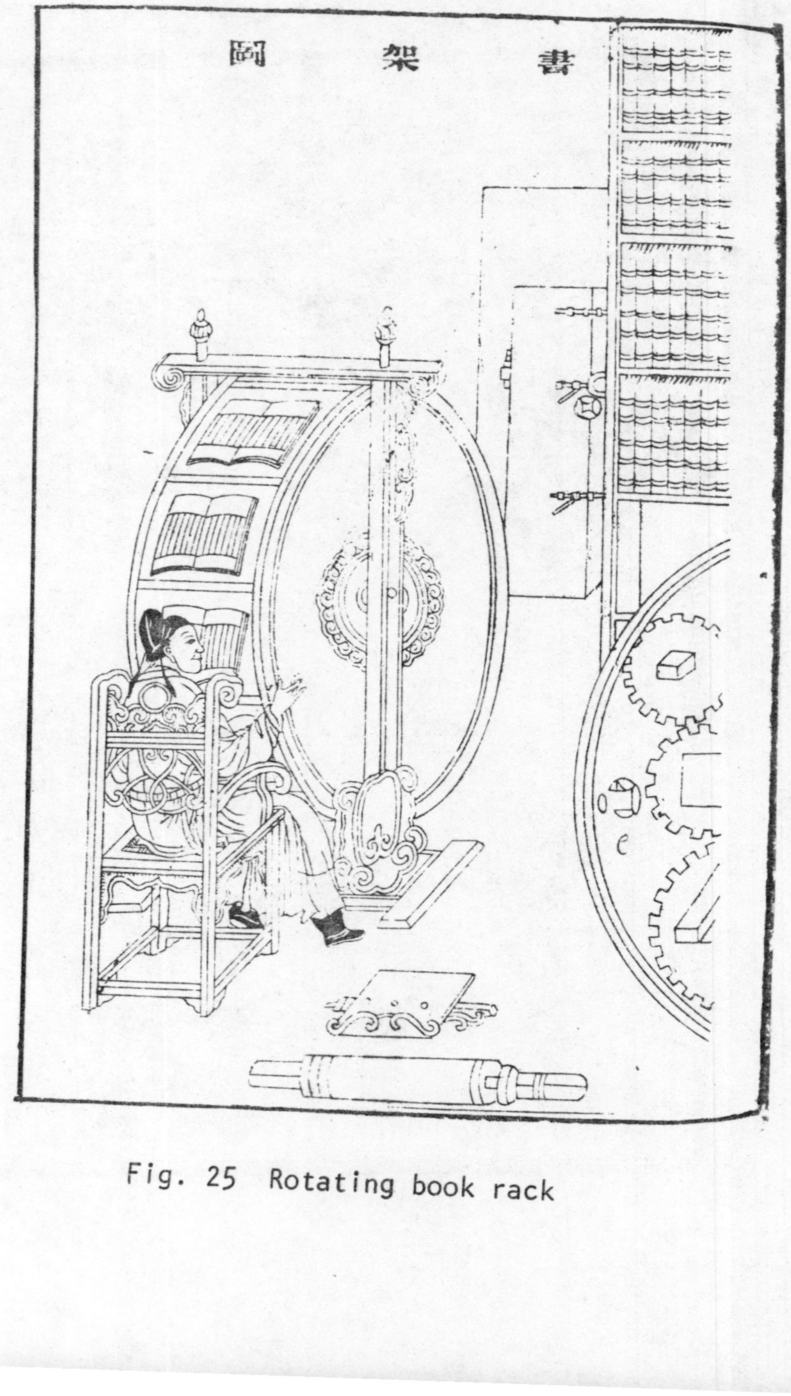

Fig. 25 Rotating book rack

Section XI

THE AGE OF FERMENTATION: THE CH'ING DYNASTY

Outline

Lasting from 1644 to 1911, the Manchus' Ch'ing dynasty halted the progress of the Chinese economy because of the narrow-mindedness and decadence of the imperial clan and Manchu officialdom. The Manchus originated as one of the three main branches of the Jurched people of Manchuria who had founded the Chin dynasty in the twelfth century. The Manchus' branch was settled in the Chien-chou area. They were united in the late sixteenth century by the chief Nurhachi who in 1616 proclaimed the Latter Chin Khanate. Before long, with his 60,000-man army (organized into eight banners of 7,500 men each) he defeated the Ming and occupied Liaotung. Within thirty years, having changed their dynastic name to Ch'ing in 1640, the Manchus took advantage of Ming decadence, the rise of internal banditry and the treason of Ming officers like Wu San-kuei to enter China and occupy Peking in 1644.

The period from then until 1911 was one of the greatest import in world history. This was the age of popular awakening, of the scientific and industrial revolutions, of mercantilism's expansion of world trade, the rise of democratic states, of imperial expansion in an age when no nation could remain isolated and advanced nations came to rule over the economically less developed states. The entire world's economy was revolutionized by this new era of capitalism. The nations transcended the limits of their traditions, as England did in producing a democratic revolution in 1649-53, as France's Louis XIV did in shaking Europe, as Russia did with its Europeanization after 1689, and culminating with the American and French revolutions in the eighteenth century. By this time England had established the base for the industrial revolution, the imitation of which was one of the main aims of the Meiji Restoration of 1868 in Japan. By the end of the eighteenth century England and America had established the base for their modernization. Democracy and industrialization flourished together.

But what were China's accomplishments during this period? The Manchus had still not transcended their barbarous pastoral origins. Their government's decadence and self-satisfaction led to a policy of isolation and unwillingness to seek progress. But from the Opium War on China could not remain self-sufficient, and the economic power of Europe and America deeply penetrated China. At this point China's economy began to change and gradually enter the road to modernization.

Factors Moving China's Economy Toward Modernization

In Nurhachi's time the Manchus treated captured Chinese like slaves and once in power the verbal forms of the master-slave relationship were in large part retained, and real persecution was practiced through such devices as the literary inquisition. Punishments were crueler than those of Yüan and Ming times. Power was increasingly centralized, local appointments having to be made by the central, not regional authorities, and no man could serve in his home province nor have any relatives serve with him. Key posts were reserved for Manchus, showing the essentially colonial nature of the regime. Unlike the Mongols, the Manchus made extensive use of Chinese officials, and thus they were rapidly sinicized but also became decadent and corrupt, and corruption spread from the top down to local government. The corruption of such men as Ho-shen, who dominated the government for twenty years in the Ch'ien-lung reign, significantly affected the national economy.

There was an unprecedented growth of tax-free manors, 80% to 90% of them belonging to the Manchus and largely used to support the imperial clan, other Manchu clans, and the banner forces and to establish garrison fields. Aside from the land confiscated from the Ming imperial estates, land was also taken away from ordinary commoners and removed from the tax rolls. Nothing was done for the improvement of this medieval agricultural system at a time when other nations were progressing into modernity in their agricultures.

An important reason for our lack of economic progress was the dynasty's intellectual isolationism. The British East India Company, founded in 1600, succeeded in entering the China trade by the late seventeenth century, but by the end of the following century they were limited to the one port of Canton and obliged to trade solely through the Co-hong middlemen merchants, largely because of the dynasty's isolationism. This isolationism was an obstacle to the new spirit of free trade and anti-feudal absolutism which dominated England in the aftermath of the Napoleonic Wars. Two English diplomatic missions in 1793 and 1816 had failed to win either free trade or equality of status for English. This failure made inevitable the Opium War and China's subsequent vulnerability to international imperialism under the unequal treaties.

Though the Portuguese were the first to bring opium into China, the British East India Company gained a monopoly over the trade after 1780. All through the eighteenth century England suffered from an unfavorable balance of trade with China. Only a few novelties, like clocks for the upper classes, could be sold. Aside from such items as silk and tea, large amounts of Chinese cotton were sold to England especially early in the century, as the English cotton industry, not yet industrialized, could not compete with the Chinese product. The resulting deficit was met by exports of silver to China until the rise of the illicit opium trade put the deficit on the Chinese side beginning in 1828.

In 1833 the Ch'ing court banned the export of silver. Its determination to suppress the opium trade by the sending of Lin Tse-hsü onspecial assignment to Canton ran up against England's determination to preserve the trade so as to avoid a return to its earlier trade deficit with China, the current surplus also contributing to the fiscal health of Britain's Indian colony. The British Lord Palmerston also wanted to use the occasion to open China to trade in general. The Chinese, not realizing British strength, were also prepared to risk war. When the British won the struggle, China was obliged to accept the Treaty of Nanking.

The opportunities for the West to trade with China thereby provided were the occasion for the first penetration of capitalism into China and the beginning of the transformation of its economy. But the placing by the unequal treaties of the collection of foreign customs duties into the hands of foreigners contravened the principles of international equality and free trade. The 5% tax on all goods in foreign trade, regardless of their type, hindered China's economic development. English management of the customs service often reduced or abolished the tax for foreigners but not for our countrymen. Foreign goods, unlike domestic products, were exempt from any further internal taxation. As further military losses to the foreigners piled up higher indemnity obligations, the proceeds of other tax sources such as the salt and likin were diverted to their payment and placed under control of the already foreign-dominated maritime customs.

The use of foreign capital to construct railroads caused no great harm to China. Though of profit to these foreigners, railroads were of still greater profit to China. Those Westerners who built railroads for aggressive purposes did not limit their mischief to the economic aspects. After 1895, Russia, Germany and France forced Japan out of her newly won position in Liaotung and Russia took the initiative by winning a railroad right-of-way across Manchuria for a shortcut for the Trans-Siberian railroad. In exchange China's Li Hung-chang won a secret treaty of defense against Japan. In 1897 Germany won railroad and mining concessions in Shantung. Russia's riposte was to occupy southern Liaotung so as to build the South Manchuria Railway. Russia's occupation of all Manchuria during the Boxer disturbances evoked the Anglo-Japanese treaty which made possible the Russo-Japanese war of 1904 and Japan's takeover of southern Manchuria. The latter in turn, led ultimately to the eight-year defensive war against Japan after 1937. The mischievous effects of these events were certainly not solely connected with their economic aspects.

The most harmful aspect of the foreigners' economic aggression against China was their snatching of mining rights. Such attempts increased after the Boxer disturbances and brought China closer to colonial status.

After 1895 Japan established textile factories in China, and America and England, under the most-favored-nation clauses of the treaties got similar rights. By 1911 there were over 160 foreign-owned factories in China. Foreign postal, inland waterway shipping, and banking establishments grew in strength from the 1860's. China's foreign trade balance tended to grow worse after 1842, but deficits remained manageable (and balanced by some surpluses) until after 1890.

Sun Yat-sen characterized China's position then as being that of a "semi-colony" whose situation was worse than that of a full colony. Sun estimated that China's losses to all forms of foreign exploitation amounted to no less than two billion yuan annually.

Though the people were being impoverished and society unsettled, this economic agression had its good side. Knowledge was increasing, superstitions were being smashed, and the medieval feudal self-sufficient economy, which could no longer be maintained, was disintegrated and the millenia-old "changeless" economy and society were fundamentally revolutionized. It was an age of economic renaissance and fermentation.

Tseng Kuo-fan was among the earliest of the intellectuals to realize the need for fundamental change after the Opium War, and from such men came the T'ung-chih Restoration. Men like Tseng and

Prince Kung, though without much experience with or knowledge of the West, understood the practical usefulness of Western science and technology. During the T'ung-chih period, Germany and Italy completed their unification and America resolved its civil war, adding three more to the great powers of England, Russia and France who had been aggressing against China.

Of the T'ung-chih era leaders Li Hung-chang had the most positive and progressive attitude toward Western technology, the older leaders tending to despair that their generation could ever grasp these things' principles. In 1864 Li wrote Prince Kung to deplore China's obtuse technological backwardness. If the Japanese, the piratical dwarfs of Ming times, could send missions abroad and learn to build weapons and steamships for themselves, so too could China, Li argued. Emphasis had to be placed on getting men who could build machines and acquiring machines to build machines so that dependence on foreigners could be minimized and China could engage in self-strengthening.

In 1861 foreign warships were purchased and British naval officers were put to work training a new army in Tientsin. The T'ung Wen Kuan (School for Translators) was established in Peking to encourage the new studies. In 1863 Li established a foreign language school in Shanghai and in 1865 Tseng and Li set up the Chiangnan Arsenal in Shanghai was a translation bureau attached to it. Eventually students were sent abroad. Mining operations were begun, military and naval academies established, a telegraph line begun. Though these men were the pioneers who set the precedent for all later modernization, they did not succeed in reaching their goal of self-strengthening. The buds they produced were plucked before they could flower and theirs' was only an age of fermentation.

In general, the West sacrificed equality of distribution for productive efficiency; China sacrificed productive efficiency for equality of distribution. Ours was an economic policy of negative self-limitation; theirs one of positive progress. Hence China ultimately lost its initial superiority to the Western economies, and in the age of imperialism suffered the ruin of its villages' handicrafts and increase in its urban unemployed.

The old remedies unavailing, a new tide of thought ultimately arose among China's intellectuals. Tseng Kuo-fan's predecessor as head of the Hunan Army had despairingly said after seeing his first steamboat, "This is not something our generation can understand." But Tseng had enough experience of the foreigners to understand something of the basis for their superiority. In his later years Tseng devoted his energies to having steamship machinery constructed and students sent abroad. Many of the most important men of the late nineteenth century were either from his original staff or from among these students.

Tseng had absorbed the characteristic Confucian passion for economy and simplicity of life and exhibited these virtues in his personal life. He also advocated frugality by public authority so as not to overburden the people. Of agricultural origins himself and having witnessed the destruction of agriculture during the Taiping Rebellion, he quite naturally emphasized agriculture over commerce in his economic thought. Commerce, he argued, had been far less adversely affected by the rebellion. In addition to requesting tax remission for the lower Yangtze provinces, he used Chu Hsi's cooperative granary scheme in Hunan, financed by contributions from the wealthy and charging 10% for loans of grain to the poor. In 1868 he supervised the building of dikes using foreign machinery. Use of the likin tax had spread to meet the fiscal needs of suppressing the Taiping Rebellion. Tseng advocated its extension to Shanghai, partly on the grounds that it was a lesser evil to burden commerce with this unfair tax than to further burden agriculture.

Having seen the efficacy of foreign arms during the rebellion and having come to understand China's weak diplomatic position through dealing with the foreigners after the rebellion, Tseng took as his motto "Study the barbarians' techniques so as to control the barbarians." Tseng's aim in constructing steamships and cannon was to simultaneously train Chinese in the techniques of their construction so as to ultimately not have to depend on the skills of foreigners. The students whom Tseng had so long argued ought to be sent abroad finally left in 1872, a month before he died.

Tseng was a transitional figure, a conservative in his attempt to preserve the old society, but in his old age a reformer in his adoption of foreign economic techniques.

Li Hung-chang, Tseng's younger disciple, built on the foundation Tseng had established. In 1873 Li argued that the coming of the Western imperialists was without precedent in the three thousand years of Chinese history, and that it would be possible to eventually neutralize their power only by mastering their own techniques for manufacturing weapons of war. He soon realized that weapons manufacture required iron and steel production which in turn required mining. Continued penetration by foreign capitalism evoked new emphasis on light industry and spinning and weaving factories. At first officially managed, such industries eventually became merchant-managed government-supervised establishments with an aura of mercantilism about them. Up until 1895 most such innovations came about under Li's inspiration.

During the 1870's arsenals and shipyards were set up in Shanghai and Nanking. In 1880 a north-south telegraph was built and railroad construction requested. During the early 1890's spinning and weaving mills were established in Shanghai.

When these proved insufficient to avoid defeat at the hands of the French and then the Japanese, Li was accused by critics like Liang Ch'i-ch'ao of shortsightedness, of having concentrated on acquisition of foreign weapons at the expense of fundamental reform. Li acknowledged the limitations of his reforms but insisted that military strength had to be the basis for all further improvements. His main handicap was to be limited by the institutional arrangements of the Ch'ing and the shortage of men with appropriate talents.

Chang Chih-tung was politically less powerful than Li but his equal as an economic builder. Chang contributed greatly to traditional scholarship's support during his numerous regional tours of duty as a civil official. He also encouraged railroad building, mining and silk processing. His motto was "Chinese learning for the substance, Western learning for practical use." Neither could be neglected, but neither should be misused. Traditional studies would cultivate the spirit within and hence preserve China as China. Western studies would be used in the material world but would not interfere with classical studies and hence not interfere with the cultivation of the traditional virtues. The principles of the sages, the lessons of history on how to control disorder, were all still valid. Western improvements would merely supplement the deficiencies of Chinese practice.

By admitting some Western ideas as legitimate Chang went a step beyond Tseng and Li, though from our perspective he still seems a conservative. In 1901, in the aftermath of the Eight-Power Intervention, Chang made several recommendations: (1) The sending of large numbers of men abroad to study the sources of the foreigners' strength. (2) Wholehearted changeover to foreign models of military organization and equipment. (3) New policies to encourage agriculture (the basis of the economy) through new techniques and tax forgiveness for opening new land. (4) New policies to encourage industry through patent rights, tax abatement, and the establishment of modern commercial and criminal law codes to provide a climate of security within which Chinese capitalists could develop. The creation of large-scale corporations would result. The lower costs of production would yield within a decade lower prices competitive with those of the foreigners.

(5) Use of the silver yüan to limit exchange abuses by officials and facilitate the flow of money in commercial life. (6) Establishment of a stamp tax to be placed on the great majority of foreign goods not yet taxed. (7) The establishment of a modern postal system with its local offices under chou and hsien management. (8) Intensified translation of foreign books. Unfortunately, the Dowager Empress remained a conservative at heart, and none of Chang's proposals was adopted during the next five years, except his proposal for greater study abroad to substitute for the defunct examination system.

Kuo Sung-t'ao, the dynasty's first ambassador abroad, was eventually impeached by conservatives for his reports from London calling for reform along Western lines. He pointed out that most of the new devices which ensured Western superiority hardly dated back to the early years of the century, especially the railroad and telegraph which were most important for the state's security. Kuo realized that military affairs ran a distant second to economic factors in making the West wealthy and powerful, and hence he recommended that, like Japan, China should have its overseas students emphasize the learning of economic techniques. But this was an idea for which the men of Li Hung-chang's generation were not yet ready.

Another diplomat, Hsüeh Fu-ch'eng, argued that China's traditional favoring of the scholar over the inventor and industrialist would have to be reversed and specialization be encouraged. He warned that unless the productivity of Chinese labor was increased by industrialization, China's large labor force would not be able to match the low prices of foreign goods, even within China. Railroads had to be built for internal security and to encourage trade by Chinese entrepreneurs who should be further aided by tax holidays of three years for new enterprises.

Ma Chien-chung was another diplomat protegé of Li Hung-chang. He argued that the path to wealth and power lay through a mercantilistic policy of having exports exceed imports, exports to be encouraged by loans funnelled through a Ministry of Commerce from foreign sources to Chinese enterprises. He also advocated use of foreign capital for railroad building but paid less attention than Hsüeh to the problem of avoiding consequent foreign control. Like the Western mercantilists he wanted to encourage mining of gold and silver and urged Li Hung-chang to preserve the mineral resources of the far north from Russian takeover. Ma called for the complete abolition of the likin as an unfair burden on Chinese but not foreigners' commerce, but this tax was not to be abolished until 1931.

The reform faction led by K'ang Yu-wei rose briefly to power in 1898 in the wake of the failure of the self-strengthening movement to stop imperialist encroachments, but it only remained in power for a hundred days before it was overthrown and six of its members were martyred by the court reactionaries. Though K'ang lived on until 1927 he was henceforth without influence.

The society K'ang envisioned in his book Ta T'ung Shu (The Great Harmony) was a hybrid between Confucian notions and various Western ideas, adding up to a species of anarcho-communism. Under the Great Harmony there would be no states, no class or racial divisions, no war or poverty. His economic principle was the elimination of private property and establishment of public production. All agricultural land would be owned publicly, and public authorities at the national, regional and local levels would decide what was to be grown and by what means to meet actual needs. Private property would also be forbidden in industry and communications. Using industrial methods under these conditions of absolute equality, a day's labor might be completed in three or four hours or less and the balance of a day devoted to leisure and study. Private commerce would be replaced by a Ministry of Commerce which, on the basis of its knowledge of local population sizes and varying needs, would assure equitable distribution through its regional and local branches. There would be no bad goods or cheating merchants, merely transportation men, clerks and accountants.

In practice, K'ang had more modest goals: to establish the administrative basis for capitalism while preserving the Confucian moral values in politics. In his Ten-thousand-Word Memorial to the Kuang-hsü emperor, he called for a large number of reforms: issuance of paper money backed by gold and silver in the public treasury, building of railroads financed by public subscriptions to avoid foreign control, allowing the people to build modern machinery rather than attempting to keep monopoly control in government hands, encouragement of mining engineering and establishment of a 5% flat rate tax on production, the minting of silver coins and ultimately gold ones so as to eliminate foreign coinage from the domestic market, and establishment of a government run postal system in conjunction with the railroad network.

To nourish the people K'ang urged the establishment under government supervision of agricultural societies to diffuse the knowledge to be obtained from foreign agricultural treatises, the establishment of a network of workmen's academies to diffuse new techniques among the population, establishment of commercial institutes, followed by lowering of export taxes to encourage commercial growth, and encouragement of migration to the northwest and Manchuria to relieve poverty. Such migrants would receive special training.

It was essentially a democratic capitalism that K'ang called for in his immediate reform proposals. But unlike England and France, who had to go through long and bloody revolutionary experiences before establishing their capitalist systems, K'ang proposed to merely take advantage of foreign threats and the good will of an emperor to impose such changes on a still feudalistic-aristocratic court. Hence his failure. In its aftermath, K'ang remained loyal to the dynasty in the manner of a true Confucian, losing thereby the allegiance of those Chinese abroad who were turning to revolution, but without himself ever regaining his position within the dynasty.

T'an Ssu-t'ung and Liang Ch'i-ch'ao were K'ang's chief disciples. T'an, though a brilliant thinker, wrote little on economics.

During his fourteen-year exile in Japan after 1898 Liang broke with K'ang to become a republican. Unsuccessful in politics after the revolution, Liang turned to teaching and writing in his last years. But his scholarship too was limited by his presentist assumptions. He was, however, very influential among late Ch'ing and early republican young intellectuals.

He believed in the creation of a "new people" through education as being more fundamental than political reform. He argued that China's poverty was not due to lack of land or labor but their unprofitable application to production of goods which did not themselves produce additional goods. This unprofitable notion was based on the concept in the Ta Hsüeh (Great Learning) that producers must be many and consumers few. Traditional Chinese industry could not compete with that of the West after the industrial revolution, was decaying inexorably, and yet its replacement by modern industry was not evident. China lacked both advanced technology and sufficient capital. Hence Chinese commerce could only be a subsidiary of foreign commerce.

In agriculture, Liang noted Chinese special crops like tea and sugar could no longer compete with equivalent foreign products, and ordinary crops were barely sufficient for domestic consumption even in good years. In bad years and because of tax increases farmers were steadily driven off the land, leading to a repeating cycle of poverty causing disorder causing still more poverty.

Liang advocated the application of the principles of sixteenth-century European mercantilism to contemporary China, arguing that any resulting diminution of economic freedom would be more than compensated by increased national wealth. In fiscal policy he advocated strict control of expenditures to meet only genuine needs through a carefully prepared budget, a state monopoly on salt sales, encouragement of a modern native banking system and going on a gold exchange standard as the closest China could approach a full gold standard.

Though no reactionary (he introduced St. Simon's ideas into China), Liang was often inconsistent, praising Kuan Tze and Wang An-shih but denigrating Sun Yat-sen for partisan reasons. A self-confessed dilletante, his contributions to economic thought were not great.

Yen Fu did not participate in the 1898 Reform. He had received a modern education in China and then in England, serving as a teacher upon his return. Though he was among those calling for fundamental domestic reform after 1895 (he argued that 70% of the reason for China's defeat was domestic), he did not win favor and remained restricted to a life of wide-ranging scholarship.

It was as a translator of Western works that he helped lay the base for China's renewal. He especially emphasized the works of the English political and economic philosophers, like Mill, Spencer, Adam Smith, and T. H. Huxley who had laid the basis for modern Western capitalism and democracy. He was a proponent of the evolutionism of Darwin, Huxley and Spencer and its application to both individuals and societies. China would grow competitive with the Western powers not by simply imitating their innovations but by instituting economic and political democracy which would enable the Chinese as individuals to become competitive with Westerners. He opposed mercantilism and favored Adam Smith's laissez-faire, though he also approved of state monopolies over the postal service and telegraph and state pioneering in new industries which could not yield immediate profit. Population growth could bring disaster unless production grew proportionately. Though two or three decades of sustained effort would be sufficient to retrieve China's position, Yen feared (and his fears proved justified) that such efforts would evoke hostile countermeasures by the imperial powers.

In youth and middle age Yen believed firmly in fundamental reform, but in his later years, seeing the destruction of the first world war, his faith in modernization was shaken, and he reemphasized the value of China's traditional Confucian thought.

By the last years of the Ch'ing, reformers had gone beyond their earlier limited concern with armaments and steamships as the requisites for modernization and much work was done in railroad building, mining and manufacturing. Sheng Hsüan-huai may be taken as representative of the official managers of such enterprises and Chang Chien of the mercantile-managed enterprises.

Sheng was originally merely a minor official. He rose in status and wealth as a bureaucratic manager of modern enterprises like the telegraph, railroads and mines under the sponsorship of Li Hung-chang and Chang Chih-tung. His scheme for a great national railroad system was aborted by the revolution. He advocated abolition of the likin tax, raising of the tariff to 10%, establishment of a modern banking system, creation of a silver coinage and a unified money system with mints in Canton, Hupei, Tientsin and Shanghai to produce a range of coins which would become the sole medium for payment of all forms of taxation.

He did not want the modern banking network to be officially managed lest abuses arise. It should be owned and managed by public spirited merchants. It should be allowed to issue paper notes and, if successful, would ultimately make possible the establishment of a central state bank. He initially argued that a special corporation ought to be set up to build railroads, dominated by private Chinese capital and management, but with some government and foreign capital as well. By 1911, however, he changed his mind. Because of corruption which had appeared in privately managed railroads, he advocated national ownership of the main trunk routes, limiting merchant-gentry ownership to local lines. Sheng remained adamant against local opposition to his plan to nationalize the trunk routes, and this led to the riots in Szechwan which provided the opportunity for the Wuhan uprising to take place and the consequent overthrow of the dynasty.

Chang Chien was an early exception to the general opinion among the gentry that modern industry ought to be an official responsibility. Rather, he argued, achievement of high office ought to come after a man had achieved success in business. Giving up prospects for an official career, he returned to his native Nant'ung region in the southeast to pioneer a modern cloth industry and eventually set up a network of additional businesses and social services, like primary and vocational schools, with his profits.

He also advocated governmental reform, including establishment of a convertible hard currency, establishing a network of provincial banks as the tax reception agencies, rationalization of the tax system, establishment of vocational schools and colleges, and encouragement of local corporations for mining and local railroad lines.

Agriculture, in Chang's view, remained the foundation for manufacture and hence trade and military power. In addition to tax holidays for newly cultivated land, agricultural corporations should be encouraged as the modern way to mobilize capital for technological improvements. Unlike traditional advocates of the primacy of agriculture, Chang held that commerce, particularly cloth and iron manufacture, must be the instrument for improving agriculture. When in charge of agriculture and commerce in 1913, he made this a formal policy.

Chang opposed socialism, arguing that wealth and poverty were ultimately the consequence of differences in intelligence and energy among different people and that China's traditions of social harmony could allow it to avoid the class jealousies that had plagued Western countries without resort to socialism.

All of the above men could only propose partial remedies. It remained for Sun Yat-sen to offer the fundamental revolutionary resolution of China's dilemma by recognizing that the very existence of the Ch'ing dynasty was an obstacle to true reform.

Mr. Sun's education was entirely modern. He was entirely free from the inhibitions of a traditional education. He was also a convinced revolutionary. He even viewed his training as a physician as a means to modernity rather than an end in itself. In 1894 he wrote a letter to Li Hung-chang calling for large-scale imitation of the West as the only true path to national resurgence. Education, Sun wrote, must be along Western and practical lines, particularly for officials. The state must actively encourage mechanization of agriculture and the opening of new land so that population would not outstrip production. Unprofitable activities based on superstition must be replaced by use of ever better developed technology based on the replacement of animal energy by steam and electricity. All internal tariffs must be abolished and only a tariff on imports retained so as to encourage the growth of the economy. Only a rail network would be capable of fully opening the interior to modernization.

This first stage of Sun's development of his economic thought emphasized production rather than distribution, but it already established the economic realm as more primary than the political or military, something Li Hung-chang could not conceive.

Sun's ideas on the people's livelihood first began to crystalize during his travels in Europe from 1896 to 1898. He noted that even though the West had solved the problem of production, it had not solved the social question of distribution. If China could solve that question, it could modernize without running the ultimate risk of revolution which now faced the West.

The goal of people's livelihood was to assure equal distribution of society's wealth, and most such wealth was in land. The land's value was increased by the labor put into it, but the landlord reaped an unearned increment from this increased value which ought to revert to the public. Though China's landlords were largely small-scale, early action was necessary to head off big landlordism. The ideal behind equalization was the same as that of the ancient well-field system, but the practice had to be different. Formerly men had been scarce and land plentiful whereas now the reverse was the case. Equalization could be achieved by taxation or by the state buying excess land from private landowners thereby limiting but not destroying the right of private ownership of land. The recent land-to-the-tiller program of land reform on Taiwan fulfills Dr. Sun's goals. It is fundamentally different from the Communist "land reform" which makes the state the single great landlord of the country.

As Sun originally envisioned it, the present land value would remain the property of its owners, but the boundless increase in land value after the revolution would be taken over by the state, to be used for needed increases in social services. Right after the revolution the price of the land would be determined and thereafter its tax or purchase price would be proportioned to increases in its price so as to nationalize its monopoly rent. Landowners would set their own price for their land. Should they undervalue it, what they save in taxes they will more than lose when the government buys them out at the low price they have themselves set. Conversely, if they overprice their land, they will pay an excessive amount of taxes. The principle here is simple and its administration easy. Hence the age-old problem of eliminating corruption in the collection of taxes is in principle solved by this reform. By levying only a single tax on the value of land, the non-usage of land would be discouraged as even unused land would be taxed. Moreover, the efficient use of labor and capital would be encouraged because improvements on the land would not be taxed.

The application of this single tax in Canton city alone, Sun argued, would provide government with enormous revenues to encourage electrification and roadbuilding without further burdening the people. Rural land bought by the state could be equitably redistributed among cultivators. It would be easier, Sun reasoned, to institute this reform before modernization had driven up the price of land all over China to the degree that Shanghai land prices had risen during the preceding forty years. If this great increase in monopoly rent was reserved for public use, the growth of great capitalists and resulting social inequality, like that of Europe, could be avoided. If not checked, the landowner usurps the profit justly belonging to capital and the wages due labor.

Sun was advocating a land-to-the-tiller reform as early as 1907, a decade before the Russian revolution. Even then he distinquished between improvements on the land, which should be privately owned, and the natural land itself the value of which should be publicly held.

Sun realized how short China was of capital for building railroads and canals, opening mines and financing machine industries and hence, though he understood the danger of creating invidious class distinctions, he was willing to see private Chinese and foreign capital engaged in such enterprises. By 1919 Sun had worked out what amounted to an economic plan for China (before the USSR had adopted this method) which envisioned the state undertaking those enterprises which individual capitalists were unable to take on.

Sun denied that class conflict was the source of social progress, and though he believed that the struggle for existence was the cause of progress, he denied Marx's principle of materialism. Social progress could only take place when the majority gained profit. Nor did Sun accept the Marxian theory of surplus value. A factory owner need not reduce his workers' wages to gain a profit. The history of the preceding seventy years had demonstrated Marx's inaccuracy as a prophet.

Land Distribution and Agricultural Credit Policies

The Manchus behaved like their Chin dynasty ancestors and the Mongols with regard to the land. They usurped land, particularly the imperial and official manors of Ming, for distribution among the imperial clan and the eight banners. The Ming manorial system was already extensive enough to have displaced many peasants. The large number of unproductive and often non-office holding bannermen exacerbated the situation. The provincial horse stations of the local banner garrisons also took much land from cultivation. An attempt in 1725 to set up a Mencian well-field system for landless bannermen failed within a decade largely because of the bannermen's tendency to sell the land to outsiders. Each manor had an hereditary head whose main duty was to forward the rents from the excess of which he supported himself.

Imperial manors originated from voluntary cession of private lands as well as from confiscated Ming imperial manors. The Manchu banner lands were concentrated in Chihli. The lands of the Mongol and Chinese banners were spread among the other outlying provinces. One class of manors in Chihli and Manchuria served to nurture the official troops of the eight banners. The eight banner manors were not supposed to be alienable, but in 1853 this rule was abrogated as too difficult to enforce.

The garrison-fields institution went back to the first century B.C. when it was used in Kansu to ward off the Hsiungnu. It continued to be used for a variety of purposes through Ming, but under Ch'ing its functions had been largely taken over by the banner system; by the eighteenth century it was abolished in all but name and formally abolished in 1898.

Official fields awarded to worthy families, like the descendants of Mencius and Confucius, and to support poor scholars were tax exempt. Monastic and temple lands had been largely confiscated by the state in late Ming. During Ch'ing they never recovered to the size of the T'ang churchly estates.

By the end of the Ch'ien-lung reign Manchu and Chinese officials had become corrupt. The population had increased to three hundred million and a shortage of uncultivated land had appeared. Rebellions were caused by both political and economic hardship from as early as the 1770's. The Taiping Rebellion of the 1850's was the culmination of this trend. Most of Hung Hsiu-ch'üan's followers, including his chief lieutenants, were impoverished farmers, unemployed artisans, petty merchants and dissatisfied intellectuals.

According to the Taiping rules all land was the possession of the Heavenly Father and Heavenly Elder Brothers and was bestowed equally on all by the Heavenly Emperor. According to the Taiping regulations of 1853, land was classified in nine grades and was to be distributed in proportion to the size of families, men and women being counted equally. All surplus product was to revert to the Taiping state. No goods were to be held as private property. An equitable conscription system and a network of churches and local treasuries were established. Footbinding and slavery were made illegal. All these reforms were in accord with peasant demands. But after taking Nanking Hung abandoned these utopian goals to establish a traditional dynastic structure which soon degenerated into bloody factionalism and ultimately led the peasant masses to abandon the movement.

To stabilize the chaos into which the countryside had fallen since late Ming, the early Ch'ing rulers reinstituted the pao-chia system and attempted to regularize certificates of landownership, especially for those who opened up new land. Attempts were made to discourage slaughter of draft animals and acquisition of land by officials. Loans of draft animals and tools were also made. Pioneers of remote territories were given housing and travel subsidies. As a consequence, 1.8 million mou of new land was opened annually from 1662 to 1766.

Ever-normal relief granaries were established. Rich men were rewarded for contributing to local cooperative relief granaries, but a tendency to retain reserves of 70% kept the granaries from selling enough grain to reduce prices sufficiently during times of high prices. In 1723 new rules attempted to remedy this defect.

By the 1850's rebellions had depleted grain reserves and after 1870 grain imports were necessary to supplement domestic production, ending China's self-sufficiency in food.

After the Taiping Rebellion rural pawnshops which made short-term loans increased in importance. Some attempts were made regionally to limit their interest rates, but the government had traditionally been connected with their profitability through taxes on their business. In the last years of Ch'ing there was an abortive attempt to set up modern rural credit banks, but only one branch was actually established. Though ostensibly based on French and Japanese models, the new bank actually more closely resembled the traditional pawnshops in its use of pledges and was so viewed by the peasantry.

Commerce

Before the Manchu conquest four customs stations had been established by them on the border with Ming. As money was plentiful and goods dear, trade was also encouraged with Korea. During the first generations after the conquest attempts were made to limit corruption in the collection of commercial taxes through published regulations. But even in its years of prosperity the Ch'ing gave formal precedence to agriculture, the fundamental activity.

The development of Ch'ing internal commerce may be divided into three phases: the first, when commerce was nurtured under the K'ang-hsi emperor; the second, when commerce was flourishing, with prosperity, steady prices and many rich merchants under the Ch'ien-lung emperor; the third, when commerce was decaying, with internal rebellions and foreign competition under the Chia-ch'ing and Tao-kuang emperors.

In addition to the capital there were four great commercial centers: Chuhsienchen near K'aifeng in Honan, the crossroads for waterborn traffic from the south; Ching-te-chen in Kiangsi, the center of production for porcelain which had a national market; Hankow in Hupei, the center for the Yangtze valley's trade; Foshan-chen in Kwangtung near Canton on the Pearl River, the gate to South Asia. Hangchow and Soochow served the flourishing trade of the lower Yangtze. The various provincial capitals were also centers of provincial commerce. The richest merchants were the Shansi bankers and Yangchou salt merchants.

The English, who had been trading with several coastal cities since the late seventeenth century and were gradually restricted during the eighteenth century to Canton, late in the Ch'ien-lung era sent a mission to the capital to unsuccessfully request wider trade opportunities and the opening of diplomatic relations. The Russians, who had unsuccessfully been seeking trade relations since Ming times, ultimately achieved the first Sino-foreign treaty late in the seventeenth century and improved terms of trade in a new treaty in the eighteenth century.

The Cohong system was established late in the K'ang-hsi era. Its thirteen Cantonese merchant members' monopoly over foreign trade was later given official recognition, thereby limiting foreign trade to Canton. Its members determined prices, collected taxes and a 3% commission on the trade. The hong merchants rented thirteen buildings, called factories in English, for the foreign merchants to reside in on the riverbank in the southwestern suburbs of Canton. Of the fifty-six firms resident in them, thirty-one were English. Foreign warships, women and firearms were banned from the settlement and even the merchants could only remain there during the trading season.

The customs office, called Hoppo by the foreigners after the Hu Pu or Board of Census under which it was placed, was supposed to collect a 16% import and 4% export tariff in addition to charging for various services like translators. But the Cohong nominally collected 30%, and total exactions were often many times the official rate.

Imports largely consisted of opium, cotton cloth, ivory and woolens; exports of silk, tea, brocades and granulated sugar. Tea was the most important export, but as a consequence of Chi'ien-lung's banning of private exports, exports tended to decline in quantity toward the level of imports which came to be dominated by opium. The English had replaced the Portuguese as the chief suppliers of opium which had been formally contraband since the Yung-cheng era and which was again banned early in the nineteenth century. During the eighteenth century the English had come to dominate the Canton trade, but later the other European states and America again began to enter the market. The attempt to really ban opium in the 1830's led to war with England, the opening of five ports to foreign trade, and the opening of an era of unrestricted foreign trade.

Treaties with America, France and then several other states followed the treaty with England in 1842. A new wave of treaties opening more ports followed the renewed conflict with England and France of the late 1850's. Tariffs were limited and diplomatic representation in Peking granted, with each nation gaining all the privileges given to any other. Influence over Vietnam was lost by war to France, and over Burma to England. More territory and privileges were lost in war to Japan in 1895. Still more privileges had to be granted after the Boxer Rebellion and the Allied occupation of Peking. Only in 1911 did England agree to end the opium trade by 1917.

Modern Enterprises

China's traditional manufacture was organized on either a family or guild base. Even large-scale enterprises like iron smelting or salt making were essentially families writ large. Only natural sources of energy like wind or water power were used and were linked to direction by men doing physical work. This differs profoundly from modern industry with its use of steam and electrical power directed by men's intelligence rather than their brawn.

China's development of modern enterprises may be divided into two periods: the beginning stage up to 1895 and the flourishing stage after the Sino-Japanese War. Before 1895 the capitalist countries concentrated on commercial penetration of China, and within China attention was largely paid to steps to overcome military weakness. After 1895 the capitalist countries had reached the stage of imperialism and were ready to export capital rather than just goods. Hence they now took over spheres of influence and invested in railroads, mines, factories and banks. The merchants and officials of China now realized that concentration on military modernization had not prevented defeat by Japan, and they undertook modern enterprises to match the efforts of their foreign competitors within China.

The Ch'ing authorities, defeated by the foreigners twice between 1839 and 1860 and having required the aid of foreign weapons to put down the Taiping Rebellion, concluded that military modernization had to be carried out. Hence a number of arsenals and shipyards were built with the aid of foreign advisers between 1862 and 1881, the first being set up by Li Hung-chang in Shanghai in 1862. Soon realizing that arsenals and shipyards required auxiliary supporting enterprises, the first modern mine, the K'aip'ing Corporation was established in 1878. The first Chinese steamship company appeared in 1872. The telegraph began in Tientsin in 1878 and the railroad in 1881, as did the telephone under English auspices in Shanghai. The early enterprises were all closely linked to military needs, were entirely officially managed, and gave little emphasis to domesticating among Chinese the techniques involved.

It was only after successive defeats at the hands of the French, Japanese and then the Allied force occupying Peking that the inadequacy of this approach was finally appreciated. From 1882 to 1894 the official-dominated enterprises began to be supplemented by merchant-managed official-supervised enterprises, and the modern production of commercial (as opposed to military) products may be said to have begun with these firms. Foreign goods had already begun to adversely affect Chinese handicrafts, and it was proposed to keep profits from such goods from flowing out of China by beginning their production domestically. Cotton goods were especially emphasized, but mining and iron smelting were also encouraged. As official supervision inevitably proved inadequate, foreign engineers were usually called in, but they tended to neglect training of Chinese and usually served as an entering wedge for domination by foreign capital. In 1893 electric power generation began in Shanghai under foreign auspices.

After China's defeats in 1895 and 1900 foreign capital took advantage of the spheres of influence their countries had won to separately and jointly make extensive investments, even to exploiting China's cheap labor and raw materials in the interior to produce goods for sale in the cities on the coast. Though these enterprises inhibited native Chinese competition, they also taught native capitalists and laborers techniques hitherto not understood, and large-scale cloth, tobacco, glass, iron and publishing enterprises also began to be established by Chinese capitalists for the first time. Railroads began to expand, and the earliest Chinese modern bank, under joint official-merchant control, was founded in 1897. In 1896 a Chinese-managed postal service was begun.

The government began to reorganize itself to accommodate modern industry, establishing a Ministry of Commerce in 1903 and beginning work on a modern commercial law code. In the aftermath of the Boxer defeat, military vengeance was out of the question and the indemnities had so weakened the government fiscally that it had no choice but to collaborate with the merchants in a variety of ways, including the establishment of several vocational schools. Lower class opposition to the foreigners had been defeated with the Boxer movement. The upper classes now took over this opposition, though they exercised it through peaceful economic competition, in particular through beginning to invest in local rail lines to limit the degree of control by foreign capital. Chinese investment in modern cotton mills and in silk and wool production also increased. Investments in Yangtze steamships, cement works and ironworks appeared. In 1907 the Ching-te-chen porcelain works came under private control. Several state banks were established and the rail network largely completed. Foreign, particularly Japanese, investments continued to expand.

The Fishing Trade

Fishing originated in prehistoric times in conjunction with hunting. From Neolithic times on it was gradually subordinated to agriculture and again became a large scale activity only in the Ch'ing dynasty. Fishing is mentioned as a subordinate activity in Shang. Emperor Shun is said to have engaged in it. The Chou Li gives the title of an official in charge of its supervision. Ssu-ma Ch'ien describes fishing and salt making as being the original main activities in Shantung which Kuan Chung used as the basis for Ch'i's enrichment. Fishing was important in all the eastern and riverine states of late antiquity. Commercial fish farming in ponds was carried out. Fish could be preserved by boning and drying. By Ch'in times fish oil was used for lamps.

Thereafter fishing was thoroughly subordinated to agriculture. Most fishermen were poor inhabitants of coastal areas, and government took little notice of them compared to salt manufacturers. In Ming times, given the threat of Japanese pirates, attempts were

Fig. 26 Fishing

made to organize fishermen into groups of eight to ten boats which would cooperate in fishing and occasionally be used for grain transport, by analogy with the pao-chia system used on land. The Ch'ing saw the beginning of the modern fishing industry. The many new activities occurring on the coast stimulated the government to extend the organization of fishermen begun by Ming.

It was only at the end of the nineteenth century that earlier orders to establish provincial fishing administrations began to be carried out even fitfully. It was early in this century before the first modern fishing companies were established as joint state-private concerns by several regional governments. This was a progressive step in the process of assuring the people's livelihood.

Communications

A communications revolution is the most efficacious weapon for transforming a nation's economy. Modern communications make possible the full unification of a nation's economy. During Ch'ing the traditional land communications instruments, horse and wagon, which had their greatest development in the postal system, were revolutionized by the railroad. The first Chinese railroad was set up just outside Peking over a one li track by an Englishman in 1866, but it was soon torn up because of popular fears. In 1876 another Englishman set up a 1.3 mile line between Wusung and Shanghai, but it was bought up and torn down by the government the next year. A horse-drawn line was assented to in 1880, the first rail line built by Chinese. It was motorized in 1882 by an English engineer.

Popular and Court opposition to railroads overwhelmed the minority who understood their value for both defense and commerce until the defeat by France in 1885 increased the latter's number and influence. In 1889 Chang Chih-tung called for construction of a line from Peking to Hankow. Such a route, he argued, would be secure from border dangers and would pass through several provinces, enhancing their economies. It would be the most effective route for hurrying soldiers to deal with any internal rebellions and as an alternate to easterly water routes for supplying the capital. Finally, it could be built in several relatively inexpensive stages.

With the Court's assent, China's railroad era at last began when construction began on the 1,213 kilometer long Peking-Hankow line in the late 1890's. It was completed some seven years later. A Peking-Fengt'ien line had been completed earlier. A line south from Tientsin under Anglo-German control was not completed before the fall of the dynasty, but another line from Peking to Changchia-k'ou was finished using only Chinese capital and completely designed by Chinese engineers. Lines from Nanking to Shanghai (entirely under foreign control), Shanghai to Hangchow, a narrow gauge line from Shihchiachuang to T'aiyüan, a line from K'aifeng to Loyang, and several lines in Manchuria and in the southeast were completed. In Taiwan, a line from Taipei to Tainan was not completed until after the Japanese takeover, though most of the work was done earlier under Chinese auspices. In all, fourteen lines were completed under official auspices before the fall of the dynasty. Four private lines were in various stages of completion. In addition, the Japanese built the South Manchurian, the Russians the Chinese Eastern, the Germans a Shantung line, and the French a Yunnan-Vietnam line.

The two-thousand-year dominance of sail, the Chinese state's control over shipping and the domination of Chinese shipping by Chinese were all ended by the coming of the foreigners' steamships. Steamships first appeared on the China coast in the mid-1830's and on the rivers in the late 1850's. By the 1860's steamships were appearing regularly on the coast and along the Yangtze and English and American steamship companies had been formed in China. The 3,000 traditional sailing vessels on the Yangtze were reduced to 400 by the late 1860's because of this foreign modern competition.

In 1862 several Chinese merchants bought four steamships to use as grain transports, and in 1868 Kiangsu officials built steamships for the same purpose. Both attempts were unsuccessful. In 1872 Li Hung-chang won approval for China's first official shipping line along the coast, and in 1873 a Yangtze line was established. The same year the official shipping line was reorganized under merchant management. In 1885 Sheng Hsüan-huai reorganized the line again as a joint state-private enterprise which it remained until into the republican era. There were also a number of other local joint state-private shipping lines.

Though the pioneering foreign shipping lines were overwhelmed by their Chinese competition, several new foreign lines were established linking China to the outside world but with extensive routes within China as well. Most were English and Japanese. There were also American, German, French and Italian lines.

Steamships were being built in China by the 1860's. During the first decade of this century the Kiangnan shipyard built nearly 150 warships and merchantmen. Though not as large as the one at Kiangnan, the Foochow and Taku shipyards were of considerable size. These three facilities, built by Tseng Kuo-fan, Tso Tsung-t'ang and Li Hung-chang respectively, were constructed only with great difficulty against many handicaps, but they served as the foundation of the modern Chinese shipbuilding industry.

In 1878 the first modern post offices in the capital, Tientsin, Yent'ai, Niuchuang and Shanghai were established under the direction of an Englishman. At the turn of the century the system was extended down to the provincial and _hsien_ level, and by the end of the dynasty an extensive local network had been established through agreements reached with several foreign post offices. The foreign post offices earlier set up within China did not, however, cease operations. After the Boxer Rebellion the Japanese started their own postal system which soon had over 160 offices. The French, Germans and Russians each had fourteen offices, the English eleven, and the Americans only one.

The Chinese electrical business started in 1879 when Li Hung-chang had a Dane install a telegraph line between Tientsin and Taku. Within a few years it was extended down to Shanghai and made a joint state-private enterprise. By the end of the dynasty a nationwide network of over 600 stations linked by over 120,000 _li_ of line had been established. Undersea cables were also run along the coast and to Japan. By 1905 wireless telegraph stations were being established as well.

The first telephones were installed in Shanghai in 1881 by the English. The first Ch'ing government-run telephones, in Tientsin, were destroyed by the Boxers. Upon Sheng Hsüan-huai's advice telephone service was placed under the telegraph administration. By 1907 the network reached from the capital to Canton, and the Shanghai system had been bought out. That year both telephone and telegraph were placed under the newly established Postal Ministry. Most of the telephone companies were under provincial management, but several, notably in Foochow, Wuch'ang and Hankow, were privately managed.

Coinage and Monetary Institutions

Nurhachi issued his first coinage in 1616. Two mints were established immediately after the conquest. The earliest post-1644 coins were blank on the reverse, but to discourage forgery the custom was soon established of having a Manchu language inscription on the reverse. The location of the provincial mint issuing the coin was also inscribed. In 1646 all Ming coins were called in for reminting, but in 1685 their use was again permitted. During the Shun-chih reign the weight of the coins was intermittently increased from 1.0 to 1.25 *ch'ien* and provincial mints closed to discourage forgers. During the K'ang-hsi reign provincial mints were intermittently closed to reduce the quantity of money in circulation so as to preserve its value. Several regional mints were permitted during the Yung-cheng reign, but the weight of the coin was reduced to 1.2 *ch'ien* to discourage melting down.

Monetary discipline began to slip during the first part of the nineteenth century, and during the Hsien-feng reign a series of large denomination coins was ordered issued to meet the high military expenses of the time. But objections that such coins had never succeeded because they encouraged forgery led to modification of the order and only 100- and 50-cash coins were issued. Attempts to circulate iron coins were still less successful because of their inconvenient weight. During the rest of the century there were intermittent attempts to circulate heavier coins, on one occasion using imported copper. Near the end of the dynasty minting of coins with holes was discontinued, and for the first time holeless coins were circulated.

The Taiping Rebellion halted provincial coinage, and stoppage of copper imports drove up the value of existing coins and decreased the effective money supply, causing monetary disorder. Near the end of the century bronze dollar (yüan) coins were issued in the south to meet the money shortage, and they soon had national circulation. These coins' greater initial value than the silver dollar stimulated their overproduction in the provinces and their consequent depreciation in value.

Small denomination silver coins were minted regionally during the late nineteenth century, but the central authorities never succeeded in carrying out plans to do so themselves. As other nations went on to the gold standard their silver coins tended to drift into China where their varying values caused confusion. Provincial mints began coining silver dollars in response, and the central authorities eventually consolidated these operations into several regional mints.

As silver was the standard of value in commercial exchanges, blocks of the metal had traditionally circulated as money. But lack of standardization of the weights and degree of fineness of the blocks was further confused during Ch'ing by the increasing circulation of foreign silver coins. During the first half of the nineteenth century the government licensed private silversmiths so as to achieve a measure of standardization of blocks of silver.

Paper money was used in early and late Ch'ing. From K'ang-hsi to Chia-ch'ing silver and copper coinage predominated. In late Ming paper notes had decreased in circulation. There was a paper issue during the Shun-chih reign, but the bad precedents of the Sung, Yüan and Ming caused its halt within two decades. Paper notes based on silver and copper were again issued during the Hsien-feng reign, and their number gradually increased thereafter. There were also private and foreign notes in circulation. By the end of the dynasty the notes of the new state-established banks circulated in confused competition with those of local authorities.

During the late eighteenth century certain Shansi dyestuff merchants began to branch out into the business of discounting notes for other merchants and by mid-nineteenth century a number of merchants in other trades were doing the same thing. There were three major groups, each with many branches. Because of the difficulty of transporting specie, merchants preferred to make payments to each other with notes issued or backed by these houses. By the 1870's they were also handling the transmission of tax revenues for the government. They did much business with very limited capitalization and made large profits through turning over other people's money. Their organization was quite simple as they depended on their customers' trust for their business. They were partnerships or single proprietorships with unlimited liability. Their informality of structure was characteristically Oriental. Though they survived the loss of their government business to the new state banks after 1900, most were wiped out by the 1911 revolution which made it difficult to call in their loans to meet the claims of their depositors.

Several money-changing houses in the Yangtze valley were able to compete successfully with the Shansi note houses by making profits from differences in exchange rates. The money changers of Shanghai dated back to the eighteenth century but grew in number and size after the mid-nineteenth century to 105 houses. The panic of 1882 ruined half of these. Some of them could pay high interest to depositors because highly profitable short-term loans were made to opium traders, but ruinous competition among those engaged in this practice led to their collapse and affected those not engaged in it as well. Collapse of a foreign-promoted rubber speculative fever in 1909 ruined many more money changers.

From the 1850's on a number of foreign banks opened in Shanghai. Chinese resentment at discrimination against them by these foreign banks led by 1896 to the establishment of the first Chinese-owned modern bank. From then until the end of the dynasty seventeen more modern banks were established, and in 1906 the first state bank was set up and soon evolved into China's official central bank.

The Taxation System

To win popular acquiescence taxes were lightened after 1644. All surtaxes on land were abolished. Henceforth tax rates were ordered to be revised every decade by the central government and the tax schedules published, with copies at the local level for public inspection and comment. After several partial tax remissions, the K'ang-hsi emperor froze the size of the tax census registers. The registers were kept at that level for the remainder of the dynasty. The Yung-cheng emperor combined the head and land taxes to simplify administration. There were several tax remissions during the Ch'ien-lung era because of government revenue surpluses.

The government's fiscal situation was completely reversed by the foreign exactions and domestic rebellions of the nineteenth century. Inhibited by the earlier self-imposed limits on the tax system, informal exactions, including those on merchants, had to be resorted to. Such exactions on the rich salt and foreign trade merchants had been used in the Ch'ien-lung era. More profitable was the selling of gentry status and ultimately official office not only to rich merchants but to the gentry as well. The defeat of the Taiping Rebellion required letting the provinces exact a variety of local taxes. Hence by the end of the dynasty there was no longer a unified national tax system. Beginning as "contributions" these new levies became indistinguishable from taxes. They removed in fact the prohibition on increasing land taxes. These land tax increases went to local authorities, salt and excise increases to the central authority.

In anticipation of the end of revenues from opium imports in 1907 preparations were made for a modern commercial tax code, but one was not put into effect before the end of the dynasty. The new military and educational responsibilities placed on the provinces after 1895 caused still greater multiplication of taxes and greater divergency among provinces. Nationally, the maritime customs and salt taxes had to be dedicated to paying off foreign loans and indemnities, and attempts to replace this lost revenue with miscellaneous new taxes were generally unsuccessful. The land tax remained most central, followed by the maritime customs, likin, salt and ordinary excise taxes.

Private land included alienated banner fields and land held by minority peoples as well as ordinary privately held fields. Official fields paid rent rather than tax. There were also imperial, imperial clan, banner, and garrison fields in the north and northwest. There were schedules of punishment for officials who illegally acquired land. Tax holidays for newly opened land were available so long as it was registered, but the rich and powerful could easily corrupt local officials so as to keep land permanently off the tax rolls.

In early Ch'ing the size of the mou was redefined, but the new definition was only applied to newly opened land. Hence the measure varied chaotically from region to region. The land registers remained essentially those of the Ming all through the Ch'ing. Local fears and inertia and the expense of a complete resurvey caused this. Hence except in name no equity in assessing taxes was possible. A variety of systems of billing landowners was used at different times and under different circumstances. Abuses, such as collecting taxes in advance and excess collection, were nevertheless numerous. The two annual collection periods were at different times in different regions.

The land tax subsumed five categories within it. The most important ones were a combined land and head tax levied in kind and cash at a ratio of eight to two but collected in different amounts in various provinces, and a grain transport tax levied in kind in proportion to a province's distance from the capital and sent to either the capital or T'ungchou to supply banner garrisons or officials.

In the 1880's Liu Ming-ch'uan succeeded in compiling a land survey of Taiwan despite the armed opposition of some of the major landowners whom the reform was designed to force to pay a higher proportion of the land tax than they had done hitherto. So complete a resurvey had not been carried out anywhere else during Ch'ing, and Liu only succeeded in Taiwan by personally supervising the entire operation with the aid of a few reliable assistants and, on one occasion, by fighting a pitched battle with his opponents. Nevertheless the reform made possible the completion of the Taipei-Keelung railroad and the opening of steamship routes to Hong Kong and Shanghai which, in turn, permitted the blossoming of Taiwan's economy.

Males from sixteen to sixty years of age, graded by wealth into three categories (with considerable provincial variations) owed a labor service tax commuted into money. The head tax was included in the land tax and was fixed at the census level of the early eighteenth century. This led the government to lose interest in keeping accurate census records. The pao-chia system, which gave some population information, was mainly designed for taxation and internal security purposes. Though local governments were supposed to hire labor service men, in early Ch'ing a limited number of men could be levied for militia duty. In the early nineteenth century such men were allowed to avoid taxes on thirty mou of land, and hence this cannot be considered a true corvée.

There was also a variety of locally levied corvées from which city residents and gentry were exempt and which could be commuted, giving local officials and clerks many opportunities for corrupt practices.

Though the early Ch'ing salt laws resembled those of the late Ming, trouble was postponed until the Yung-cheng reign by keeping the tax rate low. Rates were still kept low during the Ch'ien-lung reign, but the salt merchants were not well controlled and their exploitation of the people continued to grow worse through the end of the dynasty.

Some salt was entirely handled by officials, some partly or wholly by licensed merchants who often used their influence to pass their positions on hereditarily. From mid-Ch'ing on such merchants tended to have a free hand in disposing of their salt and to have all the tax associated with it pass through their hands. For thirteen years after 1792 free sale of salt by unlicensed merchants in some areas was permitted. The normal salt tax was divided into several components, assessed at different rates in different areas. In addition salt was subject to the likin which averaged more than twice the normal tax rate and made salt prohibitively expensive in areas far removed from production centers. There was an elaborate hierarchy within the Salt Administration to oversee the trade.

Ordinary excise taxes of early Ch'ing resembled those of the Ming. From the Ch'ien-lung era on they steadily rose and were levied on goods traveling by sea as well as by land. After 1842 these taxes were labeled "ordinary" or "old" taxes to distinguish them from the new maritime customs in the treaty ports. After 1901 those collected within 50 li of a port were placed under the maritime customs administration. The ordinary excises were collected by appropriate officials from the circuit (tao) level on down. They were levied by category of goods at a nominal rate of 5%, though in practice the rate varied widely by locality. This variation gave the foreigners an excuse to gain exemption for themselves until a uniform national rate was published, something the dynasty never succeeded in doing. Exemptions were also permitted for goods needed in disaster areas and for some small scale shipments.

The likin was first applied in 1853 in Yangchou to goods in transit along the Grand Canal at the rate of fifty cash per shih of grain. It was soon widely applied by the regional authorities fighting the Taiping rebels at a rate of 1%. Few merchants were affected, and it was understood to be only a temporary war tax. But after the war the tax was extended to more goods, and the rate increased to as much as 5%. Local control led to extensive corruption, and the nature of the tax greatly hindered the development of internal commerce, leading to repeated calls for its abolition. In addition to fifteen categories of goods, likin was also assessed on seven more products, notably salt, tea and wine.

The early Ch'ing prohibition against foreign trade (to defend against Cheng Ch'eng-kung and other pirates) was lifted in 1685, and four ports were opened of which Canton became the most important. Its trade was supervised by a special imperial supervisor limited to a one-year term so as to discourage corruption. Foreigners were restricted to Canton and were annoyed by the extraordinary exactions which were also exacted against Chinese merchants at the other ports.

New maritime customs houses were established in the treaty ports after 1842. The tariffs were collected by each nation's consular officials, and while this ended the old abuses, the tendency of each consul to favor his own nation's merchants led to an agreement in 1851 for the Ch'ing government to again administer the customs. Renewed abuses led to the establishment in 1854 of an Anglo-French-American directorate to administer the collections. Between 1862 and 1907 forty-eight customs stations were established, both on the coast and in the interior.

By treaty the rate on imports was limited to 5%, but the exemption of many goods and the tendency of prices expressed in silver to drop reduced the effective average rate to 4%. The rate was increased to 5% and the number of exemptions reduced when the customs revenue was dedicated to payment of the Boxer indemnity. The regulations of 1902 exempted grain, precious metals and specie currency, printed matter, goods for the use of the Ch'ing and foreign governments, travelers' personal goods and other minor goods. Before 1858 only opium and saltpeter were contraband. Thereafter the ban on opium was lifted, a ban on salt imports imposed, and certain military goods imports permitted.

The rate on exports was also 5%. Specie and coins, printed and educational materials, and some other goods were exempt from duty. The export of weapons, medicine, salt, copper, iron, food (except for vegetable oils) was banned.

The Treaty of Peking with Russia in 1860 allowed tax-free trade at three places. Later treaties gave Russia still more duty-free or reduced-duty privileges. A treaty with Japan in 1905 gave the same advantages to Sino-Korean trade as had been earlier granted to Russia. A treaty in 1866 reduced tariffs for France, and a similar deal was made for the Burmese-Yunnan trade in a treaty with England in 1894.

Goods in internal commerce often paid in ordinary excises and likin a tax several times greater than their price. The treaty with England in 1858 provided that English goods, after paying the maritime customs, pay only an additional tax of 2.5% in lieu of these exactions. This advantage, provided only to foreign goods, placed severe handicaps on the development of native Chinese commerce and was the greatest reason for its inability to develop. The duty placed on opium by an agreement in 1887 became the largest single revenue producer for the maritime customs, an indication of the extent of the harm done by the English to our people. Maritime customs revenue tripled in the last quarter of the nineteenth century and the first decade of this century, but with foreign goods penetrating every corner of our country, how could it not be impoverished?

The Late Ch'ing Destitution of the People's Livelihood and the Explosion of the National Revolution

Ch'ing began to decay from the middle of the Ch'ien-lung reign. The quality of the emperors had begun to decline as early as the K'ang-hsi reign. The Manchu officials' avariciousness, always present, grew beyond bounds during the Ch'ien-lung era, as evidenced by the twenty-year career of Ho-shen whose private fortune was said to equal ten years of ordinary tax receipts. Local officials took their cue from their leaders and the quality of the Chinese officials also steadily deteriorated. In 1800 Hung Liang-chi wrote that the level of honesty and morale among officials had deteriorated noticeably during the previous several decades and that clerks had become more numerous and avaricious, unchecked by equally avaricious officials.

The great increase in population had caused a turn for the worse in economic conditions. The population had exceeded 300,000,000 by the latter part of the Ch'ien-lung era. Hung Liang-chi feared that population was greatly outstripping the land supply and that the situation was exacerbated by the maldistribution of land. Prices, he claimed, had already increased significantly because of the pressure of increased demand on fixed supply.

A series of popular rebellions from the late eighteenth century on had been ostensibly responses to official persecution, and the Manchus had not been able to put down the strongest of them without the aid of the local militia.

After China's first defeat at the hands of the foreigners in the Opium War, further defeats followed one after the other during the rest of the nineteenth century.

There had been only indirect contact between Occident and Orient before Ming-Ch'ing times. Chinese silk making techniques had been transmitted to Byzantium in the sixth century A.D. The technique for making paper, though transmitted to Central Asia by the eighth century, did not reach Europe until the twelfth century. The magnetic compass reached Europe in 1302, some two centuries after its use for navigation was first recorded in China. Gunpowder was in use in China by the time of the Sung-Chin war in the 1120's but first appeared in Europe in 1354. Block printing began in mid-T'ang, movable-type printing during Northern Sung, but in Europe not until 1438. Hence it can be seen that China was not inferior to but rather a stimulus to the West. It is only in the last century or two that the West has jumped ahead in commerce and science and, not realizing that we too have our learning, has treated us like Africa's savages.

By the time of the Opium War, the drain of silver had driven up the price of an ounce of silver to 1,600 cash. This disturbed both trade and tax collection. The loss of the Opium War caused still larger silver drains. Yet the T'ung-chih Restoration, coinciding as it did with the American Civil War, the start of the French Third Republic and Japan's Meiji Restoration, had a chance to make a true renovation of Chinese life, but this was spoiled by the obduracy of the Manchus, particularly the Dowager Express. Her and a minority of courtiers' ignorant behavior during the Boxer uprising is further evidence of this. Though the Ch'ing authorities seemed to learn their lesson from the Boxer debacle, the reforms they backed were only superficial. Chang Chih-tung concluded in the end that no fundamental change would be made.

The upheavals of the last half of the nineteenth century produced Mr. Sun Yat-sen, a great popular savior. He was born in 1866 in Kwangtung province to a family which had fought for the Ming in the seventeenth century. It had vowed never to serve as officials under the Manchus and hence had devoted itself to farming ever since. From childhood Sun had heard stories of the Taiping rebellion, whose leader was a Cantonese, and deeply admired the man and the movement. Because of the depth of foreign influence in Canton, Sun was able to learn English from a missionary at an early age. He was, therefore, suited by background and training to lead a revolution against the Manchus and, in the interests of the peasant majority, to use Western as well as Chinese ideas.

Sun's determination to overthrow the Manchus was fixed in 1885 in the aftermath of the loss of the war with France which in his view had demonstrated the regime's inability to either prepare for war or exploit the limited tactical success it had won in Vietnam. The inability of Li Hung-chang to accept Sun's advice in 1894 confirmed him in his view that a revolution against the Manchus was the only course which would save China. His organization of the Hsing Chung Hui (Revive China Society) followed hard on the humiliating defeat by Japan. During the following decade and a half he extended his activities to overseas Chinese, traveled abroad and tried to unify all the indigenous anti-Ch'ing organizations within China under a common leadership.

The Hsing Chung Hui's successor organization, the T'ung Meng Hui (Association of the Joint Oath), was particularly successful among Chinese students overseas, especially in Japan. It was notable for the oath its members swore in writing not to abandon the goal of creating a new China nor to leave the organization until that goal was achieved. Membership was open to all classes, and its officers were democratically elected.

Its constitution called for establishment of a republic after the overthrow of the Manchu government. Social and economic institutions were to be changed so that any increase in land values consequent upon republican reforms would revert to the nation. Ownership of land would thereby be equalized. In other words, the San Min Chu I (Three Principles of the People) were already embodied in the constitution of the T'ung Meng Hui. These principles were to be achieved in three stages: the stage of military government, which would defeat the Manchus and foreign imperialists, and within three years set up local administrations to begin removing such abuses as opium smoking and foot binding; a six-year transitional stage during which representative government would be set up locally; and a final stage of full constitutional government.

The Three Principles were publicized in the T'ung Meng Hui's Min Pao (People's Journal), published in Tokyo from 1907 to 1910. The Three Principles, the journal argued, explained Europe's rise to dominance, but though China had to adopt the first two, it was by tradition closer than Europe to being able to resolve the problems of People's Livelihood.

By winning over members of the new army in Nanking and Wu ch'ang, Sun and his associates were undermining the heart of the Manchus' power. While Sun was organizing support in America, his followers unsuccessfully attempted a revolution in Canton in April of 1910. The martyrs of this revolt nevertheless already demonstrated the Nationalist movement's later ability to bind together men from all classes and occupations. The Canton rising also helped inspire the successful revolution the following year which was able to take advantage of the disturbances associated with the government's railroad nationalization proposals.

Within three days after October 10, 1911, the revolutionaries were able to win the garrison of Wuch'ang to their side and take over the area, and the whole nation rapidly responded. Within a month Shanghai and Nanking were won over and with them the whole of the south. Sun Yat-sen was in Denver, Colorado at the time of the Wuch'ang uprising. He quickly returned to China by way of Europe and arrived in Shanghai in December. At the beginning of 1912 he was installed as provisional president of the new republic. Though not all battles were over, he immediately set to work on such reforms as the abolition of opium use and footbinding and the unification of the fiscal administration, thereby setting the standard for the new order. Hence we call him the Father of our Republic of China.

Appendix A

Précis of Mark Elvin, The Pattern of the Chinese Past. Stanford: Stanford University Press, 1973.

Part I

THE FORMATION OF THE WORLD'S LARGEST ENDURING STATE

Empires and Their Size

Empires tend to expand until their technological superiority and politico-military efficiency are balanced off by the burdens of increased size (delayed and more costly communications, a more complex, costly and harsher bureaucracy). Size, however, also yields more and more various resources. In China these factors tending to limit size and cause fragmentation were not strong enough to create permanent disunity. The evolving tradition of unity and relative isolation from competing high civilizations in turn strengthened geographical and cultural unity. Geographical unity was also ultimately encouraged by a revolution in transport and communications (Ch. 10).

Among the consequences of unity were manorialism without feudalism, cities larger than Europe's but without Europe's autonomy, and absence of the cultural diversity which results from dividing a civilization into a competing system of states.

The Early Chinese Empire

Prior to Eastern Chou, the Yellow River valley was divided into local principalities. Its agriculture was dominantly slash and burn. Lords' estates were worked by slaves-serfs; the rest of the land by peasant collectivities. The first land tax is recorded in Lu in 594 B.C. The appearance during Eastern Chou of fallowing, manures, and iron tools lessened the number of workers per mou and encouraged the dissolution of peasant collectivities. Land became private property and serfs became free peasants. This happened more quickly and thoroughly in Ch'in.

The first empire's rotational conscription of peasants for military service and the related tax collection system were imperiled by the growth of huge estates owned by officials and merchants and worked by tenants or slaves. Hence Han Wu-ti attempted to reduce the aristocracy's size, tax trade and capital, confiscate estates (making the state the biggest landowner) and establish state monopolies in salt, iron, and wine. The tradition was begun of executing the politically suspect and selecting bureaucrats from the lower classes. Though he realized it ran counter to the goals of his domestic policy, Wu-ti moved against the Hsiungnu. Public lands may have been allocated to cultivators in lifetime tenure. They were also used to reward officials, leading to the creation of new latifundia.

During Eastern Han, slaves, about 1% to 10% of the population, were likely too expensive to use as agricultural labor, but were at times used in manufacturing. Eastern Han was too indebted to estate owners to prevent them from quasi-enserfing most of the formerly free peasantry, as happened to coloni on contemporary Roman estates. The government's weakness and the collapse of conscription (ca. 46 A.D.) forced local self-sufficiency. Walled defenses around the camps of great estates spread for the first time from the frontiers to the interior. Barbarians were invited inside the frontiers, as in Rome.

The Crisis of the Third Century A.D.

China's division into three kingdoms paralleled the division of the Roman empire into three parts. Ts'ao Ts'ao was the era's greatest innovator. His state colonies provided the government's fiscal base; his hereditary military households made up the core of the army. The state colonies were a public version of the magnates' private estates. The stratification of society induced by the military households' ubiquity resembled late third-century Rome's creation of a caste society.

These innovations soon decayed. State colonists evaded their obligations by entering trade or by not registering. Chin assimilated colony land into its state land and allocated it to cultivators. But this did not work well either, as the elite preferred to usurp land for livestock and pasturage which were still economically competitive with cereal agriculture in northeast China and were more prestigious.

China's situation was parallel to that of fifth-century Byzantium. There were many more big estates in the Western Roman empire, which collapsed, than in the Eastern Roman empire, which did not. As in Rome, in early fourth-century China barbarians were becoming increasingly sinicized and hence still more dangerous.

Sino-Barbarian Synthesis in North China

The armed camps in the interior of north China, though novel, still reflected the characteristically Chinese idea of a "properly ordered society." Ideally a camp's leader was a superior man whose deputies were senior local leaders supported by their own communities. This hierarchy was to be cemented by moral unity and legitimated by equity in resource allocation.

The Hsienpi and allied Hsiungnu victors in the fourth-century intramural barbarian conflicts initially tried to keep themselves as a separate military elite, living off the production of Chinese cities and farms. But they were steadily urbanized and drawn into large-scale farming and manufacture, often for the market, and melded with the richer Chinese families. The provinces were dominated by local magnates who also were often hereditary local officials.

Attempts to control these landowners led by the late fifth-century to the Equitable Fields system, an attempt to limit large holdings to service tenure. Local loyalties were to be fragmented by basing registration on deliberately artificial units. For the upper elite this was usually just a "paper revolution," but initially the state was merely attempting to establish the principle of central control over land. Middle landowners could evade limits by gaining additional allotments for their slaves.

By mid-sixth century, sinicization permitted the moving of the capital from the grazing-arable frontier south to Loyang. The use of professional tribal warriors was replaced by a local militia system (similar to the Roman temones and capitula) which for the first time for the Toba Hsienpi combined farming and fighting. By 581 this system provided a force big and well-supported enough to reunify the empire. Sui Wen-ti, though deeply sinicized, was "not ethnically or spiritually fully Chinese."

The Middle Empire

Sui's soldier-peasant militia resembled that of the Byzantine Heradian dynasty. The Yangtze became the empire's granary, playing the role of Egypt in the Roman-Byzantine empire. The Grand Canal was China's Mediterranean. Eventually the canal system rendered obsolete the militia's self-supply system. Sui's and T'ang's militia were commoners registered in the Equitable Fields system. As in Byzantium, the health of the militia depended on the functioning of its Equitable Fields base. Both T'ang and Byzantium made increasing use of body armor (T'ang as a defense against the powerful crossbow) and of elaborate drill maneuvers. Hence it was necessary to replace dependence on barbarians and mercenaries with the use of a tough, professional militia.

Serious attempts to keep big estates from subverting the Equitable Fields system were made by limiting the size of office lands estates. But lack of land made it hard for the state to distribute even the legal quotas. Attempts to move local officials every three years (before they could develop local vested interests) kept them so insecure that they retained incentive to corruptly usurp land. Equitable Fields never worked in rice growing areas, hence migration south increased. Slaves, though still important in agriculture, were not allotted land during T'ang. They lacked surnames, could not marry free people, and there were lesser penalties for murdering them.

T'ang's eighth-century collapse was partly caused by reaching a point of diminishing returns in military campaigns beyond the empire's bloated frontiers. By the late seventh century these extensive campaigns had already disrupted militia schedules. Development of the canal system removed justification for a dispersed, self-supplying militia. Overissue of nominal honors (hitherto reserved for the militia) debased the militia's social status. After 674 the militiamen lost tax-exempt status and hence membership became less attractive to the elite. Even before the An Lu-shan rebellion, rotating militia units had been replaced by frontier armies under permanent leaders. After 755 the loss of central control led to the breakdown of the Equitable Fields in a way parallel to the rise of European seigneurialization.

Manorialism Without Feudalism

The Sung reunification was accompanied by an economic-technological revolution which cheapened the military and administrative costs of unity and so integrated society that fragmentation thereafter was rendered much less likely. Only then did China's evolution diverge from that of Europe.

China got manorialism but without a feudal political-military superstructure. By the tenth century much of the peasantry had been enserfed on large private manors. That there was a distinction between serfs and free peasants is illustrated by a questionnaire circulated in 1180 by Chu Hsi, which has separate categories for tenant-serfs and "families cultivating land belonging to others." Admittedly few other contemporary documents make the distinction this clearly, but attempts (such as that by Tan Kyōji) to define free tenants as serfs not fully provided for by their masters cannot get around Chu's clear distinction between serfs and tenants.

Tenant-serfs are tenants bound to the soil. They appear in the records only in the tenth century. Several decrees in Sung and Yuan times attempted to mitigate bondage to the soil, but likely had little impact. Probably serfdom tended to grow harsher with time, with serfs bonded to masters, not the land. In parts of west China the state even helped enforce such bondage by ordering the repatriation of fugitive tenant-serfs if they had been enticed away by other lords and their original masters were not cruel.

Tenant serfdom likely originated in several ways: (1) As in Europe, by the partial liberation of slaves. This would account for the greater harshness of Sung than T'ang manorialism. (2) Poor free peasants might be enserfed when they sold their land. (3) Coercion or inducement of free peasants into quasi-serfdom by offering them attractive terms. There was also a limited flow of peasants from serfdom to freedom through manumission.

There was much regional variation in the percentage of the population in serfdom. Chetung, for example, had greater social equality because of its relatively infertile land. Serfs were usually not enrolled on population registers, and many of those registered (in some areas 70%) rented some land. But though it is not possible to estimate its role exactly, "the manor was the dominant institution in most of the Chinese countryside." This is indirectly confirmed by the eleventh-century decision to entrust local government to units of from five to 250 households, led by the wealthiest members of each unit. This system was based on a rural hierarchy and only collapsed in the seventeenth century when manorialism also collapsed.

Some manors were scattered; others were compact. Most frequently both forms were combined: a compact demesne worked as a unit under a manager was associated with allotments run separately by rent- and service-paying tenants. Demesne workers were even regulated by water clocks set up in the fields. Most irrigation projects were administered by manors individually or in combinations. Each tenant-serf family was normally an independent economic unit which might even trade in the market.

There were many differences from medieval European manorialism. China had many free peasants, there was free sale of land, manorial justice was not legally recognized, and landowners were not members of a special military class. But the Chinese system could have converged with Europe's if (as Li Kou actually proposed in 1052), landlords had been allowed to establish private armies and were given official rank for successfully routing local bandits. Even so, manorialism may have siphoned off enough wealth from the state to account for Sung's "incapacity to survive unconquered."

Iron, Gunpowder and the Mongols

The Sung economic revolution permitted it to establish the greatest army the world had yet seen. By 1160 government arsenals were turning out 3.24 million weapons per year. Northern Sung had 300,000 soldiers in and near the capital, a like number on the Liao frontier and 450,000 on the Hsi Hsia frontier. Han would have been ruined by even one such army. Though it could afford such an army, Sung was nevertheless conquered piecemeal, mainly because its high technology was diffused across the frontiers to its enemies.

Sung was possibly using coke (coal was definitely used as fuel to heat the blast furnaces) to produce at least 40,000 and likely 125,000 tons of iron per year. This iron technology diffused to Liao and then Chin. The combination of abundant iron with barbarian cavalry was too much for Sung. Liao did not totally armor all its cavalry. Chin used armored halberd-carrying horsemen as shields for its bowmen. The Chinese were chronically short of horses.

The Chin conquest deprived Sung of its best iron and coal resources. Worse, Chin let iron flow freely to the Mongols. The

Mongols used a variant on Chin's cavalry technique: their front cavalry shield was divided into sections through which archers could move. They also used improved stone throwers and evolved Sung fire-lances into true guns.

The Supremacy of Logistics Under the Ming

Ming faced no serious external threats. Even the fifteenth-century Oirats wanted only trade and/or ransom of needed goods. By the sixteenth century, the "Japanese pirates" were mostly Chinese traders made outlaws by Ming's own regulations.

Ming and Ch'ing absorbed a relatively small proportion of China's GNP for administration and defense, likely only 15% to 20% which shows that the Sung jump in economic productivity had proved irreversible. Costs were further reduced by the civil service examinations, which enticed the elite to pay for its own preparation.

The Sung-Yuan military innovations were also maintained, but Ming made no fundamental military breakthroughs. Development of the cannon was hindered by metallurgical limits. A more fundamental cause of this stagnation was the lack of sustained competition with equals such as faced Europe and the daimyo of sixteenth-century Japan. Ming could successfully meet its limited barbarian competitors with superior logistics mobilizing the resources of a vast empire.

The Ming founder could not afford to keep up the army (twice the size of Northern Sung's) which had conquered his empire, but feared the consequences of its demobilization. Hence he established the military as an hereditary caste settled in colonies composed of full-time soldiers and soldier-farmers who supported the former with one-half of their grain output. This system lightened the civilian tax burden. There was a tendency to increase the proportion of soldier-farmers to soldiers and to supplement their support with grain transported to the colonies by merchants in exchange for salt certificates. The merchants in turn tended to settle their own tenants on the frontiers, as the grain they produced was cheaper than grain transported from the interior. But after 1492 all grain brought to the frontier was paid for with silver, and merchant fields disappeared.

The military colonies decayed during the fifteenth century. They tended to attract Mongol raids, received less state support, and incurred greater burdens. Officers tended to turn colonies into their private manors, and the state acquiesced in this to assure adequate grain. The fifteenth century also witnessed a partial, albeit in part inadvertent, pull-back from the frontier which proved irreversible. Thereafter reliance was placed on the rebuilt Great Wall which was now higher, had more towers, and was supported by cannon, with camps built right into its structure. The wall formed a double line in northern Shansi.

By the early fifteenth century the establishment of military colonies in Liaotung allowed closure of the sea supply route to the north, though it was briefly revived in the 1590's to meet Hideyoshi's invasion of Korea. The new Grand Canal had four times the capacity of the sea route and permitted the supplying of Peking, the new capital. It also represented a technological breakthrough, with an elaborate system of locks using water from the Wen and Ssu rivers. The canal was thirteen Chinese feet deep and thirty-two feet wide. After 1500 canal traffic declined, mainly because the hereditary soldier labor force absconded. This was probably a consequence of the decay of serfdom.

But Ming was not destroyed because of decay. It was merely an accident that ruined it a century and a half after internal decay began. The coincidence of the rise of the Manchus, internal rebellions and epidemics caused a decline of military manpower. The Manchus, by themselves no match for China, carried out their conquest by using Ming generals. Their infantry was vulnerable to firearms, hence the ability of the Three Feudatories to nearly reverse the conquest in 1673 to 1683.

The Manchus deemphasized firearms within their own armies after the conquest. Muskets could still not match the crossbow. They also feared dispersal of firearms among the civilian population and tried to ban their use until the mid-eighteenth century when bandits began using them and ordinary civilians would have been defenseless without them. The Manchus accepted defeat in the Opium War because China, like Russia in the Crimean War, though too big to be conquered, feared the strain of continued war. In particular, the Grand Canal was vulnerable.

Part II

THE MEDIEVAL ECONOMIC REVOLUTION

The Revolution in Farming

Between the eighth and twelfth centuries agriculture was revolutionized. In the north better milling techniques led to wider use of wheat instead of millet. The most significant improvements were in the south's paddy-rice agriculture. The dam, sluice gate, noria and treadle water-pump led to manorial dominance, as only manors tended to have the resources to exploit these innovations. (Similarly, the European manor of the twelfth and thirteenth centuries was best able to exploit the ax, better plows and horse harness.) Political unity eased the spread of these new techniques as did printing of illustrated agricultural treatises such as the works of Lou Shou and Ch'en Fu and the Yuan figure Wang Chen.

The growing market for grain stimulated consolidation of the manorial system, just as the early nineteenth-century growth of international grain markets intensified Russian serfdom. There is some evidence of serfs paying money rents, though payment of a fixed quantity of grain was more usual. Some tenants, therefore, were directly tied to the market.

On the land there was now better plowing and more manuring. A plow capable of turning over the sod had been developed in the north by the third century and was adapted for use in the wet fields of the south by the ninth century. A variety of new seeds, including quick-ripening types, had appeared. Seeds and cultivation techniques were finely adjusted to differing soils. Increased possibilities of marketing had stimulated crop specialization. Dovetailing of crops and double-cropping wiped out seasonal unemployment in many areas. Only the use of wind power in farming was to antedate this medieval economic revolution.

Though thirteenth-century China had the world's most sophisticated agriculture, there was still much disparity among regions. That Northern Sung's population of over 100,000,000 could grow to about 160,000,000 to 250,000,000 by 1580 was the result of a more general use of Sung techniques.

The Revolution in Water Transport

During T'ang there were still difficulties in building all-weather roads, but by Sung times stone and brick were used to surface not just intracity but intercity roads. The government post took eight to fourteen days to traverse the route from Ch'angan to Canton in T'ang and Sung times. Hence by mid-T'ang the statesman Liu Yen could receive information quickly enough to adjust central government policies to the shifting local prices of commodities. The reports sent regularly from the capital by agents of late T'ang regional commandants evolved by Sung to the official gazette, "the world's first national newspaper."

The volume of shipping was "impressive." The 2,000 river vessels built in mid-eighth century by the Salt and Iron Commission had alone a carrying capacity equal to one-third that of the mid-eighteenth century British trading fleet. By Sung, junks were being built with iron nails, were waterproofed with t'ung oil, were fitted with watertight bulkheads, and carried sea anchors, axial rudders, sea floor sampling scoops, depth lines, compasses and rockets for defense. After 1000 A.D. even foreign merchants preferred to travel in Chinese ships.

An estimate in 1487 that inland water transport was 30% to 40% cheaper than land transport, and that sea transport was 70% to 80% cheaper than land transport probably holds for Sung times as well. But losses at sea were high, especially for smaller ships, and the northern seas were not reliably mastered until the seventeenth and eighteenth centuries.

The double canal lock was invented in the eleventh century. Its use at the juncture of the Grand Canal and Yangtze at Chenchou saved 500 workers and 1,250,000 cash annually over the amount needed earlier to drag ships over ramps and permitted the use of ships of three times the carrying capacity as before.

Though shipping was largely a family enterprise, partnerships were also common. These were usually dissolved after each voyage, but some were more permanent. Some fleets were as large as eighty ships and were run by delegated managers. The Southern Sung policy of requisitioning ships for the navy induced combinations of up to sixty merchants to build ships in collective ownership, half the ships going to the government. Brokerage was the most efficient way to assure steady cargos for ships without engines (and hence on loose schedules). By Yuan there existed standard threeway contracts linking hirers, brokers and shipmasters.

The Revolution in Money and Credit

Ch'in and Han used copper money widely, but it tended to disappear during the age of disunion, except during periods of political stability. By the early sixth century use of cash was sporadic and confined largely to big cities even in the stabler south. By Sui times the economy was likely no more monetized than during Han.

The money shortage persisted into T'ang. Though at the peak

of production 300,000 strings were minted annually in the early eighth century, the amount was reduced to 100,000 strings by 834. Copper was in short supply. Because minting and transport cost twice the face value of coins, provincial mints were established, but these permitted lack of uniformity and debasement and hence problems in paying taxes in cash, which in turn required payment in other commodities.

By the eleventh century the volume of money was much greater and its use reached down into villages even for very modest transactions which had been carried out via barter during T'ang. Sung coins were used as far away as Southeast Asia and Japan.

Why this monetary revolution? In part it was because "international trade" among the Chinese states during the Ten Kingdom era disciplined their coinage policies. For example, when Min began to use lead coins, its trading partners had to follow suit to avoid loss of their copper for inferior Min lead. The copper shortage led to a grim search for new ores, the banning of copper utensils or decrees lowering their prices to keep people from melting coins to manufacture them. Even free coinage was tried, though this was ruined by debasement.

The use of iron, lead and even pottery coins to substitute for copper during the tenth century was really the beginnings of a primitive fiduciary currency: "Paper" money made of other materials. Bills for the transfer of cash were known by T'ang times: food tickets issued to the militia, the eighth-century government-issued "flying cash" (based on the flow north of tax money and the flow south of money into the tea trade), deposit shops honoring depositors' checks for a fee, and the issue of promissory notes by gold and silversmith shops (which was very close to true money).

Sung initially acquiesced in Szechwan's use of iron currency and drained copper from the province. In 979 copper was permitted to return, but a subsequent fiat giving iron parity with copper led to the latter's disappearance which opened the way for sixteen officially recognized merchant houses to issue paper promissory notes. By 1072 abuses led to government takeover. The state's notes were issued against public money deposits, had three-year expiration dates (because the paper would wear out within that period), and were fully convertible, except for a discount at issue. Expiration dates were soon eliminated, and a cash reserve was set up as backing, but the notes were not yet inconvertible.

By mid-eleventh century the state succumbed to temptations to overissue paper to pay for the wars with Hsi Hsia. A note of 1000 cash face value was worth only 940 to 960 cash by the 1070's. Under Chin notes almost completely displaced cash. The Mongols even issued five- and two-cash notes. They used silver and gold as their reserve. By mid-thirteenth century removal of reserves to the Yuan capital from the provinces and overissue led to inflation, the cure for which was correctly diagnosed by one minister as being cuts in government spending.

During Southern Sung and in the contemporary north private paper was also very important as currency. There were commodity bills for tea, flour, bamboo and wine; wooden chits issued by tea houses and brothels, and the tax-free ordination licenses of monks. Credit was built into the production process; for example, in the twelfth century capitalists in the hemp cloth industry would advance loans to spinners in the countryside by way of brokers and collect their cloth later in the year.

The Revolution in Market Structure and Urbanization

In Han times, by requiring that some taxes be paid in specified commodities, the government drew even many isolated communities into the market, but nevertheless only the upper classes were significantly affected by commerce. This narrowness of the commercial sector rendered it easy for government to control and even cruelly exploit merchants.

This pattern continued on through the T'ang. But by late T'ang the limitations placed on official markets had stimulated the appearance of local unofficial markets which became numerous enough to oblige a slackening of official controls on the old markets. In turn, the new linkages of the rural economy to the market via trade in necessities was exploited and regulated by the state through the creation of an internal customs network.

The peasantry was becoming a "class of adaptable, rational, profit-oriented, petty entrepreneurs" engaged in commercial timbering, oil pressing, sugar growing and processing, fish farming in ponds, etc. Such specialization often required the importation of food into non-food specializing rural regions. A network of local markets fed into three main regional markets: K'aifeng serving north China; the Lake T'ai cities serving south China; the Ch'engtu plain cities serving Szechwan.

Commercialization, though incomplete (vide the quasi-serflike status of much of the managerial class), could also be strikingly sophisticated. There were various business associations. Business functions (trade, warehousing, brokerage) became highly specialized. The wealthy tended to disperse their capital among specialized agents within this structure rather than concentrate it under their direct control. Yet there were some large individual operations, like that of the Southern Sung ironmonger Wang K'o whose establishment of several thousand workers was comparable to the eighteenth century Urals iron works.

By the twelfth century there were enough large cities for crowd diseases to become important. About 6% to 7.5% of the population (ca. 6,000,000 people) were in cities over 100,000. In all, at least 10% of the population was urbanized. But because of the power of the imperial state these cities never developed the independence of their later European counterparts.

Hence, unlike Europe, the manor and the urban market were kept from conflict. Indeed the market's existence rendered the manor more attractive for its potential productivity.

The period from 1300 to 1900 saw the end of the earlier trend toward the growth of great cities. By 1900 a smaller proportion of the population lived in the largest cities, but there were many more small and medium-sized towns than earlier, thereby lessening the gap between town and country. Though one may explain urbanization as being caused by technological improvements in agricultural and non-agricultural segments of the economy, it is equally plausible to reverse the causation, and credit the appearance of large urban markets for stimulating agricultural growth.

The Revolution in Science and Technology

The invention of printing and wide dissemination of books (to a significant degree under state auspices) "made medieval China the most numerate as well as the most literate nation in the world."

In medicine, by the thirteenth century there was a conscious search for novelty. Old remedies were systematically questioned and often rejected for new ones. The state certified doctors by examinations and devoted much attention to matters of public health, like drainage systems in cities and quarantine rules during epidemics. Local "officials often tried hard to raise the level of medical practice" by distributing medical texts. "Medicine was one field of science at least in medieval China where a gentleman might without fear of social stigma aspire to be an expert." Even toothpaste and the toothbrush were in use.

In the thirteenth century Ma Chih-chi gave the first description of eruptive typhus. Influenza was first described during the Sung, as was schistosomiasis, a disease caused by parasites which enter through the skin while working in irrigated rice fields. The spread of irrigated rice agriculture, accompanied by increased use of human manures, may have increased the risk of this disease which by the twentieth century affected 10% of the population south of the Yangtze. This may explain the "declining economic vigour of South China in later traditional times." The first Sung dissection was performed in 1045, and in 1113 an illustrated anatomy text was published whose drawings were transmitted to the West by the Persian Rashid al-Din al-Hamdani. Mercury poisoning was recognized by the eleventh century. Malaria was linked to the influence of swamps. Some believed that infection was the cause of disease, hence the quarantine of Hangchow during the 1181 and 1187 epidemics. Others believed that prior body weakness was the cause. Previous medical theory was systematized, revised and linked to many more specific drugs and diseases than before.

Unlike the West during the seventeenth-century scientific revolution in physics, however, the Chinese failed to resolve the internal inconsistencies in these theories, perhaps because medicine is much more complex than planetary motions. Though it seemed a more practical science, the Chinese were unlucky to have picked on medicine for such extensive work.

Mathematics in north China, under barbarian as well as Chinese rule, was linked to Taoist numerical mysticism. Li Yeh, who was a scholar in Shansi after the Mongol conquest, used location in an array (matrix) to indicate powers of an unknown. Southern mathematics was more practical. Indeterminate analysis was used for constructing calendars. A late thirteenth-century introduction to mathematics drew many of its examples from contemporary city life.

By Ming times nobody understood the advanced positional algebra of Chin and early Yuan, perhaps because of the intervening disruption of north China. In seventeenth- and eighteenth-century Japan this early work showed its potential fruitfulness with Seki Kowa's invention of determinants and Ajime Chokuyen's development of calculus, though the former used a written notation perhaps learned from the West.

In Sung astronomy much larger instruments yielded greater accuracy, and a clockwork mechanism was invented. In metallurgy coal and perhaps coke were used in blast furnace technology. In military technology gunpowder was developed into a true explosive, flame-throwers and poison gas were developed, and the Mongols used previous Chinese work and Chinese technologists to produce a true cannon. In textiles, a machine described in a 1313 work automatically spun silk and later hemp into thread. It is very like an eighteenth-century European machine described in Diderot's Encyclopedia. Further progress in textile machinery after Yuan was not blocked by inadequate science but by a "weakening of those economic and intellectual forces which make for invention and innovation."

Part III

ECONOMIC DEVELOPMENT WITHOUT TECHNOLOGICAL CHANGE

The Turning Point in the Fourteenth Century

For still "largely inexplicable" reasons the medieval economic revolution ended with a sharp economic decline between 1300 and 1500 after which only a slow recovery occurred. From the mid-fourteenth century on the economy's dynamism disappeared. Why? In part because the expanding frontier began to "fill up," in part because reduced overseas trade cut off supplies of foreign silver and reduced foreign contact encouraged society to become "inward looking," in part because philosophers turned from the investigation of nature to introspection and intuition.

In 1290 the proportion of the population in the north reached its nadir, about 9% to 10% of the total. Thereafter the proportion of northerners began to increase. This was a long-term trend, not just a response to the Mongol conquest. The south had begun to fill up, its old frontiers becoming densely enough settled to send out migrants themselves. By the eighteenth century there was no longer any place promising for migrants to move to, except for Manchuria which remained closed until 1860.

Up until this point was reached, migration to new regions

would increase productivity in both the old and new regions, even without technological advances, as the new regions would relieve population pressure on the old settled ones and further stimulate the latter via trade. After 1300 increased production only kept pace with population growth. There was no real technological advance. Even the novel crops from the New World occupied only about 7% of the total acreage. Soy cake was one of the few new types of fertilizer.

Why was there no boom in production of the new fiber cotton big enough to break out of these limits? Feasibility of machine spinning had already been demonstrated for hemp. A cotton-based industrial revolution did not occur because the "relative glut of raw cotton . . . did not last long and could not, under the economic circumstances of late traditional China, be re-created."

By the sixteenth century cotton was in short supply in the lower Yangtze and by early Ch'ing the region had to import most of its supply from north China. After 1700, when cotton manufacture began in the north, the south had to turn to Manchuria and before the end of the century to India. There was no way to raise the already high domestic productivity in cotton agriculture. Hence China had no opportunity equivalent to Britain's access to New World cotton which permitted a tripling of production between 1741 and 1775. There were too many Chinese, and China's commercial network was too good to permit any local anomaly to develop into an industrial revolution in cotton. Industrialization of cotton manufacture would have had to draw its supplies at the expense of handicraft cotton production, and this would have yielded no net increase in production.

The closure of foreign contacts overtly harmed Fukien and removed its former intellectual stimuli. The works of Ptolemy and Euclid were known in Peking by the late thirteenth century and had been translated by early Ming but had "no lasting impact."

Imports were first taxed in the mid-eighth century. The Court asserted priority of access to imports, but others could deal with foreign traders. In 979 Sung established a state monopoly over some imports but soon allowed officially licensed private trade in these goods. On balance, however, both Northern and Southern Sung encouraged foreign trade. The Mongols banned foreign trade totally by 1309 but allowed a limited reopening in 1314. The Ming founder set up a purely tributary trade but tried to ban overseas travel by Chinese. By the mid-fifteenth century even coastal shipping was banned. Within a century growth of illegal trade forced relaxation of the ban, but in the mid-seventeenth century it was reimposed and the Manchus initially continued the ban so as to isolate Coxinga (Cheng Ch'eng-kung) on Taiwan. The ban was again relaxed by the early eighteenth century and then gradually restored until by 1757 only Canton was open to foreign trade through the officially licensed Cohong monopoly.

Extension of the Grand Canal to Peking by 1415 removed Ming's incentive to maintain its navy and its seaborne trade, especially in the flimsy (because cheap) and hence dangerous government vessels. The ban was maintained thereafter because the government feared development of independent centers of power. But this policy was economically disastrous. The shortage of good money it engendered contributed to the post-fourteenth century recession. Earlier, the Mongols' "reckless issue" of inconvertible paper currency had drained silver into West Asia, further contributing to the early Ming liquidity crisis. Hence, without foreign trade, Ming had to stick with an inconvertible paper currency which must have greatly alienated the people. The situation was mitigated by the silver brought from Japan and South Asia by the semilegal and illegal foreign trade of early Ming and by New World silver in the sixteenth century.

But too much of southeast China's energy was wasted in dodging the authorities. Only the local gentry had sufficient power to defy the ban, and they connived in smuggling so thoroughly that they developed a vested interest in keeping the ban formally in effect. In 1547 to 1549 the Chekiang governor Chu Huan was impeached for successfully enforcing the ban. There followed a great increase in "piracy," apparently attempts by small and middle merchants to break loose from the big merchants and gentry. The ban was finally lifted in 1567. The very size of the empire made the ban possible in the first place. States the size of those of Ten Kingdoms times could not have afforded such isolation.

The fourteenth century was also a divide in philosophy. Sung Neo-Confucianism asserted the world's reality against the Buddhist claim that it was an illusion. Hence it was good to study Nature. But then how to explain evil? If human nature and li (理) were good, then some portion of ch'i (氣) had to be bad or at least "unclear." This, however, drove li out of Nature and rendered philosophy vulnerable to Wang Yang-ming's intuitionism which made "Nature ... a derivative of man's consciousness." Hence, by the seventeenth century even practical scientists thought of knowledge "as an ordered progression from the empirical/analytical study of phenomena to an intuitive grasp of the working of Mind or Spirit as the ultimate reality."

The seventeenth-century scientist Fang I-chih looked down on Western thought for never reaching this ultimate reality, and hence he did not take seriously its empirical/analytical side. Fang merged the mind of the individual and the mental aspect of the universe. This merger, he argued, made it possible to finally reach ultimate reality after the study of particular phenomena had enlightened the individual's mind. But such an assumption had the disastrous effect of enabling Chinese science to always be able to explain any puzzle by shortcircuiting the progression up to ultimate reality. Fang himself, however, was cautious about how much of the universal mind an individual's mind could link up with.

The Disappearance of Serfdom

Manorialism and serfdom were still dominant during Ming and early Ch'ing but with declining vigor. They disappeared during the eighteenth century. The manor lord was replaced by the landlord and pawnbroker; status relationships were replaced by financial relationships; the gentry ran rural projects as professional managers and not as interested landowners.

During early Ming very large manors were given to the new nobility, and it proved impossible to take these back. Manors also increased through exercise of private force and by voluntary commendation (t'ou-hsien) to escape taxes. The extent of serfdom cannot be measured; tenants were sometimes treated like serfs. Only the official classes could legally hold serfs, hence others would hide their holdings.

There is evidence that by mid-Ming the manor lord was no longer obliged to aid his tenant-serfs in time of disaster. Does this make them mere tenants? Without a written bond, serf status was not legal. In the sixteenth century the master-serf relationship seems to have become more precarious, needing kindness by the master for it to be kept up. As local networks of markets grew more dense during the sixteenth and seventeenth centuries, tenants and serfs tended to meet in them and forge a common class interest. Hence the seventeenth century peasant rebellions much more overtly aimed at "overthrowing the existing status order" than did those of the mid-fifteenth century and in fact really helped do so. In part this was because they coincided with the uprisings of roving bandits in the northwest (though men like Litzu-ch'eng were not interested in a status revolution) which ultimately destroyed Ming.

The Manchus considered serfkeeping as socially dangerous because it encouraged murder of serfowners. In 1681 they banned selling of tenants along with the land. Land in any event was now less profitable than trade, pawnbroking and urban real estate. By the eighteenth century, land accounts for only 2% to 20% of those great fortunes for which detailed breakdowns are available. By that time in many areas, such as Kiangsu, tenants habitually resisted paying rent. Pawnbroking was easier and more profitable.

With land less attractive, the Chinese bent toward equal inheritance asserted itself and manors were gradually fragmented. Landowners were increasingly drawn into the more numerous and attractive towns, weakening their control over sefs, especially as they tended to use local government officers at the lowest level to collect their rents. As in Tokugawa Japan, free tenants proved to be more efficient than serfs in irrigated rice agriculture, though there is no actual evidence of landowners freeing serfs for this reason. The south Chinese pattern was to separate rights to the subsoil from rights to the surface, and hence for long-term tenancy to become de facto permanent tenure. By the early twentieth century one-third to two-fifths of the lower Yangtze and four-fifths of the land in north China was farmed by tenants holding their land in permanent tenure.

The end of manorialism contributed to a population explosion. In 1580 there were about 200,000,000 Chinese and in 1850 about 410,000,000. This in turn contributed to increased social and geographical mobility and to the movement of rural power to institutions or the rich in towns and cities. Serf females were often kept unmarried, as those who reared girls had to pay their lords for the privilege. Hence the end of serfdom increased the supply of females who had children. Though monasteries remained disproportionately wealthy, the number of monks leveled off before the end of the fifteenth century.

By the 1930's, according to Communist documents, it could take only three years to achieve landlord or rich peasant status. "Everywhere there was a constant competition, without benefit to society as a whole, in which the fortunes of individual peasant families continually rose and fell," producing a society "both egalitarian and riven with mutual jealousies." Even landless managers of clan, temple and association land could become wealthy.

Until the mid-seventeenth century, landowners were still responsible for local public works. But their disappearance from the countryside led to takeover of these tasks by local clerks and village officers, and later, in the eighteenth century, by local gentry. In the late sixteenth and early seventeenth centuries the Ming local administrative apparatus began to be dismantled piecemeal, region by region. Labor service supervisors and mutual-responsibility tax collectors disappeared. Clerks became so corrupt that local rich men avoided service jobs. Since the early sixteenth century, service jobs had often been performed by men from the poorer classes who could not stand up to the clerks but who had to be used because fewer rich rural landlords were available.

The gentry were not drafted to be local managers. Hence magistrates had to consult with and defer to them. The gentry worked through lower-level professionals, as on the Rural Compact Boards, who were usually lower class and lived off squeeze. Gentry did not hold gentry status because they owned land, though such status might be reflected in land ownership. In order of ascending importance, local power resided in trade, finance, education and institutional position.

Rural Markets and Rural Industries

Around the seventeenth century, market towns, especially in economically advanced areas, began to multiply faster than the population increased. Judging from Shanghai county, this seems to correlate with the rise in interregional trade guilds in the county seats.

Large scale putting-out (as in the Sung hemp industry) disappeared by late Ming, apparently because the market mechanism was now so elaborate as to make it unnecessary, even for cotton manufacture. Though without capital, a peasant had daily access to a market to buy raw materials and sell his or her finished product. (The argument for the absence of putting-out is, it must be conceded, ex silentio.) The first evidence for putting-out in cotton comes from the late nineteenth century.

The cotton industry was based on subsidiary, seasonal labor, an "enormous reserve of unused productive capacity." Merchants operating through the market had "no direct involvement" in the production process. A rise in demand simply temporarily mobilized this unused potential, permitting no reward for technological innovators. In slumps, peasants could spend more time farming. Hence there were no penalties to drive the inefficient permanently out of the business. Four groups interacted in this mix of "organizational fragmentation and structural rigidity": cotton cloth merchants, contractors, artisans and perhaps landlords of the places where the work was done.

Cotton's institutional arrangements appear to be typical of Chinese industry in general. Merchants were rarely involved in financing production except in some very competitive markets or in fields where raw materials were very expensive. The raw material for silk was expensive and the looms for weaving it could be very elaborate, needing two or three men to operate. Hence when demand grew during the eighteenth century, twenty-loom shops became uncompetitive and putting-out evolved, financed by "account houses" which were isolated from producers by two or three levels of intermediaries.

Though in general production increased, the separation of production from commerce indicates that China was not evolving toward an industrial revolution.

Quantitative Growth, Qualitative Standstill

Some Ming-Ch'ing industries operated on a massive scale: the porcelain works of Ching-te-chen and the ironworks on the Hupei-Shensi-Szechwan border which used charcoal rather than coke, transported ore and wood over long distances and employed thousands of workers. Then why was there no industrial revolution? The development of the cotton, iron and silk industries shows there was no shortage of capital or restrictions on markets to account for the "drying up of mechanical invention."

Was industrialization aborted by political hazards and government rapacity, causing the middle class to hide its capital by entering the gentry? The government did occasionally "hunt and fish" the merchants. Yet officials often were involved in commercial life, at least indirectly through agents, and this led to a "symbiosis between bureaucrats and businessmen." By the nineteenth century guilds were taking on governmental roles, particularly during the Taiping crisis, as did the Ten Guilds of Hungchiang in western Hunan, almost all of whose leading members also held official rank. Such men represented an urban elite based on commerce and government more than on landholding and were not members of "a disadvantaged caste."

The Ch'ing government abandoned Ming's forced inconvertible paper currency. It opened new copper mines and imported Japanese copper. Paper money did reappear as demand for money increased, but it was the entirely private "cash bills" of money shops. The only drawback to the late imperial monetary system was its excessive multiplicity of forms which required an "army of assayers and exchangers," but this was preferable to a liquidity shortage.

Were enterprises too small-cale and shortlived? No. Though commercial law was mainly a matter of privately enforced custom within guilds and trust among non-friends was rare, up to a point contracts could be enforced in courts of law, and kinship ties and partnerships could support very large enterprises. Much use was made of networks of branch offices, as by the Shansi banks, which allowed large fortunes to be put to work quite flexibly. There are records of businesses lasting for centuries, as did a 240-year old Suchou drygoods store.

None of the conventional explanations of Europe's industrial revolution are controverted in China, but an industrial revolution nevertheless failed to occur, even though the Ming and Ch'ing economies still showed resourcefulness. New World crops were adopted; the simpler Western contraptions (guns, clocks, telescopes, microscopes) were imitated; zinc-smelting, multicolor printing, and sailing in northern waters were perfected. The use of damp cellars for spinning cotton in the dry north was discovered. Cotton was manufactured nationwide. Welldigging spread into the north. The gybing sail windpump, the bulletproof vest and soybean cake fertilizer were invented. Entrepreneurship and new institutions (money shops, remittance banks, denser market networks) were all present.

But it is also necessary to consider the availability of resources, capital and labor. Many resources were drying up: wood, fuel (especially on the coast where weed and reed fields had been converted into paddy), fiber (though cotton gave more fiber per acre than hemp, good cotton land was also good food-growing land), good farmland and metals. Population growth and technological standstill exacerbated shortages. Even simple wooden machines became too costly for many peasants. The Yüan government had to donate wood to peasants so they might construct water pumps. The high cost of metal may have prevented the wide use of the Western cylinder and piston pump later on. Roads, though good, were often designed only for pedestrians and wheelbarrows because fodder land was so scarce that men were cheaper to use for transport than animals.

Waterways were so much cheaper than land routes that areas without waterway potential remained underdeveloped. Even eighteenth-century British-style land transport improvements would not have made land transport competitive enough with water transport to make the improvements worthwhile. Backward landlocked areas remained backward for this reason and also because areas with water transport attracted developmental interest away from them.

Because of the high degree of sophistication in water transport only marginal improvements were possible. No big advance via simple improvements, like the American Erie Canal of 1825, was possible because such technology had long since been in use. Only a "large jump forward" into steam power could have made any significant difference.

A similar "technological discontinuity" would have been needed in agriculture. Higher yields would only have been possible by industrial-age techniques like chemical fertilizers and pesticides and machinery. Even additional traditional inputs were often not available. In the 1930's Hopei and Shantung agriculture would have done better with more animal manure, but manure was in short supply because grazing land was scarce, and grazing land was scarce because a dense population needed more crop land.

Demographic pressure also brought increasingly poor land into use, reducing the proportion of the total in paddy. Hence figures showing static overall productivity may mask much higher productivity on the best land. According to Dwight Perkins' figures, agricultural productivity rose from 140 to 224 catties per mou from 1368 to 1600. By the 1770's it dropped to 200 c.p.m. and then rose again to 240 c.p.m. in mid-nineteenth century. The initial rise most likely represents mainly recovery from the Mongol devastation. From 1600 to 1850 there was not much of a rise unless Perkins underestimated the amount of land in use in 1600, which would lower productivity for that date. This is possible because much arable land was concealed from the government during late Ming.

Yet yields in the 1920's were well above Europe's just before the industrial revolution; France got 9.5 bushels per acre of wheat around 1800, but in the 1920's China got 14. Hence the Communist attempt during 1956 to 1959 to increase output by applying more traditional technology and labor increased neither yield per acre nor per worker. By mid-eighteenth century Chinese writers like Hung Liang-chi recognized that a point of diminishing returns had been reached. J. L. Buck has shown that in this century yields per acre are constant for all farm sizes, but yields per worker are higher on larger farms with fewer workers.

Why did the population keep growing? The population peaked in the twelfth century, fell until the fourteenth century, rose again until the late sixteenth century, dropped until 1650 and has apparently been rising since. From the twelfth to the nineteenth century, the population increased threefold to around 400,000,000. Disease was the biggest check; there were epidemics in the periods from 1586 to 1589 and from 1639 to 1644 and which led to a 35% to 40% population decline between 1585 and 1645. This eased land pressure until around 1800. Cultivated land doubled in quantity from 1600 to 1850, but its average quality fell. There were no big epidemics from 1644 to 1756 which allowed population to increase. Cholera epidemics began around 1820 to 1822, just when population pressure on the land again became critical.

Manchuria's population doubled from 1905 to 1940. From 1919 to 1932 its land in use more than doubled and its cereal output increased three and a half fold. This was done by traditional techniques, except for the institutional novelty of the large land development company. Because initially Manchuria was well short of a point of diminishing returns in its agriculture, it could provide a base for industrialization under the Japanese in the 1930's.

The rest of China was "almost incapable of change through internally generated forces." For China to have tripled its cotton consumption as England did from 1741 into the 1770's, would have been beyond the entire planet's resources. The modern West's role in China has been to "ease and then break" this "high-level equilibrium trap," at first through the treaty ports, especially Shanghai, and then by percolating new techniques into the interior. The new methods "made possible new combinations of traditional elements." Steamships on the major river and coastal routes stimulated business for junks on subsidiary routes. The telegraph allowed traditional banks to form themselves into more efficient networks. Imported cotton yarn was used in a new Fukien handweaving industry. Foreigners bought Hunan and Szechwan t'ung oil.

Conclusion

Compared to China, early modern Europe enjoyed what Alexander Gerschenkron has called the "advantages of backwardness." China may have been too mature to progress rapidly. Late imperial China's complex hierarchy of urban centers may not have been a prelude to modernization but an alternative thereto. The disproportionate development of the fewer Sung cities might have been better suited to encourage modernization, as was the case for the similarly disproportionate position of early modern London and Paris in the economies of England and France.

Original contributions, in a Western language at least, to our knowledge may be claimed for these topics: (a) the origins of the Equitable Fields; (b) the origins of Chinese paper money; (c) the role of the late Ming epidemics; (d) the structure of the late traditional cotton industry; (e) the argument that serfdom and serf-like tenancy from Sung to early Ch'ing were not minor and that their disappearance led to the evolution of a new type of rural society; (f) the thesis that between 800 and 1300 something akin to an economic revolution took place, after which growth slowed relative to China's earlier pace and that of contemporary Europe.

Chinese technological creativity has deep roots and its re-awakening may astonish us. But industry must advance fast enough to let agriculture break out of its trap, and to do this industry must enter foreign trade. It can do so effectively, but if it does, it will disrupt the regime's control over thought and information. We cannot tell if this will be "potentially lethal or merely troublesome."

Appendix B

Translation in Précis of Fu Chu-fu (傅筑夫) and Li Ching-neng (李競能), Chungkuo fengchien shehui nei tzupenchuyi yinsu ti mengya 中國封建社會內資本主義因素的萌芽 (The Sprouts of Capitalistic Factors Within China's Feudal Society). Shanghai: Jenmin ch'upanshe, 1956.

WHAT ARE THE SPROUTS OF CAPITALISM?

Though it had its idiosyncracies, China's society went through all the stages prescribed by objective historical law. As Chairman Mao has pointed out, even without foreign intrusions after the mid-nineteenth century, the sprouts of capitalism already existing within China's feudal society would have slowly developed into full capitalism. Already present within Chinese society were money, production and consumption capital, capitalists and their agents, and proletarians. Commercial capital was already serving as the leading edge of capitalism. At first capitalist relations were merely localized, with labor subordinated only in form, not actuality, to capital. It is from such sprouts as these, as Engels points out, that capitalism eventually burgeons to become the central and unifying factor in the economy.

THE DEVELOPMENT OF CHINA'S MERCANTILE ECONOMY DURING T'ANG AND SUNG

As Marx tells us, the mercantile stage is the necessary precondition for capitalism. The mercantile economy involves production as well as trade. Trade was already somewhat developed by Warring States-Ch'in times, and there were large-scale accumulations of commercial capital. Ssu-ma Ch'ien wrote that by Han "for a poor man to seek riches, agriculture is not as good as artisanship, and artisanship is not as good as trade" (Shih Chi, 129). Though foreign trade, by land and by sea, was highly developed, it was largely in luxury goods and isolated from the rest of the economy. Commerce depended on guile and was subject to the whims of the state. It was without roots and not only unable to serve as the base for capitalism, but was also a hindrance to society.

T'ang represented the peak of China's feudal economy. Though the feudal natural economy was still the most important sector, the mercantile sector began to make great strides forward. By the mid-eighth century T'ang's internal economy had in many respects transcended its earlier forms. Markets were fixed and urbanized. Articles of everyday use now entered the market. Merchants specialized and were grouped in markets by specialty. Craftsmen also traded in their own products, at least locally. Middlemen with considerable capital as well as money changers became numerous. Bills of exchange came into use. There were also rural markets operating down to the village level. The monetary system was shifting from a bronze-cloth basis to specie, particularly silver. Improvements in commercial and transportation techniques were mutually stimulative.

Foreign trade grew, particularly the land trade with the nearby states of Central Asia. Occasionally this trade drained so many goods from China that the state had to suspend it. A significant number of private fortunes were created. T'ang's sea trade provided the base for still more extensive development later on. Arabs were the most important people in this trade. Maritime excise taxes became a significant source of government revenues.

Tea, which had become ubiquitous in its use by mid-T'ang, was a notable agricultural specialty. The "flying cash" paper notes were mostly used by the far-ranging tea merchants. Tea also now began to be exchanged for horses at the frontier markets. One T'ang source lists fifteen districts specializing in tea production. Most of the actual cultivators were hired laborers. They worked by the hundreds in large tea gardens owned by the rich, usually of the official class. We do not know whether most of these laborers were free. The skilled workers engaged in drying and processing the tea leaves were recruited from a wide area, and they were often paid in tea which they then sold after dispersing from the gardens. Their status still had a feudal aura about it.

Tea seems to have been the only product significantly commercialized. Officially controlled artisans for the palace and army were still in the central position in the labor force. This practice went back to Chou times and had spread with the evolution of the economy. Production materials for these official artisans came from taxes in kind. Artisans served prescribed periods of apprenticeship with close supervision either directly or indirectly by the state.

State interference in the salt and iron industries after mid-eighth century greatly restricted the private sector in these trades. This was because some of the state monopolies in these trades did not produce for the market and kept many of their techniques secret. Even in those activities like the salt trade, which produced for the market, the state's aims were primarily profit for itself and the subordination of commerce to agriculture. But because the scale of operations was so great, there was advance in the division of labor and increasing sophistication of techniques. Nor did state production prevent a significant increase in the size of the private sector. Rural and urban commercial production were already separately organized.

In manufacture there was specialization by craft and region. In textiles, silk, hemp and wool were distinct trades. The scale of manufacture was, however, comparable in smallness to that of the producers' guilds of medieval Europe, i.e., it was still pre-capitalist in form. Little is known about the forms of management and status of labor of the large-scale private firms.

As would be expected in a period when feudalism was at its peak, the several forms of labor service tax constituted the most important forms of labor in the T'ang state industries, though at times hired labor was used to supplement it. Free labor existed, as is shown by the numerous names used for various kinds of hired laborers. Laborers were hired by the day, month, or by piece rate. Some artisans owned their own tools. Some traveled about offering themselves for hire. Some had their own fixed places of business. But, as Marx and Engels say was the case in medieval Europe, free labor was scattered and without power or cohesion, merely an aid to a feudal order in which a natural economy was still central and the state was still emphasizing agriculture.

Hence one may not yet speak of the sprouting of the factors of capitalism. Present, however, was the foundation for economic development in the period from Sung to Ch'ing.

Late T'ang and Five Dynasties was a period of feudal chaos and warfare. Economic decay was not halted until the early Sung reunification and consequent pacification of village life provided a breathing space for society. Thereafter growth was renewed and the mercantile economy took a step forward.

Sung commerce was much greater in scale than T'ang's. The T'ang urban markets operated only during daylight hours and were closely supervised by the state. Locations of the markets and the type and quality of the goods sold were all specified. By Sung such restrictions were gone. Free markets operated day and night. There were also temple markets. Southern Sung went even further. There were big urban markets thronged with both local and traveling merchants. Local trade, especially Southern Sung's, was also much more developed than during T'ang. Many rural markets which had been formally organized as garrison centers (<u>chen shih</u> 鎮市) during Northern Sung, became significantly large urban centers, often county seats, by Southern Sung. These were also the loci for considerable accumulations of monetary capital.

Though the forms of state regulation of foreign trade still resembled those of T'ang, the scale of the trade was much greater, reaching its peak during Southern Sung. Even by Northern Sung there were many more tax offices and sub-offices than during T'ang. Canton was still the biggest port, but by late Northern Sung and early Southern Sung Ch'üanchou was beginning to become the new center, ultimately because of its nearness to Hangchow, the Southern Sung capital. It attracted merchants from more than fifty countries dealing in several hundred kinds of goods. Because imports exceeded exports, there was a monetary drain and a serious internal monetary crisis. Nevertheless a flourishing foreign trade continued through late Yuan. But because it was still controlled by feudal lords and rich merchants, this trade was not able to displace from centrality the feudal natural economy, and capital accumulation and the development of internal commerce was still hindered.

Tea was still the chief commercialized agricultural product, but the scale of the trade greatly exceeded that of T'ang. The state took over marketing and even had its own tea plantations and processing plants, some using water power. Labor was still either conscripted or recruited and hence was still basically feudal. There were many more varieties of tea than during T'ang, requiring specialized processing techniques. Tea was no longer a subsidiary agricultural product but the center of mass-use specialized industry.

Sugar became an important commercial item during Sung. Though still a part of agriculture, it was also becoming an article of interregional trade. Its processing required specialized tools and shops of twenty and more workers, with some division of labor. There were other specialized trades during Sung but, unlike sugar and tea, they all produced for local markets only.

Sung handicraft industries were much advanced over T'ang's. Though we do not know the nature of labor relationships, there was division of labor. The scale of operations of both private and public mining and smelting was much greater in Sung than in T'ang. By Northern Sung coal was used in smelting iron. Some smelters had as many as 500 or 600 workers. One public mint employed 300 day laborers and could turn out 10,000 strings of cash daily, 270,000 strings in a nine-month period. Of course this mint was completely feudal in its management. Private mints also flourished and there was no way to stop them. Private manufacture of bronze implements also flourished.

Silk weaving was carried out on a big scale. State enterprises were feudal in organization and larger than private ones. Both used division of labor. Printing was a new industry during Sung. Aside from the National Academy in the capital, there were printing centers in Chekiang, Szechwan and Fukien. In addition to books, printing was used to produce paper money and commodity bills. Not only did the new technique promote a higher level of culture, it also encouraged the division of labor.

Porcelain manufacture also became a large-scale industry during Sung. There were both state and private kilns. There was a big export trade in porcelain. So large-scale an industry must have required division of labor, but little evidence of this survives.

Shipbuilding was also more developed than in earlier times. State and private shipyards built large, complex vessels, using special skills and mechanical aids to supplement human muscle power. Though there was an extensive internal and external waterborn commerce, shipbuilding techniques were linked to military use and never strongly affected society at large.

All of the above are merely samples of the proliferation of commercially produced goods during Sung and illustrate the possibility that existed for production capitalism by factory owners. State manufacture was still extremely important and still used conscripted craftsmen. Farmers and official slaves were still important sources of labor. But hired labor was more generally in use than in T'ang, particularly when official labor was insufficient or during emergencies. Conscripted labor was in decline because of the inconvenience of bringing conscripts from a distance and disturbing their businesses. Many would abscond. Hence conscripted labor was inefficient and costly to maintain. It was better to collect a labor service tax and use it to hire men. This is what Wang An-shih proposed in his Service Avoidance Tax. There are many references to private hired labor, but most such laborers were not engaged in production and the methods of organizing hired laborers were tainted with feudalism.

Especially by Southern Sung, the mercantile economy was much more developed than during T'ang. Though still limited to urban areas and not affecting the bulk of the rural natural economy, it was nevertheless now large-scale. It involved not just accumulations of monetary capital but a diversified commercial output which produced the sprouts of capitalism and served as the historical precondition for capitalism's development. There were already factories with systematic division of labor. Of course many factories were state-owned and hence completely feudal in nature, but quite a few were private and these produced a variety of commercial goods. Hired laborers were becoming ever more numerous. It is possible to say that by Southern Sung in the Soochow-Hangchow region there were sprouts of capitalism in the cloth trade, though we still lack sufficiently detailed materials to describe it adequately. Nevertheless the base was present for Ming-Ch'ing developments.

THE SPROUTS OF THE FACTORS OF CHINESE CAPITALISM DURING THE MING-CH'ING TRANSITION

Yuan represented a period of pause, with different sectors of the economy unequally affected. The policies of the early Ming centralized feudalism encouraged revival of commerce to a level above that of Southern Sung. The period from early Ming to mid-Ch'ing was the high point of feudal society's economic development, the period when sprouts of capitalism clearly appeared.

The lower Yangtze silk cloth trade was first to revive and show sprouts of capitalism. Even during Yuan much wage labor was being used in factories owned by the rich. Laborers worked long hours and were much weakened thereby. They were mobile and shifted jobs to get better wages. This shows that labor was commercialized, being bought and sold freely. By mid-Ming this phenomenon spread more widely down to the smaller commercial towns of the lower Yangtze and their surrounding agricultural areas. Small family weaving enterprises would frequently bring their products into the commercial towns to sell to traveling merchants. Some of these weavers prospered, expanded production and hired laborers, thus becoming capitalists in their own right. Commercial capital entered the production process by making contracts in advance to buy small operators' output.

These sprouts developed further by late Ming as many officials, landowners and rich merchants began to invest in the trade. In addition many unsuccessful weavers were losing their production capital and were being forced to become wage laborers. In 1601 in Soochow there was an uprising of such laborers.

Cotton, which had come up from Lingnan during Yuan, became widespread during Ming. By early Ming part of the land tax in kind was being paid in cotton. Cotton manufacture provided another task for cottage industry and advanced the mercantile economy. By mid-Ming cotton had become the most common clothing fiber. The trade centered in the Sungchiang area, including Shanghai. By mid-nineteenth century about 70% of the rural population of this region was involved in the cotton trade. By the eighteenth century 20% to 30% of the land in Chihli was devoted to cotton culture. By Yuan times there was already elaborate equipment for processing cotton, including a two-man cotton gin. During Ming techniques continued to improve. There were spinning machines run by foot treadles and capable of spinning three or four threads simultaneously.

In Ming-Ch'ing Sungchiang commercial capital was entering cotton cloth production and gradually transforming itself into production capital. Sungchiang was also a cotton merchandizing center. The contract purchase system allowed rich merchants to dominate the local markets and oblige the actual producers to make what the merchants wanted. A putting-out system also evolved in the cotton trade, with cloth being contracted out by a main house to various specialists for different stages of its processing. Finished cloth was also contracted out to family workshops, which often possessed their own tools, to be sewn into stockings.

Mining and smelting also progressed. From early Ming a special tax of one-fifteenth was paid on such products. The amounts paid over the course of years show the great size and growth of this industry. The late Ming technological encyclopedia T'ien-kung k'ai-wu's narrative indicates that iron smelters were of considerable size. Growth continued into Ch'ing. A Ch'ing era blast furnace in Kuangtung had 300 families living nearby and employed over 200 men to service the furnace. There were many large iron complexes in this area, each using detailed division of labor and large-scale blast furnaces working around the clock. Kuangtung iron and its products were exported as far as Hunan and the lower Yangtze. A similar scale and complexity of operations was achieved in other handicraft industries such as porcelain, salt, sugar, wine, paper and shipbuilding.

These sprouts of capitalism were also reflected in other sectors of the economy. Conscription of labor in state enterprises gradually disappeared. In early Ming there were still over 230,000 hired state craftsmen. By mid-Ming many were defaulting on their quota of labor and were being allowed to pay a tax in lieu of such labor. By late Ming such default continued and because the continuing expansion of the commercial sector rendered conscripted labor's productivity ever less than that of hired labor, the dynasty went fully over to the use of a labor exemption tax and then increased its rate, using the proceeds to hire labor.

The spread of commercialization increased the avariciousness of the ruling strata. A monetary economy was fully dominant by Ming times. Taxes and rents were collected and computed in money, not kind, after mid-Ming. Peasants now had to sell their crops in the market to get cash to pay their taxes. They also began to buy necessities in the market as well, thereby beginning the destruction of the natural economy and creating regional specialization. The raising of silkworms and mulberry trees was one notable specialty, particularly in Chekiang and Szechwan. Most of the profits from such specialties went into the hands of rich landlords.

Tea held a special place in China's agricultural economy. Its production increased at an unprecedented rate during Ming-Ch'ing. During Ming it was an important source of state revenues. The government set up many offices to manage its production and distribution. Under state auspices production increased greatly and spread to new regions. Much tea was exported to the northwest in exchange for horses, and from the seventeenth century until the 1880's increasing amounts were sold to Europe and America.

Sugar production also increased in amount and variety. By Ch'ing, Canton was its center, with as much land devoted to it as to grain in some areas. Dyeing and dyestuff production increased along with the cloth trade. Indigo was the most common dyestuff, its culture spreading from Fukien all through the empire. Production of vegetable oils also spread. Tobacco appeared in late Ming, coming from Luzon to Fukien and then becoming much more diffused as the habit of smoking took root during early Ch'ing. A variety of fruits were also increasingly grown for the market.

After mid-Ming hired agricultural labor in commercialized areas became comparatively common and relations between landlords and peasants changed. By late Ming many peasants were forced by feudal exploitation and usurious exploitation by commercial capital to go out and sell their labor, either by the year or month, in order to live. Many worked in commercial agriculture. Such laborers were related to landowners by a cash nexus, as is shown by the increasingly numerous complaints about their productivity made by landowners.

Though such evidence indicates that commercialization of life was somewhat developed in comparatively advanced areas, this only represented the beginnings of the transformation of a predominantly feudal natural economy. Small-scale farming and artisanship were still the dominant forms of economic organization. Nevertheless the scale and complexity of urbanization were much greater than before Ming. There were many smaller cities apart from the capitals, with rich inhabitants possessing capital on a capitalistic scale. Merchants were dealing in materials of production, both manufactured and agricultural, not just finished goods. This was a fundamental distinction from the commerce of previous eras.

Money was becoming increasingly indispensible, especially for the elites. By mid-Ming there were seventeen and more families with capital of from 500,000 to 1,000,000 cash. Many of the rich invested in the commercial sector and by their oppression of small craftsmen and farmers further concentrated wealth. Several dozen large commercial cities developed. Peking and Nanking were economic as well as political centers. Other cities were regional economic centers specializing in various products like silk, cotton, and porcelain.

CONCLUSION

From the above we may conclude the following: (1) Though T'ang was the height of feudal development, it also saw the establishment of commerce and commercial production to a sufficient degree to serve as the base for later sprouts of capitalism. (2) Sung's (especially Southern Sung's) commercial economy was more developed than T'ang's. Commerce was already yielding rather large-scale accumulations of monetary capital. There were large manufacturing enterprises, with division of labor and with hired labor becoming daily more evident. These all reflect the steady proliferation of petty commercial producers. Perhaps in a few areas (Soochow-Hangchow) in Southern Sung, the sprouts of capitalism had already appeared. (3) During Ming-Ch'ing, the feudal natural economy still held the dominant place in Chinese society, but the commercial economy had risen to a high level from the T'ang-Sung base.

In the Soochow-Hangchow silk trade, Sungchiang's cotton looms, and in the metals, porcelain, papermaking and shipbuilding handicrafts trades in various areas, the elements of capitalism had already sprouted and developed. In these trades, on one hand petty commercial producers differentiated into capitalist enterprise owners and hired laborers and, on the other hand, merchants managed production directly via delegated commercial capital.

This high level of commercial development and the sprouts of capitalism in some handicrafts were also reflected in other aspects of China's social economy, most importantly in official manufacturing's substitution of the hired labor for the conscripted labor system, the development of cottage manufacture in agriculture and the gradual increase in hired labor, commercial capital's rapid increase and participation in commercial production, the concentration of monetary wealth in a few men's hands, and the appearance of important economically specialized regions. All these are related to the sprouts of capitalism in important industries.

But we must forcefully point out that the development of China's feudal social economy was extremely uneven; the sprouts of capitalism appeared in only a few regions and industries where the commercial economy was highly developed. For the most part villages were still in the grip of a feudal natural economy. Though China's feudal system had begun to loosen in late Ming, the economic links between small-scale agriculture and handicrafts were still extremely close, and these became a serious obstacle to the general spread of the commercial economy.

Aside from this, the rulers of China's feudal monopoly system were still quite strong. Official industries continued to exist and develop. Various sorts of taxes and feudal management and oppression were all at that time serious obstacles on the road to development of privately managed industries. All of these are the basic reasons for the failure of capitalism to develop and for primitive capital accumulation to be delayed in its appearance. During Ming-Ch'ing, though sprouts of capitalism developed within Chinese feudal society, the historical basis for development to a capitalist society was not prepared. Hence by mid-nineteenth century the whole of the feudal system of production had not yet been destroyed.

Of course this does not mean that China's feudal society was incapable of developing into a capitalist society. The sprouts of Chinese capitalism were slowly progressing. If there had been no capitalist intrusion from abroad, China too would certainly have been able to slowly develop from a feudal to a capitalist society.

DYNASTIC TABLE

(Keyed to Chou Chin-sheng's periodization of Chinese economic history)

PERIODS AND DYNASTIES	DATES
I. The Mythical Period	
1. The Yellow Emperor (Huang Ti 黃帝) [Traditionally viewed as the ancestor of the Chinese race. Traditions vary as to his predecessors, but most include the "culture hero" rulers Fu-hsi 伏羲 (trad. 2852-2738) and Shen-nung 神農 (trad. 2737-2696) among them.]	trad. 2697-2596 B.C.
2. [Four mythical rulers]	trad. 2597-2357 B.C.
3. Yao 堯	trad. 2356-2256 B.C.
4. Shun 舜	trad. 2255-2206 B.C.
5. Yü 禹	trad. 2205-2198 B.C.
6. Hsia Dynasty 夏代 [Said to have been founded by Yü's son.]	trad. 2197-1766 B.C.
II. The Founding Period	
1. Shang-Yin 商殷	trad. 1766-1122 B.C. (perhaps actually only c. 1500-c.1100)
Shang 商	trad. 1766-1400
Yin 殷 [Name changed when capital moved]	trad. 1400-1122
2. Western Chou 西周	trad. 1121-770
III. The Age of Metamorphosis	
1. Eastern Chou 東周	770-249
Spring and Autumn (Ch'un-ch'iu) 春秋	770-403
Warring States (Chan-kuo) 戰國	403-220
IV. The Flourishing Epoch	
1. Ch'in 秦	221-205
2. Western (or Former) Han 西 (or 前) 漢	205 B.C.-8 A.D.
3. Hsin (Wang Mang) 新 (王莽)	9-24 A.D.
V. The Age of Troubles	
1. Eastern (or Latter) Han 東 (or 後) 漢	25-220

DYNASTIC TABLE (cont'd)

V. The Age of Troubles (cont'd)

2. Three Kingdoms 三國	220-265
Shu (Han) 蜀 (漢)	220-265
Wei 魏	220-265
Wu 吳	222-280
3. Chin 晉	265-430
Western Chin 西晉	265-316
Eastern Chin 東晉 [in South China]	317-420
4. Southern and Northern Dynasties (Nan Pei Ch'ao 南北朝)	
Southern Dynasties:	
Liu-Sung 劉宋	420-478
Ch'i 齊	479-501
Liang 梁	502-556
Ch'en 陳	557-588
Northern Dynasties:	
The Sixteen Kingdoms (Shih-liu kuo 十六國)	304-439
Northern Wei 北魏	386-534
Western Wei 西魏	535-557
Eastern Wei 東魏	534-550
Northern Ch'i 北齊	550-577
Northern Chou 北周	557-581

VI. The Age of Reestablishment

1. Sui 隋	581/9-618
2. T'ang 唐	618-906
3. a. Five Dynasties (Wu Tai 五代) [in North China]	907-960
Later Liang 後梁	907-922
Later T'ang 後唐 [Turkic]	923-935
Later Chin (Tsin) 後晉 [Turkic]	936-946
Later Han 後漢 [Turkic]	947-950
Later Chou 後周	951-959
b. Ten Kingdoms (Shih kuo 十國) [in various places in South China, except for Northern Han.]	
Wu 吳 [capital at Yang-chou]	902-937
Southern T'ang 南唐 [capital at Nanking]	937-975
Southern P'ing 南平 [middle Yangtze]	907-963
Ch'u 楚 [in Hunan]	927-951
Former Shu 前蜀 [in Szechwan]	907-925
Later Shu 後蜀 [in Szechwan]	934-965
Wu-Yüeh 吳越 [capital at Hangchow]	907-978

DYNASTIC TABLE (cont'd)

VI.	The Age of Reestablishment (cont'd)	
	Min 閩 [capital at Foochow]	909-944
	Southern Han 南漢 [capital at Canton]	907-971
	Northern Han 北漢 [in Northern Shansi]	951-979
VII.	The Age of Renewal	
	1. Sung 宋	960-1279
	Northern Sung 北宋	960-1126
	Southern Sung 南宋	1127-1279
VIII.	The Age of Destitution [overlaps Age of Renewal]	
	1. Western Hsia 西夏 [Tangut]	1038-1227
	2. Liao 遼 [Khitan]	916-1125
	Western Liao (Qāra Khitāi) 西遼	1126-1211
	3. Chin 金 [Jurched]	1115-1234
	4. Yuan 元 [Mongol]	1234/79-1368
IX.	The Age of Renewal	
	1. Ming 明	1368-1644
X.	The Age of Fermentation	
	1. Ch'ing 清 [Manchu]	1644-1911
XI.	The Republic (Minkuo 民國)	1912-

WEIGHTS AND MEASURES

Chinese weights and measures have varied, often over considerable ranges, at different times during the past three millenia. Even in relatively recent times there has been wide variation among different regions during the same period. The metric and English equivalents given here are for recent times only, and are intended only to make rough comparisons possible. They must NOT be used as the basis for quantitative calculations, even for recent times. For purposes of calculation consult a good history of Chinese weights and measures and make whatever allowances seem prudent for regional and local variations.

1. Linear Measures

Chinese unit	Metric equivalent	English equivalent
fen 分	3.3 mm.	0.131 in.
10 fen = 1 ts'un 寸	3.3 cm.	0.109 ft.
10 ts'un = 1 ch'ih 尺	33 cm.	1.094 ft.
10 ch'ih = 1 chang 丈	3.3 m.	10.94 ft.
150 chang = 1 li	0.5 km.	0.33 miles

2. Areal Measures

Chinese unit	Metric equivalent	English equivalent
li 厘	6.1 sq. m.	7.34 sq. yd.
10 li = 1 fen 分	.6144 are	74.43 sq. yd.
10 fen = 1 mu 畝	6.144 ares	.1647 acre
100 mu = 1 ch'ing 頃	6.14 hectares	16.47 acres

3. Cubic Measures

Chinese unit	Metric equivalent	English equivalent
sheng 升	1 liter	.908 quart
10 sheng = 1 tou 斗	10 liters	1.14 pecks
10 tou = 1 tan (or shih) 石 [not to be confused with the homophonous unit of weight. Cf. below]	100 liters	2.85 bushels

4. Weight Measures

Chinese unit	Metric equivalent	English equivalent
liang 兩 "tael"*	31.25 g.	1.1 oz.
16 liang = 1 chin 斤 "catty"*	.5 kg.	1.102 lb.
100 chin = 1 tan 担 or 擔 "picul"*	50 kg.	110.23 lb.

*Commonly used "pidgin English" terms during the nineteenth century